The Complete Guide
to Software Testing
Second Edition

The Complete Guide to Software Testing

Second Edition

Bill Hetzel

A Wiley–QED Publication

John Wiley & Sons, Inc.

New York • Chichester • Brisbane • Toronto • Singapore

Library of Congress Cataloging-in-Publication Data

Hetzel, William C., 1941–
    The complete guide to software testing.
    Bibliography: p
    1. Computer software—Testing. I. Title.
    QA76.76.T48H48   1988   005.1'4   88-6014
    ISBN 0-471-56567-9

Printed in the United States of America

10 9 8 7

Contents

Preface

The quality of systems developed and maintained in most organizations is poorly understood and below standard. This book explains how software can be tested effectively and how to manage that effort within a project or organization. It demonstrates that good testing practices are the key to controlling and improving software quality and explains how to develop and implement a balanced testing program to achieve significant quality improvements. You need to read and use this book if you want to know

- what good software testing means
- how to determine software testing objectives and criteria
- how to develop and validate a test plan
- how to select and prepare test cases
- when there is too much or not enough testing
- how to prepare testing policies and standards
- how to use testing aids and tools
- what to test before buying a software package
- what to test after maintenance and enhancement changes
- how to measure the success of your testing efforts

The book covers the discipline of software testing: what testing means, how to define it, how to measure it, and how to ensure its effectiveness. The term *software testing* is used broadly to include the full scope of what is sometimes referred to as test and evaluation or verification and validation activities. Software testing is viewed as the continuous task of planning, designing, and constructing tests, and of using those tests to assess and evaluate the quality of work performed at each step of the system development process. Both the *why* and the *how* are considered. The *why* addresses the underlying principles, where the concept came from, and why it is important. The *how* is practical and explains the method and management practices so they may be easily understood and put into use.

It is not assumed the reader has any specific prior knowledge other than some perspective and experience drawn from working on past projects. The first two chapters are conceptual and build from the reader's working experience to establish an intuitive feel for the ideas and approach. Later chapters present testing techniques, methodologies, and management perspectives.

Each chapter contains examples and checklists to help the reader understand the material and adapt it to his or her environment. Case studies taken from the author's consulting and management experience are provided throughout. They include sample reports, policy guidelines, and results actually achieved. All chapters close with a summary of key points and observations.

The book is intended for the software practitioner or manager. It may be read to provide a fresh look at the discipline of software testing or used as a reference for testing techniques that might be employed on a particular program or project. Practical information on how to manage the testing function as well as how to evaluate current project or organization effectiveness in testing is included. Finally, the book should be useful as a supplementary text to students working on software projects or in programming courses. EDP auditors and quality assurance personnel should also find the book helpful, especially in the development of testing standards or evaluation of testing effectiveness.

Part 1

The Testing Discipline

Chapter 1

An Introduction

Software Testing: A Historical Perspective

It has been said that "approximately 50% of the elapsed time and over 50% of the total cost are expended in testing a program or system being developed."[1] Testing is an activity most of us have endured or experienced, and one on which we spend a great deal of time and money. Yet we find it difficult to define it clearly. What is a testing activity and what isn't? How should we define testing? How has the testing discipline changed and evolved to where it is today?

The word *test* is derived from the Latin word for an earthen pot or vessel (*testum*). Such a pot was used for assaying metals to determine the presence or measure the weight of various elements, thus the expression "to put to the test." Today the word is very commonly employed. We grow up "taking tests" in school, and most of us have a strong intuitive understanding of what testing means. Extending the concept from a series of questions or exercises to measure the knowledge and skills of individuals to the measurement of computer systems is where most of us encounter fuzziness.

The notion of "testing programs" arose almost simultaneously with the first experiences in writing programs. The programs that ran on the first

---

1. Preface to Glen Myers, *Art of Software Testing* (New York: John Wiley, 1979).

machines had to be tested, and references to program testing in the literature can be traced back to 1950.[2] Testing was a routine activity associated with engineering and manufacturing processes, and it was quite natural to see it take shape as part of the software development process.

The early view was that you "wrote" a program and *then* you "tested and debugged it." Testing was considered a *follow on* activity and embraced not only the effort to discover errors but also to correct and remove them. A number of the earliest papers on "testing" actually concerned "debugging," and the difficulty of correcting and removing errors was long thought to be the more interesting problem. It was not until 1957 that program testing was clearly distinguished from debugging. In a lengthy review of *Digital Computer Programming*, Charles Baker took author Dan McCracken to task for not separating the two ideas. As Fred Gruenberger observed, "We don't want to be hard on Dan; his book was written when only a thousand people in the world could have called themselves programmers. But Baker's insight is applicable today, with program testing still confused with debugging, and an organized approach to the subject still lacking."[3]

During the late 1950s and 1960s software testing came to assume more and more significance because of both experience and economics. It was evident that computer systems contained many deficiencies, and the cost and impact of fixing or recovering from these problems were substantial. More emphasis was placed on "better testing" by users and development managers, and the time and resources devoted to testing and debugging increased sharply.

I organized the first formal conference devoted to software testing, which was held in June 1972 at the University of North Carolina, to bring together a broad cross section of people interested in software testing. *Program Test Methods* was published as an outgrowth of this conference and established the view that "testing" encompassed a wide array of activities all associated with "obtaining confidence that a program or system performed as it was supposed to."

A Definition of Testing

Testing is the process of establishing confidence that a program or system does what it is supposed to.

Hetzel 1973

---

2. See Ed Miller's essay, *"Program Testing—An Overview for Managers."* IEEE Software Testing Tutorial, 1980.
3. See William Hetzel, Ed., *Program Test Methods* (Englewood Cliffs, N.J.: Prentice-Hall, 1973), p. 11.

Since that initial conference many conferences and workshops have been devoted to software quality, reliability, and engineering, and gradually the "testing discipline" has emerged as an organized element within software technology. Literally millions of programs and systems have been tested with widely disparate results. Most practitioners have their own favorite stories to tell about software failures they have experienced or calamities they have witnessed. Yet it is clear that there are also many successes and, that a systematic discipline and testing methodology is now emerging.

During the last few years a number of books on testing have contributed to this growing discipline. Glen Myers wrote *The Art of Software Testing* in 1979, and Boris Beizer published *Software Testing Techniques*, in 1983. Most programming and project management texts now include several chapters on testing, and testing basics are taught in most programming courses. The subject is continuing to develop with the need from every sector of industry for more practical methods for assuring quality. The field is far from mature. Even satisfactory agreement on a definition of testing remains in question. Glen Myers states that "most people have an incorrect view as to what testing is *and that this is the primary cause for poor program testing.*" (My emphasis) He believes one should not test a program to show (or gain) confidence that it works; rather, one should start with the assumption that the program contains errors and then test to find as many of the errors as possible.

Another Definition of Testing

Testing is the process of executing a program or system with the intent of finding errors.

Myers 1979

This view of testing makes "finding errors" the goal. Myers emphasizes "that if our goal is to demonstrate that a program has no errors, then we are subconsciously steered toward that goal; that is, we tend to select test data that have a low probability of causing the program to fail. On the other hand, if our goal is to demonstrate that a program has errors, our test data will have a higher probability of finding errors and we become more successful in testing."

While Meyers's definition and its implications have been important toward understanding testing, it has gradually come to be viewed as too narrow and restrictive to accept as a definition of testing. There are many ways to evaluate (or test) a system besides executing it, and taking Myers's definition literally would mean testing would begin only *after* a program was coded. In addition, our intuitive understanding of testing is built on the notion of "measuring" or "evaluating," not trying to find things wrong. The goal in testing students is not to find what they do *not* know, but rather to allow them to demonstrate an acceptable understanding and grasp of the subject matter.

For several years now my colleagues and I have opened every testing seminar we teach by asking the participants to define what they mean by testing. We have done this enough times to observe a repetitive pattern of responses and have listed some of their typical answers.

Practitioners' Views of Software Testing

Checking programs against specifications
Finding bugs in programs
Determining user acceptability
Insuring that a system is ready for use
Gaining confidence that it works
Showing that a program performs correctly
Demonstrating that errors are not present
Understanding the limits of performance
Learning what a system is not able to do
Evaluating the capabilities of a system
Verifying documentation
Convincing oneself that the job is finished

I see all these views as correct and believe that the proper way to look at testing is as a *broad* and *continuous* activity throughout the development process. Testing should be thought of as a necessary information-gathering activity to enable us to evaluate our work effectively. Any activity that is undertaken with the objective of helping us to evaluate or measure an attribute of our software should be considered a testing activity. This includes most reviews, walk-throughs, and inspections and many judgments and analyses that are performed during the development process. The goal is to obtain reliable information about the software in the easiest and most effective manner possible. Is the software ready to use? What are the risks? What are the capabilities? What are the limitations? What are the problems? Does it perform as it is supposed to? These are the questions that an effective testing discipline seeks to answer and thus emerges the definition of testing, which I will use throughout the book.

Revised Definition of Testing

Testing is any activity aimed at evaluating an attribute or capability of a program or system and determining that it meets its required results.

Hetzel 1983

Another definition found in some of the recent literature defines testing as the measurement of software quality. What do we mean by software quality? For many practitioners the term *quality* is as elusive and abstract as is the term *testing*. Note that the elements of quality are not constant. The quality product in one environment may be inferior or unsuitable in another. This seeming contradiction goes away when we define quality to mean "meeting requirements."

A Definition of Quality

Quality means "meets requirements"

This definition establishes that meeting requirements is a criterion of quality that must be included in the guidelines we establish. If requirements are complete and a product meets them, then, by definition, it is a quality product!

The relevant factors affecting quality are broad and diverse. Quality is best viewed as a complex, overall measure of excellence, made up of a large number of distinct factors and considerations.

One broad set of quality factors has to do with function—does the software do what it was intended to do and is it easy for people to relate to and use? Another rather different set of factors relates to how well the software has been built or engineered. This includes considerations such as documentation, structure, efficiency, degree of testing, ease of understanding, and so forth.

Yet another set of factors relates to the area of adaptability—is the system easy to extend or change? Can it adapt to different environments? Can it be used in other applications, and so on?

Testing and Quality

Quality is *not* intangible.
The purpose of testing is to make quality visible.
Testing is the measurement of software quality.

These three sets of factors—functionality, engineering, and adaptability—can be thought of as *dimensions* in the software quality space. Each dimension may be broken down into its component factors and considerations at successively lower levels of detail. Identifying these factors and subfactors leads to an operational definition of quality and provides a basis for measuring whether we have it or not. As an example, the table below illustrates some of the most frequently cited quality considerations.

Typical Software Quality Factors

Functionality (exterior quality)

Correctness

Reliability

Usability

Integrity

Engineering (interior quality)

Efficiency

Testability

Documentation

Structure

Adaptability (future qualities)

Flexibility

Reusability

Maintainability

Good testing provides measures for all relevant factors. The importance of any particular factor varies from application to application. Any system where human lives are at stake must place extreme emphasis on reliability and integrity. In the typical business system usability and maintainability are the key factors, while for a one-time scientific program neither may be significant. Our testing, to be fully effective, must be geared to measuring each relevant factor and thus forcing quality to become tangible and visible.

Software Testing: A Foundation

Any proposed testing methodology must provide a means of answering the following major questions.

1. **What should be tested?**

   Of all the possible attributes that could be measured and test cases that could be tried, how does one select an appropriate subset to use in a given situation?

2. **When should testing start and stop?**

   How soon should work on test design and construction begin? What is a good test? When is a test unsuccessful, and when is it successful?

3. *Who does the testing?*

Who should carry out the testing work, and how should it be coordinated with the rest of the development process?

Conducting a test is basically a simple concept. It consists of selecting something to measure (an attribute or feature of the software); developing controlled inputs or test situations (cases) that exercise or reveal something about the attribute to be measured; simulating or executing the test situations and observing the results in comparison to a standard or an expected behavior. We consider the test to be "successful" if the observed results meet our expectation and to be "unsuccessful" or to have uncovered a deficiency if they do not.

The central issue is selecting what to test. Consider the problem of interviewing a job applicant. How does one select, from the infinite array of possible questions, the set that will provide the most effective judgment (measure) of the individual's skills and capabilities?

This is the sort of task the software tester is faced with. How long should the interview go on? What does it take to reach a satisfactory level of confidence so that a job offer might be made? Who should do the interviewing? A specialist in personnel or the hiring manager, or both in some coordinated way? All these questions have a direct parallel to software testing. The various testing methods I will discuss in Part 2 differ in how they shape or aid finding answers for the what-to-test, when-to-stop, and who-does-the-work questions.

As we will see, selecting the "right" set of test cases and resolving the "right" expected results turn out to be complex and difficult tasks. Efficiently and accurately measuring any complex object is difficult. The measurement of software quality is no exception.

Testing Practices

How do people test software today? For many organizations and practitioners the sad reality is that the answers for what to test and when to stop are not provided by a systematic testing methodology. Ad hoc, individualized approaches are the norm. It is common to find within a single organization a wide range of testing techniques and approaches—especially in the early phases of testing. Testing policies and standards defining how testing work is conducted, what is to be tested, who is responsible, and providing for ongoing tracking of testing effectiveness and cost are rare in our experience—they exist in fewer than one out of every ten organizations.

Most organizations conduct at least three distinct levels of testing work. Individual programs are "unit tested," and then groups of programs are tested together in "system testing." Completed systems are then "acceptance tested." Different individuals or groups may perform these different levels, with acceptance testing usually carried out by the end user or customer. Additional levels of testing are employed in larger, more complex projects.

Three Common Levels of Testing	
Unit Testing	Testing of individual programs as they are written
System Testing	Testing of groups of programs
Acceptance Testing	Testing to verify readiness for implementation or use

Unit Testing

Deciding what to test and when to stop at the unit testing level is most often the programmer's decision. Programmers may approach unit testing from either an external (black-box) perspective with test cases based on the specifications of what the program is supposed to do or on an internal (white-box) perspective with test cases developed to "cover" or exercise the internal logic of the program. Most unit testing is informal—no records are maintained of the tests that are run, defects found, and so forth. The ad hoc approach is completed when the programmer "feels comfortable" with the program and has corrected the deficiencies uncovered without spotting any new ones.

In a few organizations, unit testing is much more formalized. Test plans describing what is to be tested and the expected results may be signed off by both designer and programmer, and specific coverage criteria such as every statement and branch (or some specified percentage) in the program being exercised by the test cases may be required as a standard before testing can be considered complete.

Typical Unit Testing Practices

Objective:	Confirm that module is coded correctly
Who does it:	Usually the programmer
What is tested:	Functions are exercised (black box). Code may be exercised (white box). Extremes and boundaries are explored.
When complete:	Usually when programmer feels comfortable and has no known defects
Tools or aids:	Not commonly employed
Records:	Usually not recorded

System Testing

System level testing begins when modules are brought together. Often a separate testing level, called integration testing, is carried out first to test interfaces and ensure that modules are communicating as expected. Then the system functions are exercised and the software is stressed to uncover its limitations and measure its full capabilities. As a practical matter, most system testing relies on the black-box perspective. Time precludes any significant degree of code logic study as a basis for selecting tests to be run. Some organizations have extended the notions of code coverage in unit testing and require that the extent of testing be measured in terms of the number of routines and functions exercised and that this must meet some standard value before system testing can be considered complete. System testing is much more formalized than unit testing, with records of what gets tested and the results of each test normally maintained. Automated aids are more useful and more commonly used. "Test data generators," which create test data files based on parameter inputs and "comparators" that compare two files and report on the differences, are finding increasing use. Extension of program library systems to accommodate test cases and data is also common.

Typical System Testing Practices

Objective:	Assemble modules into a working system. Determine readiness for acceptance test.
Who does it:	Team leader or test group
What is tested:	System requirements and functions; system interfaces
When complete:	Usually when majority of requirements met, no major defects remaining
Tools or aids:	Library system and test case library. Test data generators, comparators, and simulators
Records:	Defects discovered usually logged; test cases maintained

---

Acceptance Testing

Acceptance testing begins when system testing is complete. Its purpose is to provide the end user or customer with confidence and insurance that the software is ready to be used. Test cases or situations are often a subset of the system test set and usually include typical business transactions or a parallel month of processing. Tests are quite often conducted informally, with little record maintained as to what is tested and what results are obtained.

Typical Acceptance Testing Practices

Objective:	Evaluate readiness for use
Who does it:	End user or his agent
What is tested:	Major functions, documentation, and procedures
When complete:	Usually when user is comfortable or when test set runs successfully
Tools or aids:	Comparators
Records:	Spotty; some highly formalized

The effectiveness of the testing practices outlined above varies greatly. Some organizations have established independent quality assurance and/or test groups and have given these groups authority and responsibility to address testing technique improvements. Some use tools and automated aids extensively. Others are outstanding on certain projects or levels of testing and terrible at others. Almost all report serious concerns with system quality problems that go undetected or are discovered too late in the development cycle. Most feel they need significant improvements in testing techniques and are striving to find ways to become more systematic and effective. How do you stand as a practitioner? Are your own testing methods effective? How does your testing practice compare with others'? The accompanying ten-question self-assessment quiz is designed to provide a quick gauge of your personal testing practices. Take a few minutes to complete this assessment now and find out. You may also wish to check your own assessment against typical practices found in other organizations. Appendix A contains a recent survey of practices reported by organizations attending the 1987 International Software Testing Conference. Compare your responses with those in the survey to obtain a more in-depth perspective of your organization's testing effectiveness.

A Ten-Question Self-Assessment Quiz

Answer the following questions and then score your result.

	Check One		
	Yes	*Sometimes*	*No*
1. A *plan* establishing objectives and the test approach is required.	—	—	—
2. A *log* of what is actually tested and the results obtained is maintained.	—	—	—
3. A *record* of the time spent and resources used during testing is maintained and used to calculate the cost of testing.	—	—	—
4. A *record* of the deficiencies found during testing is maintained and used to estimate the benefits of testing.	—	—	—
5. Testing is conducted as a *systematic* and organized activity according to an established and well-thought-out methodology.	—	—	—
6. Test cases and data are *saved* and maintained for reuse.	—	—	—
7. A record of operational problems is maintained and *used to* *evaluate* and improve testing effectiveness.	—	—	—
8. Test plans' designs and records are *regularly reviewed* and approved by others.	—	—	—
9. Test tools and methods are understood and employed where appropriate.	—	—	—
10. Tests are designed and specified before coding whenever possible.	—	—	—

To score, give yourself 2 points for each yes and 1 point for each sometimes answer. Then *subtract* 1 point for each no answer. Interpret your personal scores as follows:

18 or higher	Don't bother to read this book.
13 to 17	Better than average; testing effectiveness should normally be quite good.
6 to 12	Average practitioner; great improvement possible.
Below 5	Testing effectiveness is seriously deficient.

To obtain some feel for overall organizational performance, give the quiz to each professional and calculate the unit or group averages. Most companies score under 10. When the quiz is administered in companies that emphasize good testing practices and claim to have effective methods installed, the average rises to 14 or 15. Remember, this is only a very quick and crude assessment; for a much more detailed survey assessment turn to Appendix A.

Related Terms and Definitions

As introduced in this chapter, "software testing" has been generally defined to include the full scope of evaluation and verification activities. Many related terms fall under this general umbrella. Some of those with which the reader may be familiar are listed below. While many have no absolute definition, the meaning shown is the one most commonly accepted. Many of the definitions may be found in the IEEE Standard Glossary of Software Engineering Terminology. For purposes of this book all of the following are part of the software testing discipline.

Verification—Evaluation performed at the end of a phase with the objective of ensuring that the requirements established during the previous phase have been met. (More generally, verification refers to the overall software evaluation activity, including reviewing, inspecting, testing, checking, and auditing.)

Quality assurance—A planned and systematic pattern of all actions necessary to provide confidence that the item or product conforms to established requirements.

Test and evaluation—As employed in the DOD, T & E is the overall activity of independent evaluation "conducted throughout the system acquisition process to assess and reduce acquisition risks and to estimate the operational effectiveness and suitability of the system being developed."

Validation—The process of evaluating software at the end of the development process to ensure compliance with requirements.

Independent V&V—Verification and validation of a software product by an independent organization (other than the designer).

Inspection—A formal evaluation technique involving detailed examination by a person or group other than the author to detect faults and problems.

Walkthrough—A review process in which a designer leads one or more others through a segment of design or code he or she has written.

Performance evaluation—The assessment of a system or component to determine how effectively operating objectives have been achieved.

Interface testing—Testing conducted to ensure that the program or system components pass information and control correctly.

Formal testing—Process of conducting testing activities and reporting test results in accordance with an approved test plan.

Software audit—An independent review for the purpose of assessing compliance with requirements, specifications, standards, procedures, codes, contractual and licensing requirements, and so forth.

Acceptance testing—Formal testing conducted to determine whether or not a system satisfies its acceptance criteria and to enable the customer to determine whether or not to accept the system.

Desk checking—The manual simulation of program execution or flow to detect errors and defects.

Operational testing—Testing by the end user on software in its normal operating environment (DOD).

Integration testing—An orderly progression of testing in which software and/or hardware elements are combined and tested until the entire system has been integrated.

System testing—Process of testing an integrated system to verify that it meets specified requirements.

Regression testing—Selective testing to verify that modifications have not caused unintended adverse side effects or to verify that a modified system still meets requirements.

Functional testing—Process of testing to verify that the functions of a system are present as specified.

Note the closeness in definition between verification, quality assurance, test and evaluation, and testing as we have defined it in the book. As parts of the overall testing discipline all of the above are treated later in the book in more detail.

Several other terms that are central to any treatment of software testing follow. These terms are elaborated on in later chapters.

Test plan—A document prescribing the approach to be taken for intended testing activities.

Test case—A specific set of test data along with expected results for a particular test objective, such as to exercise a program feature or to verify compliance with a specific requirement.

Test data—Input data and file conditions associated with a particular test case.

Expected results—Predicted output data and file conditions associated with a particular test case.

Test Validity—The degree to which a test accomplishes its specified goal.

Test Log—A chronological record of all relevant details of a testing activity.

Test Procedure—A document defining the steps required to carry out part of a test plan or execute a set of test cases.

Test Design—A selection and specification of a set of test cases to meet the test objectives or coverage criteria.

Software quality—The totality of features and characteristics of a software product that bears on its ability to satisfy given needs.

Software error—Human action that results in software that contains a fault that, if encountered, may cause a failure.

Correctness—The extent to which software is free from errors.

Software failure—A departure of system operation from specified requirements due to a software error.

Requirement—A condition or capability needed by a user to solve a problem or achieve an objective.

Specification—A statement of a set of requirements to be satisfied by a product.

System reliability—Probability that a system will perform a required task or mission for a specified time in a specified environment.

Software reliability—Probability that software will not cause the failure of a system for a specified time under specified conditions.

SUMMARY

1. Testing is *any* activity whose aim is the measurement and evaluation of software attributes or capabilities.

2. Testing is an information-gathering activity.

3. Testing is the measurement of software quality.

4. Reviews, inspections, and walk-throughs are important "tests" of the early phases of software development.

5. The central concerns for any testing method are what to test, when to stop, and who does the work.

6. Most software testing done today is ad hoc and poorly systematized.

7. The purposes of testing are to:
    *   Gain confidence that systems may be used with acceptable risk.
    *   Provide information that prevents errors from being made.
    *   Provide information that helps detect errors earlier than they might have been found.
    *   Discover errors and system deficiencies.
    *   Discover what system capabilities are.
    *   Provide information on the quality of software products.

Chapter 2

Principles of Testing

The Meaning of Principles

There has been sufficient experience in software testing to establish a few basic principles about its characteristics. Such principles help us to better understand what testing is all about and serve to provide a foundation for the methods and techniques to be discussed in Parts 2 and 3.

A principle, as used here, means an accepted or professed truth that embodies some insight about the testing discipline. This chapter presents six such principles; each is important for the practitioner and manager to understand.

Testing Principle 1—Complete Testing Is Not Possible

Many programmers seem to believe that they can and do test their programs "thoroughly." When asking about testing practices, I frequently hear expressions such as the following: "I'll stop testing when I am sure it works"; "We'll implement the system as soon as all the errors are corrected." Such expressions assume that testing can be "finished," that one can be certain that all defects are removed, or that one can become totally confident of success. This is an incorrect view. We cannot hope to achieve complete testing, and, as we shall see, the reasons are both practical limitations and theoretical impossibility.

19

Consider an almost trivial program segment to look up names in a table and print out the first entry, named "BILL." Pseudocode logic for such a segment is shown in the Sample Program Segment.

Sample Program Segment

Turn searching indicator on
Do WHILE entries in the table AND searching indicator ON.
If name = "BILL" THEN print the name and turn searching indicator OFF.
END
IF searching indicator ON THEN print message that no name "BILL" was found.

How might we test such a program "completely"? Do we test just the two situations of a table with the name BILL in it and one without? Do we test different-sized tables? Does it matter to test *where* in the table the BILL entry is placed? Does it matter what other names we use for the rest of the table? All of these are variables that could conceivably affect the proper functioning of the program and thus could *conceivably* be tested as additional cases.

Consider again the analogy of testing a student's skill in multiplication. While there are an unending number of possible multiplication problems that might be presented (my son feels he gets just such an unending number on his homework!) the practical limit of time leads the teacher to select a very small subset. From all the possible pairs of numbers, the teacher assigns ten or twenty that are "representative" and hopes they cover the different cases fairly thoroughly. Such a test is not "total" or "complete," but it is able to "measure" the student's knowledge with some reasonable confidence. We don't test more broadly because we gain very little additional measurement of ability by adding more and more problems, and at some point the time to take and grade the tests becomes limiting. In other words, what stops us is not that we conduct *all* of the tests, but rather that we find it increasingly ineffective to continue testing.

The software tester is in the identical situation. The total number of possible tests in even the simplest of situations (such as our name search) is essentially infinite. Practically speaking, it is *impossible* to try all the cases. Instead the tester must select a very small subset of the possibilities involved. The subset must be big enough to provide a reasonable measure or gauge of the performance (that is, it must provide a satisfactory level of confidence), but not so big that it becomes impractical to administer the tests and ceases to provide a significantly enhanced measurement.

Some Practical Limits to Testing

In any form of testing it is impossible to achieve total confidence. The only exhaustive testing there is is so much testing that the tester is exhausted!

Several people have demonstrated that if our objective was to "prove" a program free of defects, then testing is not only practically, but also theoretically, impossible. The proof for this will not be discussed here. Interested readers are directed to several of Manna's papers (see Bibliography) that establish the following axioms:

Some Theoretical Limits to Testing

"We can never be sure the specifications are correct."
"No testing system can identify every correct program."
"We can never be certain that a testing system is correct."

Manna 1978

These theoretical limits tell us that there will *never* be a way to be sure we have a perfect understanding of what a program is supposed to do (the expected or required results) and that *any* testing system we might construct will always have some possibility of failing. In short, we cannot achieve 100 percent confidence no matter how much time and energy we put into it!

Testing Principle 2—Testing Work Is Creative and Difficult

Anyone who has had much experience in testing work knows that testing a piece of software is not simple. Despite this we perpetuate several myths that have caused a great deal of harm.

False Beliefs about Testing

- Testing is easy.
- Anyone can do testing.
- No training or prior experience is required.

While most managers don't openly profess to believe these myths, their actions signify otherwise. Users are frequently assigned major testing responsibilities without being given any training in how to perform such work. Programmers, analysts, and project leaders have volumes of standards detailing how development is carried out, but they are left to their own resources for testing. It seems to be implicitly assumed that testing is dirty work, that people don't enjoy it, and that senior-level personnel need not get involved. In a broad sense testing suffers from the same maligned reputation as documentation and maintenance work.

Frankly, it is difficult for me to understand this viewpoint. I present the following argument:

Why Testing Is Not Simple

- To test effectively you must thoroughly understand a system.
- Systems are neither simple nor simple to understand.
- Therefore, testing is not simple.

One can't begin to design and develop an effective test until one has a detailed understanding of what a system is supposed to do. Managers routinely assign their most senior business analysts to answer such questions and have no trouble recognizing that it is difficult to understand complex systems and their interactions within the enterprise, yet they fail to appreciate that testers must have this knowledge as a *prerequisite*! Consider again our classroom student analogy. Asking untrained and inexperienced people to test software might be similar to asking parents to test their own children on what they have learned in school. The parent who is removed from the details of the subject and has only a sketchy understanding is totally ill equipped to measure student skill or grasp of material. Most of us would consider it laughable for anyone other than a teacher or a professional tester to undertake such an assessment. The software tester who is unable to fully appreciate what a system is trying to do is in just as laughable a situation, but, sadly, many of us fail to recognize it.

Testing is difficult. It is difficult because it requires a great deal of insight and knowledge as well as experience to perform effectively. I believe that all of the following are essential to success in testing work:

Essential Ingredients to Good Software Testing

- Creativity and insight are important.
- Business knowledge is important.
- Testing experience is important.
- Testing methodology is important.

This book covers the testing methodologies and provides some perspective toward understanding what our collective experience has taught us. Basic creativity and insight probably cannot be taught, and application or business knowledge must be learned on the job or as a broader element of overall career development. The need for all four points is what makes software testing so difficult. Far from *anyone* being able to do testing, it is rare to find all the ingredients in any single individual!

Testing Principle 3—An Important Reason for Testing is to Prevent Deficiencies from Occurring

Most practitioners do not appreciate the significance of testing in terms of preventing defects instead of just discovering them. As mentioned, the traditional view of testing was as an after-the-fact activity that happened after all coding was completed. Gradually, during the last fifteen years, a very different attitude has emerged: we now look at testing not as a phase or step *in* the development cycle, but as a continuous activity *over* the entire development cycle.

The Testing Life Cycle Concept

- Testing is not a phase.
- There are testing deliverables associated with *every* phase of development.

The reasons behind this changing perspective are not mysterious. Testing when all coding is complete may be likened to the teacher who gives only a final exam. No opportunity is provided along the way to "signal" to the student that he or she is in trouble, and serious misunderstandings about the subject matter may easily develop or go undetected until it is too late to do anything but fail the student. We implicitly understand that frequent tests throughout the semester help the students and prevent serious problems from developing. At a minimum, attention can be given to problems earlier with increased ease and likelihood of correction. The situation in testing software is exactly analogous. We desire frequent tests throughout the development cycle in order to obtain early recognition (or measurement) of any quality deficiencies that might be present. This permits the correction to be made inexpensively and prevents more serious problems from arising later on.

The best testing gives rapid feedback. As we complete a segment of work we want to be able to test it as soon as possible. Many have observed that the "process" of *thinking* out what we are going to test helps us to avoid certain errors or realize that deficiencies exist.

Some believe that the best possible thing we can do to prevent defects is establish the testing first! By establishing what we do to convince ourselves that something is working properly, we increase our understanding and insight about what we are working on. As Beizer puts it:

"The act of designing tests is one of the most effective error prevention mechanisms known ... The thought process that must take place to create useful tests can discover and eliminate problems at every stage of development."

Beizer 1983

My experience has firmly convinced me that to truly understand something you must know how to test it, and vice versa. (More on this in Part Two.) Students who "design" or think out the final exam they would use if they were the teacher often report a major benefit in terms of subject comprehension and aid in preparation for an actual exam. This reinforces the principle that testing plays a most important role in preventing errors or, at the very least, discovering them much earlier. One day we may well consider that the highest goal in testing is not finding defects, but avoiding them.

Testing Principle 4—Testing Is Risk-Based

How much testing would you be willing to perform if the risk of failure or missing a defect were negligible? Alternately, how much testing would you be willing to perform if a single defect could cost you your life's savings, or, even more significantly, your life?

Reflecting on such questions emphasizes that good testing is inherently risk-based. The amount of testing we should (and are willing to) perform depends directly on the risk involved. Programs or systems with high risk require more test cases and more test emphasis. Programs with low risk or limited impact of failure do not warrant the same concern.

Understanding the risk-based nature of testing is the key to dealing with the chronic problem of inadequate testing resources. As Principle 1 asserts, we are not able to "completely" test anything. Risk must be used as the basis for allocating the test time that is available and for helping us to make the selection of what to test and where to place our emphasis.

Testing Principle 5—Testing Must Be Planned

Testing Principle 5 is one everyone agrees with. The problem is that most of us do not discipline ourselves to act on it. We know that good testing requires thinking out an overall approach, designing tests and establishing expected results for each of the test cases we choose. Since we can't test everything (Principle 1 tells us we are limited to only a very small sample out of the total possibilities), we must make a selection, and the planning and care we expend on that selection accounts for much of the difference between good and poor testers.

A document that defines the overall testing objectives and the testing approach is called a *test plan*. A document or statement that defines what we have selected to be tested and describes the results expected is called a *test design*. Test plans and designs can be developed for any level of testing—requirements and designs, programs, subsystems, and complete systems.

Test Plans vs. Test Designs

Plans	*Designs*
A statement of the testing objectives	A specification for tests to be developed
A description of the test approach	A description of the test set
A set of tasks for accomplishing the testing objectives	

Plans and designs may be formal or informal. A "formal" plan is one that is written down and made available as a permanent project document. An "informal" plan is one that exists only in someone's head or as temporary notes that are not intended to be reviewed or saved. Test plans may be organized as integrated documents covering the entire testing activity or be broken down hierarchically into a series of related documents. The IEEE Standard for Test Documentation (discussed in Chapter 12) takes the latter approach. The standard emphasizes the difference between test planning and test design and stresses that test cases and procedures should be recorded in a document separate from the test plan. As used in this book, test planning refers to both the overall activity and the detailed test case design and specification.

Planning for testing (whether formally or informally) is necessary. One has *not* tested something if one has simply run a few inputs through it. The purpose of testing is to *measure* the software quality. Ad hoc or haphazard testing does not provide sufficient information to give reasonable measurements. Such testing may even be harmful in leading us to a false sense of security. It takes careful planning to select a good set of tests. The what-to-test and when-to-stop questions must be answered, and that involves examining the cost (in terms of expense to test) versus the confidence that can be gained. We know we have to be selective in deciding what to test and when to stop. Certain groups of tests are "better" than others, and by planning carefully and submitting the plan and design to others for review and critique (testing the test plan) we are much more likely to develop a systematic quality measurement.

What Makes Certain Tests the "Right" Ones?

The confidence they provide versus the cost they incur.
The likelihood of discovering problems and defects.

A second major benefit of test plans (particularly formal ones) is that they impose the discipline of working out "expected results" before test cases are run. Teachers who carefully prepare "expected answers" for the questions they are considering produce better exams and measure their students more effectively. Expected results in the test plan provide independent judgments of what systems are supposed to do and help us to spot many errors—often without even running the test.

Planning can help every practitioner to become a better tester. The implication is not that a lot of time must be invested in planning—just that some time be set aside to focus on what has to be tested and to write that down on paper. If it is not committed to paper then no one else can see it and help review it, and the opportunity for a permanent record (even for yourself) is lost.

Testing Principle 6—Testing Requires Independence

When you want an "unbiased" measurement you need an unbiased person to do the measuring. In our Testing Managers Workshops my colleagues and I conduct a test-planning exercise. Groups work intensively for several days to develop a master test plan for a selected scenario. Group proposals are then presented, reviewed, and evaluated competitively by each class participant. In every case the highest ratings for any given group have come from the group members themselves! Having participated in developing an approach, we gain so much "ownership" of it that it is impossible to view it fairly against competing approaches. This is just one example of many that could be cited in support of the principle that testing must be done independently if it is to be fully effective in measuring software quality.

There are many means of achieving independence. Some organizations have established independent testing or quality control units that report outside of the software development function. Other projects are provided with a "verification and validation" contractor who oversees the entire effort and is charged with independently verifying system quality. Other approaches can achieve the same goal without requiring different people or added organizational structure. Team approaches and periodic reviews throughout a project serve the same end. The requirement is that an independence of *spirit* be achieved, not necessarily that a separate individual or group do the testing.

What Is an "Independent" Tester?

- an unbiased observer
- a person whose goal is measuring the software quality accurately.

The need for independence is what makes the question of who does testing work so interesting. Principle 2 emphasizes the importance and need for fully understanding any system and principle 6 states the need for independence; the dilemma is that they are often contradictory. The person with the most understanding of the system may be the least independent. I will deal further with this dilemma and the resolution of who should best do testing work in Parts Two and Three.

SUMMARY

Six key testing principles:

1. Complete testing is not possible.
2. Testing is creative and difficult.
3. An important reason for testing is to prevent errors.
4. Testing is risk-based.
5. Testing must be planned.
6. Testing requires independence.

Key influences on testing performance:

1. Individual creativity and insight
2. Application knowledge and understanding
3. Testing experience
4. Testing methodology
5. Effort and resources

Designing tests discovers and prevents defects.

Chapter 3

Methodology

The Evolution of Testing Methodologies

Gradually, over the past several decades, our industry has established a basic process for developing software that has achieved broad consensus and acceptance. A *methodology* means having a set of steps or tasks, and most organizations have provided standards for software development that define a *life cycle model* and specify the steps or methodology required to carry it out.

The idea of *phases* is central to all of the software methodologies. The overall development activity is subdivided into distinct major phases, each with its own key end products, or *deliverables*. Particular phases may vary from organization to organization, but all embody the same basic steps of *analysis, design, implementation* and *maintenance* as the software passes from an idea or request in someone's mind to an operational system, to eventual replacement by some new system.

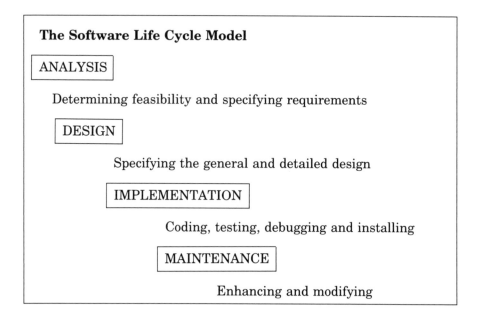

The Software Life Cycle Model

ANALYSIS

Determining feasibility and specifying requirements

DESIGN

Specifying the general and detailed design

IMPLEMENTATION

Coding, testing, debugging and installing

MAINTENANCE

Enhancing and modifying

Having an effective software methodology in place means that detailed steps are defined for each of the development phases. The steps for testing should be a component of the overall software methodology. However, in practice, testing has been poorly described and has been rapidly evolving to the point that most organizations' testing procedures are out of date and ineffective.

The early view of testing saw it as a phase of development *after* coding. Systems were designed, constructed, and *then* tested and debugged. As testing practices have matured, we've gradually come to recognize that the proper viewpoint is one that emphasizes a complete *testing life cycle* embedded within the overall software life cycle.

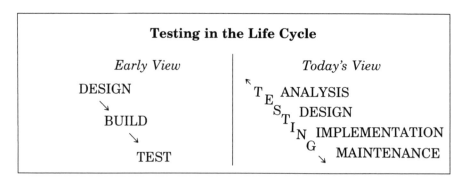

Testing in the Life Cycle

Early View	*Today's View*
DESIGN	T E ANALYSIS
BUILD	S T DESIGN
TEST	I N IMPLEMENTATION
	G MAINTENANCE

In today's view, testing is an activity to be performed in *parallel* with the software effort and one that consists of its own phases of analysis (planning and setting test objectives and test requirements); design (specifying the tests to be developed); implementation (constructing or acquiring the test procedures and cases); execution (running and rerunning the tests); and maintenance (saving and updating the tests as the software changes). This life cycle perspective of testing represents a dramatic change from just a few years ago, when almost everyone equated testing with execution. The activities of planning, designing, and constructing tests were not recognized, and testing wasn't seen as *starting* until you started running tests. Indeed, this is still the perspective of many managers and practitioners I talk with. I ask if they have started testing yet, and they assume I mean have they started executing!

The evolution of testing methodologies is brought into focus by contrasting it with the evolution of our thinking about software methodology. Thirty years ago, anyone involved with software had the job title of programmer and all the emphasis was on coding. It is not that good programmers did not perform analysis and design, but rather that those early phases were not recognized; the *real* work was not thought of as starting until code was laid down. Gradually, analysis and design were given more and more emphasis and emerged as distinct phases within the software life cycle. We concluded that it was a good idea to require that the analysis be completed and reviewed before the design activity was initiated, and that the design be completed and reviewed before coding was begun. Eventually, this process grew to become the software life cycle model we introduced earlier.

With testing, we have seen the same evolution in thinking occurring 15 to 20 years later. Initially, testing equated to just execution. Again, this did not mean that good testers did not emphasize test analysis and design, but simply that the activities were not recognized as phases with their own deliverables. Now, we recognize that we have to build or acquire tests before we can run them and that careful planning and analyzing of the test objectives and requirements must be done before it makes sense to design and build tests. What has emerged is the life cycle model for testing that looks very similar to the methodology we've grown accustomed to for software. Considering that a test set is made up of "data" and "procedures" (which are often implemented as executable test programs), it should not surprise us that what it takes to build good software is also what it takes to build good test sets!

An Example of a Testing Methodology

To illustrate one testing methodology that has gained broad acceptance within industry, I will describe STEP, *Systematic Test and Evaluation Process*, which is a proprietary methodology developed by Software Quality Engineering.

STEP provides a model process and a *step-by-step* sequence of activities and tasks for performing software testing at any level from unit testing through acceptance testing. The methodology grew from and is built upon the foundation provided by the American National Standards Institute (ANSI) testing standards (see Chapter 12). The key features of STEP are highlighted in the next few pages. STEP breaks down the testing process into three major phases: Planning, Acquisition, and Measurement.

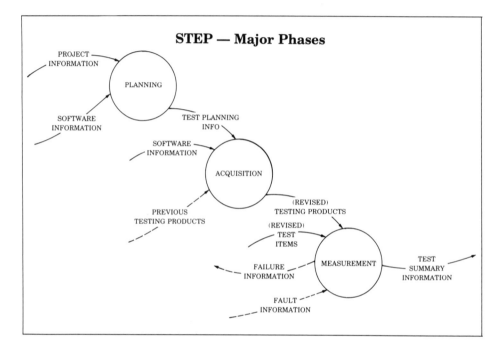

STEP — Major Phases

In Planning, information about the software to be tested and the project is used to develop testing objectives and an overall testing approach. The output of the phase is a *test plan* that serves to guide the remainder of the testing activity and coordinate the test levels. In Acquisition, more information about the software (requirements and design), along with previous testing product documentation and data, is used to specify and develop a *test configuration* for each level of testing performed. The output of this phase is the test set and its documentation. Finally, in Measurement, the test set is executed. The input to this phase is the software to be tested, and the output is *test reports* documenting the execution and measurement activity along with records of any failures or incidents observed.

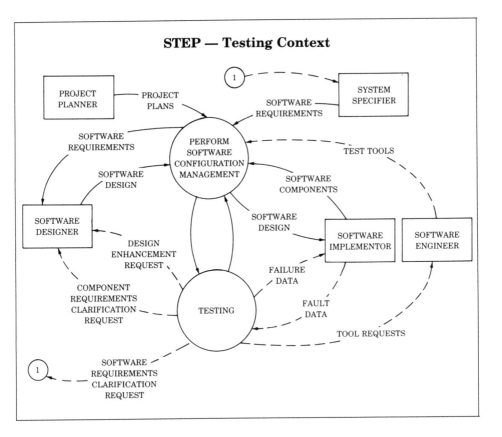

STEP — Testing Context

This diagram displays STEP's view of software testing within the context of overall project activity. The key interface is to the activity of *Configuration Management* (CM). All information needed for software testing (software requirements, software designs, code, etc.) is taken from CM. Other project activities, such as Project Planning, Requirements Specification, Software Design, and System Implementation submit information and work products to CM as work and deliverables are completed. The testing activity then has access to the software work products and can develop testing work products (test plans, test specifications, test cases, test procedures, test reports, etc.) that are, in turn, placed into CM and updated or revised as necessary.

The methodology does not imply that testing is organizationally separate from software development or engineering. In very small projects or at low testing levels (module or unit testing), all of the functions in Figure 2 (Planning, Specification, Design, Implementation, Tool Support, Configuration Management, and Testing) are likely to be performed by the same person or organizational unit. As project size and risk increases and as the testing level gets

higher, these functions tend to be separated and assigned to different organizational units.

The following data flow diagrams show the subdivisions of the three testing
phases into the following eight activities:

Major Testing Activities in STEP

PLANNING

1. PLAN the general approach
2. DETERMINE testing objectives
3. REFINE the general plan

ACQUISITION

4. DESIGN the tests
5. IMPLEMENT the tests

MEASUREMENT

6. EXECUTE the tests
7. CHECK termination
8. EVALUATE results

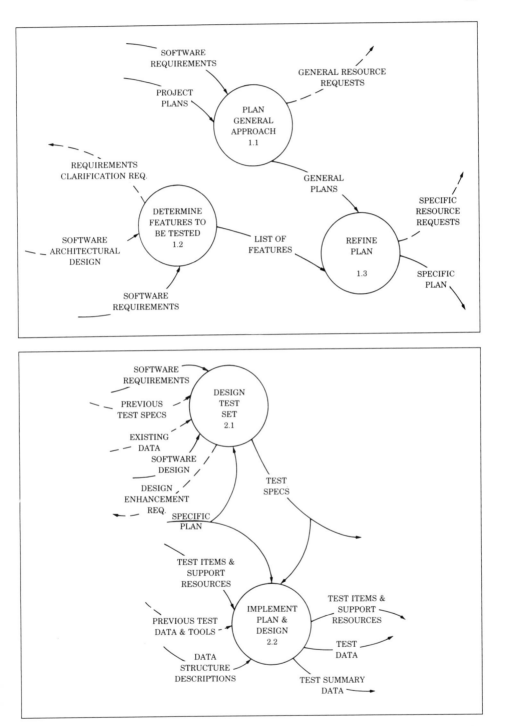

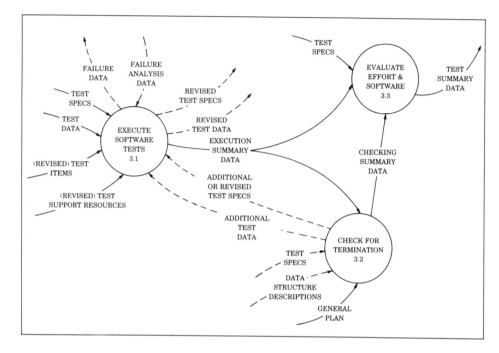

Each of the eight activities is further subdivided into detailed steps or tasks to be performed to complete the activity. The next diagram gives an example of the steps defined in the methodology for Activity 6—test set execution.

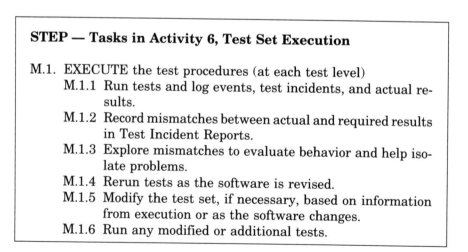

STEP — Tasks in Activity 6, Test Set Execution

M.1. EXECUTE the test procedures (at each test level)

M.1.1 Run tests and log events, test incidents, and actual results.

M.1.2 Record mismatches between actual and required results in Test Incident Reports.

M.1.3 Explore mismatches to evaluate behavior and help isolate problems.

M.1.4 Rerun tests as the software is revised.

M.1.5 Modify the test set, if necessary, based on information from execution or as the software changes.

M.1.6 Run any modified or additional tests.

Similar steps and additional detail for each of the steps are provided for the other seven activities in the methodology.

The STEP methodology also specifies *when* the testing activities and steps are to be performed and is linked to the ANSI Test Documentation Standard in specifying templates and outlines for the documents that are produced during the process. The relationship between the testing activities in STEP and the testing documents is shown below. The recommended timing is illustrated in the following diagrams.

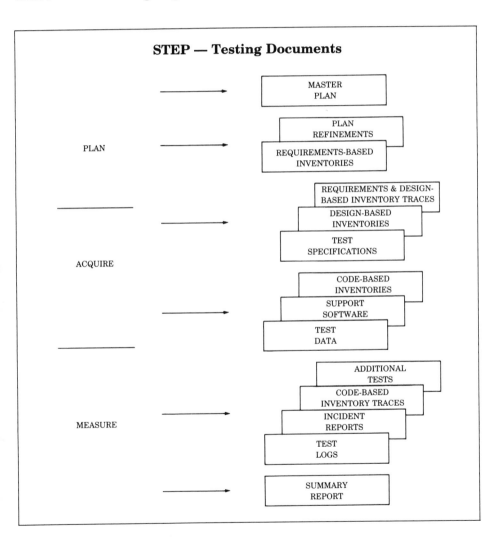

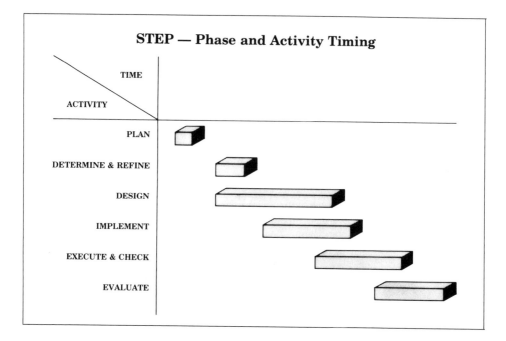

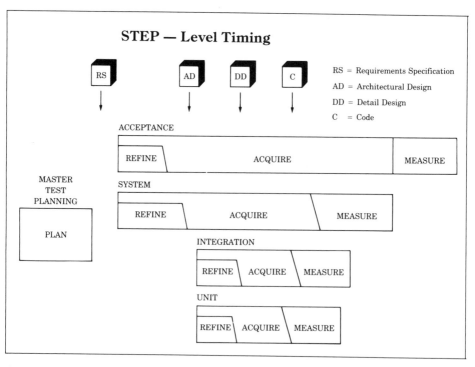

The timing emphasis is on getting most of the test design and specification work completed *before* the software is designed and coded. The starting trigger to begin the test design work is an external, or black box, specification for the software component to be tested. For the Acceptance and System test levels, the external specification is equivalent to the System Requirements document. As soon as that document is available, work can (and should) begin on the design and acquisition of the requirements-based tests (those tests that are developed from requirements). The test design process continues as the software is being designed and additional design-based tests (those tests that are developed from the software design) are identified and added to the requirements tests. As the design process proceeds, detailed design documents are produced for the various software components and modules comprising the system. These, in turn, serve as external black-box specifications for the component or module, and thus may be used to trigger the development of requirements-based tests at the component or module level. As the software project moves into the coding phase, a third increment of tests may be designed based on the code and implementation details. Thus, the methodology calls for designing tests at all levels in three separate increments—presenting requirements-based tests first, then supplementing those with tests based on the software design, and finally adding those based on the detailed code logic and data structures as implemented. Test set design and acquisition at the various levels is *overlapped*. Rather than sequentially developing the unit test set and then moving on to the system and higher level test sets, the two are developed at the same time. The reasons for all this emphasis on timing is to exploit the fact that testing work (done at the right time) will identify and prevent errors and defects in software requirements and designs. By forcing the bulk of the test design work to be completed before the software is designed and coded, we ensure that the requirements are "testable" and well thought out, and thus reveal many errors and defects.

The timing for the measurement phase follows the traditional practices we are used to. Unit testing is done first, then modules are integrated and components are tested, and, finally, the system is integrated and we can perform system and acceptance level testing. The sequential testing of small pieces to big pieces is a physical constraint that we must follow. The new contribution of the methodology is recognizing that the acquisition phase is *not* so constrained and that it is, in fact, in our interest to reverse the order and build the high-level test sets first—even though we get to use them last! The timing *within* a given test level (Figure 9) corresponds to our experience with software development. Plans and objectives come first, then test design, then test implementation, and, finally, we can execute and evaluate. Some overlap of each of the activities is reasonable as long as one is used to drive the other. For example, test design must serve to guide the test implementation.

Testing Methodology Revisited

In the preceding section, we described STEP as an example of one of the testing methodologies now in place in a number of organizations. Testing methodologies have matured and achieved proven success. It is no longer the case that we have to practice the *art* of testing and approach the activity from an ad hoc, disorganized, and uncontrolled perspective. Testing can be systematic, and appropriate models such as STEP are available. The purpose of this book is to help an organization to establish such a systematic approach and augment it with the tools and techniques needed to assure success.

SUMMARY

1. A *Methodology* is a set of steps or tasks for achieving an activity or end.
2. Software Methodologies emerged with the development of the phased life cycle model, consisting of analysis, design, implementation, and maintenance.
3. *Testing Methodology* should be a *part* of the software methodology.
4. The effective testing methodology recognizes testing as having its own testing life cycle, consisting of *planning* (analysis and objective setting); *acquisition* (design and implementation of the tests), and *measurement* (execution and evaluation).
5. Testing methodology must consider both *what* (the steps) and *when* (the timing).
6. Design of tests is best performed in three increments:
   • Requirements-based—from the external specification
   • Design-based—from the software design
   • Code-based—from the coded logic and data structures
7. Requirements-based and design-based test case design should be performed *before* software coding.
8. Testing is no longer an art.
9. STEP is one example of a proven methodology that works in practice.

Part 2

Testing Methods and Tools

Foreword: The Testing Life Cycle

The concept of a testing methodology that defines the steps and tasks to test a software system was introduced and illustrated in the last chapter. The methodology consists of procedures to follow for each major phase of work. The procedures specify what should take place during each phase of the work and spell out individual subphases and tasks in considerable detail. The intent is to bring discipline to the manner in which the testing is carried out and to ensure that required steps are completed in an appropriate sequence.

It is necessary to have a testing methodology that is closely integrated with the development process and that brings discipline to the manner in which the what-to-test, when-to-stop, and who-does-the-work questions are answered. Testing requirements at each step of development have to be defined and, in effect, a "testing life cycle" has to exist side by side with the development life cycle.

Integrating Testing within the Life Cycle

Project Initiation

Develop broad test strategy.
Establish the overall test approach and effort.

Requirements

Establish the testing requirements.
Assign testing responsibilities.
Design preliminary test procedures and requirements-based tests.
Test and validate the requirements.

Design

Prepare preliminary system test plan and design specification.
Complete acceptance test plan and design specification.
Complete design-based tests.
Test and validate the design.

Development

Complete the system test plan.
Finalize test procedures and any code-based tests.
Complete module or unit test designs.
Test the programs.
Integrate and test subsystems.
Conduct the system test.

Implementation

Conduct the acceptance test.
Test changes and fixes.
Evaluate testing effectiveness.

Part Two is organized to help an organization enhance its current testing methodology and establish an effective testing life cycle. Successive chapters discuss testing techniques that might be adopted or utilized throughout the life cycle. The reader will find the chapters useful in two ways. The broader use is in support of establishing overall testing policies and standards and extending the existing development methodology. Individual chapters may be read more narrowly to brush up on selected techniques just prior to their use—much as a reference manual might be employed. Reviews as a key testing tool throughout the life cycle are discussed in Chapter 4; techniques for testing requirements are in Chapter 5; Chapter 6 addresses the testing of designs; Chapter 7, the testing of programs or testing in the small; Chapter 8, systems testing or testing in the large; Chapter 9, the testing of software changes; and, finally, Chapter 10, the testing of software packages.

Chapter 4

Testing through Reviews

Evolution of Reviews

One crucial element in any testing life cycle is reviews. What is a review? Reviews of software began evolving as a management control tool. During any project, management requires a means of assessing and measuring progress. Are we ahead of or behind where we expected to be? Will we complete the work as planned? Such questions need to be answered reliably, and the so-called progress review evolved as the means of doing it. The manager designated various points along the life cycle and "reviewed" the status of the project at those times.

The results of these early reviews proved to be bitter experiences for many project managers who had to learn the hard way how long a project could remain at 90 percent complete! "True" progress could not be measured by counting tasks completed *unless* there was a reliable way of gauging the *quality* of the work performed and knowing that it would not have to be redone or changed later. Thus we saw the emergence of "technical reviews" to examine the quality of technical work and serve as input into progress reviews. We now see many different types of reviews throughout the development life cycle. Virtually any work produced during development can be and is reviewed. This includes requirements documents, designs, code logic, test plans, test documentation, and so forth.

What Is a Review?

A review is any of a variety of activities involving

- Evaluations of technical matter
- Performance by a group of people working together

The objective of any review is to obtain reliable information, usually as to status and/or work quality.

There are many *different* types of reviews:

• Requirements	• Procedural	• Test design
• Specifications	• Documentation	• Test procedures
• Design	• Conversion	• Test plan
• Coding	• Installation	
	• Postimplementation	

Reviews as a Testing Technique

Most practitioners consider reviews and testing as completely different things, arising from the old view of testing as a follow-on activity that involved executing test cases. When testing is thought to be the measurement of software quality, it is clear that reviews are a general class of testing methods. In the university a graduate student can expect to undergo thesis reviews as his or her research program is formulated. Such reviews are conducted to ensure that the completed dissertation will meet requirements. They "test" interim work, which passes and fails as in more traditional examinations. Our treatment of software reviews should be similar. Reviews are the *only* testing technique available in the early phases of development work, and it is essential that we view them as tests and make sure that they are effective. This means planning carefully what we will test (review), what it will take to pass (the expected results and when to stop), and who will do the work (responsibilities).

Reviews may be formal or informal. We call a review formal if the participants feel responsible for accurate evaluations and produce a written report of their findings to management. That is quite different from more informal reviews, which involve the sharing of opinions between practitioners. It is the formal review that is designed to provide reliable information about technical matters and may be considered a testing technique.

Formal Reviews

- The product is a written report of findings
- Participants take responsibility for results
- A testing technique

The Review Plan

The first step toward achieving an effective testing life cycle is to select a series of formal review checkpoints. The reviews may be placed anywhere along the development cycle. They are generally conducted as each major work result is produced and serve as completion checkpoints. The number of reviews needed and their placement in the life cycle may vary considerably, depending on the size and nature of the software project.

Some important potential review times are listed with their purpose or expected result. I find that the conduct of virtually all these reviews is important to effectively test even modest-sized software efforts.

Some Important Review Checkpoints

Review	*Typical Purpose or Expected Result*
System Requirements	Understand what the system is intended to do.
Software Requirements	Approve the requirements specification and initiate preliminary design.
Master Test Plan	Approve overall test strategy and approach.
Preliminary Design	Establish a preliminary design baseline; concur in the basic design approach for the software and the tests.
Critical Design	Approve detailed design; authorize start of coding and test implementation.
Module Reviews	Approve unit completion and release of module to formal testing.
System Test	Concur in completion of system testing and authorize start of acceptance testing.
Acceptance Test	Accept the product; approve operational implementation.

For each formal review that is established a plan is needed to structure the review and provide answers to the what-is-to-be-tested, when-to-stop, and who-does-the-work questions. At a minimum the review plan should specify:

- Who is to attend
- Information required before the review may begin
- Preconditions that must be completed before the review is conducted
- Checklists or other indications of what will be covered
- End conditions or criteria that must be met for the review to be completed
- Records and documentation to be kept.

This plan should also assign responsibility for preparing and training review participants, for scheduling and organizing the review, and for reporting results.

A hypothetical review plan follows. This is an outline plan for a review conducted at the completion of the preliminary design phase of a project. This review tests the quality of the basic design and ensures that the project is ready to proceed into detailed design work.

A Sample Review Plan for a Preliminary Design Review

Expected results

1. Approval of the basic design approach/alternative selected. (Criterion: signatures on design alternatives approval sheet.)
2. Acceptance of a preliminary design specification as the design baseline.
   (Criterion: Checklist scores above 75.)
3. Agreed-upon acceptance criteria for the critical design review. (Criterion: signatures on design test plan.)

Process

1. Input
   - Prereview packet containing participant checklists C1 to C4 and review procedures
   - Review orientation session one week prior to start
   - Prereview study of proposed preliminary design specification and list of rejected design alternatives

2. Process
   - Presentation and overview of functional specifications
   - Discussion of design alternatives considered
   - Review and approval of basic alternative selected
   - Presentation of preliminary design specification
   - Completion and scoring of review checklists C1 to C4
   - Presentation of design test plan
   - Preparation of review findings and report
3. Output
   - Decision endorsing design alternative selected
   - Formal review report including individual checklist scores
   - Approval of preliminary design specification and design test plan

Responsibility

Organizing, conducting, and reporting on this review is the responsibility of the testing manager.

Review attendees

Testing manager	Systems manager (not involved in the project)
Design architect	Two customer representatives
Lead designer	

Checklists such as those referred to in the sample plan are finding increasing use in formal reviews. Checklists ensure that a carefully selected set of questions is covered during a review.

Checklists as Tools to Aid Reviews

- Provide structure for the review
- Vehicles for recording results (individually and overall)
- A means of guiding the review activity
- Vehicles for learning from the past
- Ensure systematic and comprehensive coverage
- Tools for quantifying and measuring results

Checklists are available commercially from a number of organizations. Some of the best checklists are developed simply by collecting lists of problems that occur in various projects and adding new questions as new concerns or problems arise. Using such self-renewing checklists over a period of several years quickly improves them and ensures that the organization "learns" from its past mistakes.

Effectiveness of Reviews

How effective are reviews? The effectiveness of any testing technique depends on a comparison of the confidence obtained or defects discovered or prevented versus the cost of the test. There has been enough experience with reviews to gauge this trade-off. Those organizations that have had formal design reviews and code logic reviews (often called walk-throughs or inspections) for several years uniformly speak highly of their benefits and impact. Some of the benefits observed include the following.

What Do Reviews Accomplish?

- Reviews provide the primary mechanism for reliably evaluating progress.
- Reviews bring individual capabilities to light.
- Reviews discover batches and classes of errors at once.
- Reviews give early feedback and prevent more serious problems from arising.
- Reviews train and educate the participants and have a significant positive effect on staff competence.

Reviews are the only effective means of testing the early phases of software development. Installing a good review program is not easy. While it is easy to start conducting reviews, it is quite another matter to develop them into effective tests that are supported enthusiastically by the staff. As with any testing program, an investment of time is required. I advise budgeting from 4 percent to 8 percent of the total cost of a project for review work. Various rules of thumb exist to gauge how fast technical matter can be reviewed. Werner Frank, the president of Informatics, suggests from two to six hours per thousand lines of eventual code for design reviews and five to fifteen hours per thousand lines for code logic reviews. This is in line with what Myers, Fagen, and others have reported. However, taking such rules too literally is dangerous and can destroy the review. My view with any test is that the objectives and reasons for the test should be carefully set down and that those objectives should then dictate the time and resources required. Plans, objectives, and expected results must be the driving force behind testing work, not an artificial standard or the amount of time or money that happens to be available.

I have observed (and participated in) many bad reviews. Many practitioners harbor prejudiced views about the value of reviews because they too have been involved in many bad reviews and may never have experienced good ones. When a review turns sour, one or more of the following critical factors is almost certainly lacking.

Critical Success Factors for Reviews

Expected Results	Know the purpose of the review. What is to be tested or measured?
Responsibilities	Clearly assign responsibilities of all participants.
Individual Rights	Protect the opinions and feelings of individuals, not a committee
Attendees	The right people—some outsiders and some insiders
Structured Process	Established procedures
Moderator	Skilled and trained
Records	Written report and evaluation

Of these seven factors, the first three are the most frequently violated. What is expected from the review and the responsibilities of *all* participants must be spelled out clearly. It is important to preserve individual opinions. Perhaps the worst way to achieve accurate technical information is to "vote" and decide on the basis of the majority view. As mentioned earlier, it is the job of the review plan to deal with these factors and organize the review properly.

The Use of Metrics to Quantify Reviews

Reviews are becoming more quantitative. Scored checklists that are completed by each reviewer and then discussed and evaluated in a group setting are just one example of the trend toward more quantitative evaluation. This is part of a general movement toward the use of metrics in software quality evaluation and measurement.

The metric technique consists of selecting certain measures that are believed to be predictive of an aspect of system quality. The metric is then computed during development and used to test or measure the quality aspect of interest. In the next several chapters I will discuss a number of practical examples involving different kinds of metrics. Metrics offer a means of quantifying review results, and they are sure to gain increasing use in formal reviews at every stage of development.

Reviews of Testing Products

The emphasis so far has been on employing effective reviews to measure the quality of the software development deliverables—software requirements, design modules, etc. Equally important to the tester is the review of the testing deliverables and work products produced by the testing process. Good candidates for test reviews include the test plans, test objectives and coverage inventories, test design specifications, test procedure specifications, test procedures, test sets, and test reports.

Test Products That May Be Reviewed

Test Plan (Master and Each Level)	Test Cases
Test Design Specifications	Test Reports
Test Procedure	Inventories
Specifications	
Test Procedures	

Any work product produced can be the subject of a review. The principles of effective reviews discussed earlier in the chapter all apply as before, and, as might be expected, test reviews can be as effective or as ineffective as the software reviews.

Additional reviews need not be added to the life cycle in order to implement a test product review program. What is generally more effective is to include the test reviews within the existing project reviews. One such arrangement that I have found to work well is illustrated on the next page.

Integrating Test Reviews and Software Reviews	
Existing Review	*Test Products Included in the Review*
Requirements	Master Test Plan Acceptance Test Specifications
Design	System Test Specifications Integration Test Specifications Updated Master Test Plan
Detailed Design	Module or Program Test Specifications
Code	Program Tests and Test Procedures
Implementation	Test Result and Summary Reports

The Master Test Plan and high-level Acceptance Test Specifications should be included and reviewed as part of the Requirements Phase Review. The System and Integration Test Specifications should be reviewed along with the software design. Module or Program Test Specifications should be reviewed at the same time as the detailed design for a module (this permits the tests to be used as walk-through cases). The Unit Test Set should be reviewed along with the module code, or pseudocode, and, finally, the Test Reports and Results may be reviewed along with an overall implementation readiness or post-implementation review.

Combining test and software reviews gives emphasis to the importance of testing and measuring the quality of the test products without adding any significant burden or complexity to the overall life cycle process. Much more can be said about how to conduct good reviews. For the interested reader and those in organizations seriously committed to establishing a review program. I recommend Freedman and Weinberg's review handbook.[1] This complete volume on reviews covers the subject in depth.

---

1. Daniel Freedman and Gerald Weinberg, *Walkthroughs, Inspections, and Technical Reviews,* 3d ed. (Boston: Little, Brown, 1977).

SUMMARY

1. The definition and structuring of a testing life cycle that parallels the development life cycle is central to any testing methodology.

2. There are testing deliverables and activities within *every* phase of software development.

3. Reviews are a primary testing method—particularly during the early stages of development.

4. Reviews serve to measure the quality of interim work.

5. Formal reviews require participants to assume responsibility and produce a written report of findings.

6. The success of a review depends on a good review plan.

7. The review plan provides structure for the review, establishing objectives and results and assigning responsibilities.

8. Reviews may cost up to 10 percent of total project cost and still be an effective cost versus confidence trade-off.

9. Reviews are more important for preventing future errors than they are in discovering current defects.

10. Reviews are becoming more quantitative, with checklists and other metrics finding increasing use.

11. The most critical success factors for reviews are to clearly define the expected results, clearly establish reviewer responsibilities, and preserve individual opinions and evaluations.

12. Test products, like any other products in the software life cycle, can and should be subject to regular reviews.

Chapter 5

Testing Requirements

Requirements Testing Objectives

Requirements documents have historically been the most poorly "tested" work products in the development cycle. Only recently has the concept of testing such work products become accepted. Testing such documents involves answering two basic questions:

1. Are any requirements missing?
   - Have all needed functions been addressed?
   - Is required performance specified?
   - Is the software quality specified?
   - Is the software fully defined?
2. Can any of the requirements be simplified or eliminated?
   - Should requirements be combined?
   - Are any requirements overly restrictive?
   - Are any requirements redundant or contradictory?

Answering these two questions effectively depends almost completely on the formal review as the basic methodology. General techniques for achieving effective reviews were discussed in the previous chapter and apply to the testing of any phase. In this chapter we consider particular techniques for requirements reviews. It is essential that the phase be reviewed critically. The highest cost/confidence trade-offs derive from testing requirements thoroughly.

Testing Requirements through an Understanding of What to Test

Obtaining a statement of the requirements for a software project that is as simplified and unrestrictive as possible and yet covers the desired needs has proved to be exceptionally difficult. It is basically a task of "problem definition." As testers we have to determine whether or not the problem statement in this phase has been properly formulated.

How do we test for correct problem definition? Paradoxically, the answer is by looking at the back end and coming up with what we would test to determine that a proposed solution actually solved the problem. There is a profound advantage to understanding what we are trying to do by discovering how we can convince ourselves that we did it!

To unwind this puzzling twist of words, consider the following example. Your mother tells you that she has a requirement for you to "eat three well-balanced, nutritious meals a day." To understand and test the requirement we look at some possible tests mother might use to determine (test for) whether we are fulfilling it.

Three Possible Tests for Well-Balanced Meals

1. Adding up everything we consumed, did we meet minimum nutritional guidelines in terms of calories, proteins, vitamins, and so forth?
2. Did we eat exactly three meals?
3. Were the meals "well-balanced" in the sense that each weighed the same amount?

Test numbers 2 or 3 probably look silly because most of us would agree that mother wouldn't care whether we ate twice or four times or that each meal weighed the same, as long as we got the nutritional content our bodies require.

Notice that attention to how a requirement will be tested helps focus on the real meaning of the requirement itself and enables us to formulate it more clearly. A much better statement of mother's requirement would be simply that we met or exceeded minimal nutritional guidelines (as specified by an authority or reference) each day. Stating it in this manner makes implicit how it can be tested, and all fuzziness and confusion is removed.

Experience in our workshops and with our clients has demonstrated convincingly that to achieve a good statement of requirements you must specify the test for accepting a solution along with the statement of the requirement. When the statement and the test are listed together most problems associated with misunderstanding requirements disappear. Just such misunderstandings create most of the errors and problems within software systems.

Testing Requirements through Requirements-Based Test Case Design

Recognizing that requirements become clearer and that faults within them are recognized more readily when we understand how to test them has led to the practice of designing some test cases at requirements time. Such cases are called *Requirements Based* as they are derived solely from the external specification or requirements for the software. Since information about the software design and data structures is not available, the requirements-based tests designs may be incompletely specified. However, the purpose is to derive requirements-based test situations and use them as a test of requirement understanding and validation.

As examples, consider the following:

Example 1: Dealing with Incompleteness

When requirements are found to be incomplete, the tester can use a test case to focus the missing information and get it clarified. For example, if the behavior or response to some input is not specified, a test case can be designed with that input and the question asked, "What should the system do in this case?" Such directed questions using specific instances and cases are much more effective than general comments that the requirements are incomplete.

Example 2: Dealing with Imprecision

Similarly, when requirements are fuzzy or imprecise, a test case may be constructed and the question asked, "Is this the result I should have in this situation?" The specific instance will focus attention on the imprecise answer or result and ensure that it is examined carefully.

The STEP testing methodology described in Chapter 3 stresses completion of requirements-based test design *before* software design and coding is started.

This is based on the conviction that taking the time and effort to develop a thorough test from the requirements pays for itself many times over through improved and more validated requirements before the software design and coding activity begins.

The Requirements Validation Matrix

One effective means of organizing all the requirements and ensuring that tests are specified for each of them is through a Requirements Validation Matrix, which is a matrix of requirements versus test cases. A portion of a sample validation matrix is illustrated below.

Organizing Requirements Tests with a Requirements Validation Matrix

Requirement	Test Cases	Status
1. Provide the capability to submit a sales order for a single item.	87, 88, 102	√ √ √
2. Provide the capability to submit sales order with multiple items and multiple quantities.	81–88, 102	√ √ √
3. Generate an automatic back order for ordered items not in stock.		
4. Generate an automatic customer credit verification for a new customer.	87, 88, 103–106	√

The matrix lists each requirement and refers to the test cases or situations that have been created to test it. The test case numbers might refer to an on-line data set where the test is fully described or may simply refer back to a folder or folio number. The sample matrix tells us that test cases 87, 88, and 102 must be successfully completed in order to fulfill the testing for requirement 1. Note that test cases 87 and 88 are also used for requirements 2 and 4. Contrary to what we might first suspect, we seldom end up with unique test cases for each individual requirement. It usually takes several test cases to test a requirement effectively, and reusing some of those test cases to test other requirements is common. The absence of any test case numbers in the matrix for requirement 3 signifies that suitable tests have not yet been developed or agreed upon.

Benefits of Using a Requirements Validation Matrix

- Ensures that requirements are listed
- Identifies the tests associated with each requirement
- Facilitates review of requirements and the tests
- Provides an easy mechanism to track status of test case design and review progress
- Is easily made a part of the master test plan and can be updated throughout the project to give a record of all requirements testing

---

The use of a Requirements Validation Matrix provides a number of important benefits. The most valuable benefit arises from the discipline of forcing test cases to be designed for each selected requirement and then subjecting both the requirement and the tests to a series of formal reviews (tests). The status columns may be used to indicate the review progress. The use of these columns may easily be adapted to a particular organization or project needs. The first column might indicate that the specification team had completed review, the second that a user management team had, and the third that the test case specification was complete and ready to be used. The Requirements Review Plan would specify how the matrix is to be used and who is responsible for completing it.

Testing Requirements through Prototypes or Models

A second important strategy for testing requirements (determining whether any requirements are missing or whether the needs can be simplified) is through the use of prototypes or test "models." The technique consists simply of building a model or prototype system not with the *intent* to use it, but to test and confirm the understanding of the true requirements.

The Benefits of Models

- A picture is worth a thousand sentences,
- An example is worth a thousand pictures!

Test models are especially useful when so little is understood about the requirements that it is necessary to gain some "experience" with a working model. Such models recognize that requirements change with experience and that one of the best ways to test for proper understanding of true requirements is to use a system (or at least as much of a skeleton as may practically be provided for test purposes).

The popular practice of incremental development is an extension of the prototype concept. Incremental development simply means that the process of establishing requirements and designing, building, and testing a system is done in pieces or parts. Rather than attempting to solve a "total" problem, one selects a part of the problem and designs, builds, and *implements* a system to address it. Then, based on the experience with that subpart, one selects another part of the problem, and so on. The advantage is that requirements for later increments do not have to be specified prematurely and can be adjusted on the basis of working experience.

Some practical experience with incremental development suggests that it is best not to specify too many increments in advance. Most organizations try to define (or at least foresee) all of the increments in the initial organization of the effort. They quickly discover how much those later increments *change* as a result of changing requirements. The most dramatic changes are when the client or customer says, "I like what I have now and do not want any additional increments!" Here the testing of requirements achieved as a result of a working prototype (or stage of incremental development) has been so effective that all additional requirements are dropped and no longer seem to be necessary. As Gerry Weinberg has pointed out, not every organization is quick to recognize such a situation as positive. Project managers may feel that they have "failed" when further work is canceled. Only later might they realize that the "ability to decide when to stop is a feature, not a failure!"

Other Requirements Testing Techniques

Testing for missing requirements is aided by any effort to organize or "structure" the existing list of requirements. Indexing and organizing by function, or by affected data element or system output so that related requirements are grouped together, is always useful, especially as a preparatory step to a formal review. Checklists can also be extremely useful as reminders of commonly overlooked requirement areas or previous omissions. When requirements are grouped together they can be analyzed in a *block* for simplicity, redundancy, and consistency. With a look at the entire group, one can make an effort to formulate simpler or higher-level requirements that specify the same needs more effectively, and the unnecessary requirements can simply be dropped out.

Automated tools and support aids for requirements testing are not well developed and currently offer little benefit. Experimentation is taking place with specification and requirements definition "languages." Such languages provide a vehicle for stating requirements in a quasi-structured English and permit some forms of automated analysis. Most of the benefit arises from the discipline imposed in organizing the specification and then listing the test explicitly with each specification. As emphasized earlier, insisting on testability greatly improves the ability to understand and validate the requirements. Other automated aids include indexing programs to group related requirements, paragraph analyzers to flag confusing and overly complex sentences, and decision-table or cause-and-effect graph analyzers.

Anything that helps to make requirements more "testable" improves our ability to simplify or eliminate unnecessary requirements. Specifying requirements in the form of decision tables or as cause-and-effect graphs is an example. The use of a table to show possible conditions and specify intended actions provides an implicit test to determine success. Thus requirements provided in the form of a decision table (or as an equivalent cause-and-effect graph) are inherently testable and can usually be validated quite easily.

There is clearly no simple formula for testing requirements well. Good reviews are the essential ingredients. All the automated aids play only a minor role in actual requirements testing practice.

SUMMARY

1. Two basic questions have to be answered to test requirements properly:
   - Are any requirements missing?
   - Can any of the requirements be simplified or eliminated?
2. The primary means of testing requirements is the formal review.
3. Knowing how to test a requirement is a prerequisite to being able to validate (or test) the true need for and proper formulation of the requirement; *or*, test requirements by analyzing how to test them.

   Techniques useful in requirements testing include
   - Requirements validation matrix
   - Test models or prototypes
   - Incremental development
   - Decision tables and cause-and-effect graphs
   - Requirements grouping and analysis
4. Completing the requirements-based test design as a part of the requirements phase is the best method for ensuring the requirements are testable and understood.
5. Automated tools have little importance in requirements testing

Chapter 6

Testing Designs

Design Testing Objectives

The task of design is to find a solution that fulfills the stated requirements. There are usually many alternative and competing designs that meet the majority of the requirements. Our goal is to find the "best" such design—best in the sense that it is easier to build and use than the other alternatives and less prone to errors and failures. As in the testing of requirements, we have to answer two basic questions.

1. *Is the solution the right choice?*
   - Can the design be achieved more simply?
   - Is this the best alternative approach?
   - Is this the easiest way to do the job?
2. *Does the solution fulfill the requirements?*
   - Are all requirements addressed by the design?
   - Will the design work?
   - What are the sources and risks of failure?

Once again the predominant method of testing (particularly in the earlier stages of design) is the formal review. To test the design phase effectively, design reviews must be planned and conducted throughout the phase. The reviews must determine not only whether the design will work, but also whether the alternative selected is a good (or in some sense the best) choice available.

Design Testing through Alternative Analysis

The design process inherently involves alternatives. The first (and often the most important) testing that must take place is to confirm that the approach the designer has selected is the "right" alternative.

Many alternative "eating" regimens will meet Mother's requirement of a specified nutritional intake each day (see Chapter 4). Some of the possible designs might be:

1. Preplanned menus for every meal.

2. Eat anything you feel like, then, at the end of the day, see what (if anything) was missed and take care of it.

3. Eat one meal programmed to provide the nutritional requirements each day, and others as you wish.

4. Take vitamins and protein packs, then eat anything else desired.

All these plans provide for fulfilling the specified daily nutritional requirement. Some are "better" than others in terms of cost of food; others are better in terms of convenience or ease of implementation; still others are better in terms of overall health and effect on the body. Testing one proposed alternative is best achieved through comparison with the others. If one holds up a single alternative the only question that can be answered is whether it is feasible. To determine if it is the "best" choice, you must identify other choices and compare them critically to the preferred proposal.

In the computer software setting such alternative analysis is rarely performed. Design reviews, when they are held, concentrate on the will-it-work question, and designers quickly become locked in on particular approaches. Alternatives have to be reviewed *early* in the design process when it is still practical to change horses and pursue a different course. This implies the need for a high-level design review only a week or two after design work is initiated. Planning for such a review should concentrate on alternatives and ways of evaluating and comparing them.

Designers must describe the alternatives they considered but rejected and outline the reasons they believe a given approach is superior. My preference is to hold such a review in two parts. First, the reviewers listen to the design alternatives considered by the designer and go over various advantages and disadvantages of each. Then the session is adjourned and each reviewer is asked to come up with at least one alternative that has not yet been considered. At the second meeting of the review team, these forced alternatives are evaluated and the entire design decision is again considered. Another technique is the competitive design concept, which will be discussed in the next section.

There is no question that early and critical testing of the software design provides a high payoff. Correcting for the wrong approach cannot be done later without starting over. This is simply a case of either getting it right at the beginning or living with the consequences (or perhaps failing because of the consequences!). No other formal review point is so basic as the high-level design review, and thorough testing at this time is absolutely essential.

Forcing Alternative Analysis through Competitive Designs

An outstanding technique for testing high-level design and ensuring that alternative approaches are thoroughly reviewed is "competitive designs." Instead of being assigned to a single designer or design team, the basic task is competitively "awarded" as the result of preliminary analysis work performed by a number of individuals or teams in parallel.

One case study is particularly illuminating. The project involved the redesign of a Human Resources Inventory System in order to make it more competitive in the software marketplace and add a number of features. The requirements document was fairly straightforward, as most of the functional requirements were derived from the previous system. (New requirements involved the use of on-line displays and the new features.) After reviewing the requirements and completing a fairly careful statement describing them, the company selected four potential designers and asked each one to complete a preliminary design proposal. The designers were understood to be "competing" against each other. They were given two weeks to complete their proposals, at which time there was to be an extensive review of all alternatives and a "winning" design approach selected. The selected designer would then earn the opportunity to complete the design for the project and be awarded a special $10,000 bonus.

The review process involved a half day being alloted to each designer for presentation and discussion. Each approach was evaluated independently seven times. Four of these evaluations came from the participating designers assessing each other's work, and the three other reviews were provided by user management, EDP management, and an outside consultant. Before the presentations started each reviewer was provided with a design outline and concept paper for each of the four competing designs. Presentations were limited to two hours, with the remainder of the half day available for questions and discussion. The alternatives were ranked in terms of overall superiority, ease of implementation, functional capability, performance, and reliability. Designers were asked to provide quantitative estimates for such things as projected number of programs, lines of codes, months to develop, total cost to develop, and total cost to operate. These were also ranked and evaluated during the review.

The results were dramatic. As might be expected, each of the designers worked virtually nonstop during the two-week competitive period. Many went far beyond a high-level proposal in an effort to be as thorough in their presentations as possible. The proposed designs varied greatly, with differences as great as a factor of five on virtually every quantified measure—projected costs, lines of code, and so forth. One competing design had eighty-two projected programs and an estimated thirty-five months of effort to complete, compared with fourteen programs and six months in another! Major differences in risk, performance, function, and reliability were also evident.

Some are undoubtedly highly skeptical of the concept of competitive design testing. Managers tell me that with the pressures they are already under, there is no way they could afford to do high-level design four times; they barely have the resources and money to do it once! The competitive test cited cost, *at most*, six extra weeks of effort plus the two days spent on the review. It saved two years of effort because a better and simpler design alternative was selected, and the designers were alerted to pitfalls and mistakes that they were able to correct before the detailed design and programming started. Which strategy is the more productive?

Design Testing through Test Models

Many critical aspects of design are suitable to testing with test models or analytical simulations. The basic technique consists of building a simplified representation or model of a selected design property and then using the model to explore (or test) the underlying design. The model permits testing to take place early in the design, *before* programming has started, and ensures that the design is sound (at least with respect to the aspect tested).

Such models are used extensively to test data base design configurations, transaction sequences, response times, and user interfaces. Response time testing may be the most common and offers a good illustration. Many early system designs failed simply because the response time they eventually delivered was too slow and could not be improved sufficiently through system tuning. This created a need to test response time early in the design, and vendors responded with test models that permitted entering basic information concerning the nature of the data bases and the accesses that each transaction required. Then, under the assumption that the limiting factor was I/O time, the model could "calculate" projected response times for the different transactions under various hypothetical data base structures. Such testing permitted the design to be improved or modified early on, if necessary, and engendered confidence that the response time requirements would be achieved.

Design Testing through Design-Based Test Case Design

In the last chapter, we emphasized requirements-based test case design as the primary technique for helping to validate requirements and to recognize faults within them. In the same manner, software design errors and faults may be discovered and software designs validated by emphasizing early design-based test case design. Such cases are called *design-based*, as the information for deriving them is taken from the software design documentation.

Design-based test cases focus on the data and process paths within the software structures. Internal interfaces, complex paths or processes, worst-case scenarios, design risks and weak areas, etc. are all explored by constructing specialized test cases and analyzing how the design should handle them and whether it deals with them properly. Requirements-based and design-based test cases provide specific examples that can be used in design reviews or walkthroughs. Together they provide a comprehensive and rich resource for design testing.

Design Testing Metrics

Increasingly, formal design reviews are adopting metrics as a means of quantifying test results and clearly defining expected results.

The metrics (measures that are presumed to predict an aspect of software quality) vary greatly. Some are developed from scored questionnaires or checklists. For example, one group of questions may relate to design integrity and system security. Typical questions might be items such as the following:

Sample Integrity Questions

1. Are security features controlled from independent modules?
2. Is an audit trail of accesses maintained for review or investigation?
3. Are passwords and access keywords blanked out?
4. Does it require changes in multiple programs to defeat the access security?

Each reviewer would answer these questions, and their answers would be graded or scored. Over time, minimum scores are established and used as pass/fail criteria for the integrity metric. Designs that score below the minimum are reworked and subjected to additional review testing before being accepted.

Another example of a metric-based design test that I have seen used effectively is a test for system maintainability. An important consideration in evaluating the quality of any proposed design is the ease with which it can be maintained or changed once the system becomes operational. Maintainability is largely a function of design. Problems or deficiencies that produce poor maintainability must be discovered during design reviews; it is usually too late to do anything to correct them further along in the cycle.

To test the maintainability we develop a list of likely or plausible requirements changes (perhaps in conjunction with the requirements review). Essentially, we want to describe *in advance* what about the system we perceive is most apt to be changed in the future. During the design review a sample of these likely changes is selected at random and the system alterations that would be required are walked through by the reviewers to establish estimates for how many programs and files or data elements would be affected and the number of program statements that would have to be added and changed. Metric values for these estimates are again set on the basis of past experience. Passing the test might require that 80 percent of the changes be accomplished by changes to single programs and that the average predicted effort for a change be less than one man-week. Designs that score below these criteria based on the simulated changes are returned, reworked, and resubjected to the maintainability test before being accepted. This is just one example of an entire class of metrics that can be built around what-if questions and used to test any quality attribute of interest while the system is still being designed.

Design for Testing

In addition to the testing activities we perform to review and test the design, another important consideration is the features in the design that simplify or support testing. Part of good engineering is building something in a way that simplifies the task of verifying that it is built properly. Hardware engineers routinely provide test points or probes to permit electronic circuits to be tested at intermediate stages. In the same way, complex software must be designed with "windows" or hooks to permit the testers to "see" how it operates and verify correct behavior.

Providing such windows and reviewing designs to ensure their testability is part of the overall goal of designing for testability. With complex designs, testing is simply not effective unless the software has been designed for testing. Testers must consider how they are going to test the system and what they will require early enough in the design process so that the test requirements can be met.

Design Testing Tools and Aids

Automated tools and aids to support design testing play an important role in a number of organizations. As in requirements testing, our major testing technique is the formal review; however there is a greater opportunity to use automated aids in support of design reviews.

Software tools in common use include design simulators (such as the data base and response time simulators mentioned earlier in this chapter); system charters that diagram or represent system logic; consistency checkers that analyze decision tables representing design logic and determine if they are complete and consistent; and data base dictionaries and analyzers that record data element definitions and analyze each usage of data and report on where it is used and whether the routine inputs, uses, modifies, or outputs the data element.

None of these tools performs direct testing. Instead, they serve to organize and index information about the system being designed so that it may be reviewed more thoroughly and effectively. In the case of the simulators, they permit simplified models to be represented and experimentation to take place, which may be especially helpful in answering the question of whether the design solution is the right choice. All the tools assist in determining that the design is complete and will fulfill the stated requirements.

SUMMARY

1. Two major questions that design testing must answer are:
   - Is the solution the right choice?
   - Is the solution complete and does it fulfill the requirements?
2. Both of these questions must be answered in formal reviews of the design work.
3. Determining whether a design is the right choice inherently involves examining alternatives.
4. Methods to bring out alternatives and validate design include
   - Simulations and models
   - Competitive designs
   - Requirements and design-based test cases
5. Quantifying design testing is achieved with various metrics:
   - Scored checklists and questionnaires
   - What-if questions to measure quality attributes
6. Complex systems must be designed to facilitate testing and be provided with test windows or self-testing checks.
7. Tools are useful to organize design testing information. They include simulators, system charters, and data base dictionaries and analyzers.

Chapter 7

Testing Programs—Testing in the Small

Introduction to Testing in the Small

Program logic may be built in levels, starting with pseudocode or structured English and expanding as more detailed code is added; it may be prepared at a terminal using an on-line programming support tool; or it may simply be worked out on a coding sheet. Regardless of the manner in which the logic is developed, our task as testers is to measure the quality of coding and ensure that the program has been completed properly. The definition of *program* is not to be taken literally. What we are concerned with is testing logical pieces or units of work that arise naturally. These may be functions, subroutines, or just logically distinct parts of individual programs. The task is to test these logical units independently, that is, "in the small." Later, we combine this logic with other units that have also been tested in the small and test "in the large." Common names for testing in the small are program testing, module testing, and unit testing. Common names for testing in the large are systems testing, component testing, functional testing, performance testing, and acceptance testing. Methods and techniques for testing in the large are the subject of Chapter 8.

Testing in the Small versus Testing in the Large

Testing individual units of logic as they are coded is called *testing in the small*.

Testing groups of modules or units of work that have been assembled to form components or systems is called *testing in the large*.

Testing in the small is something with which every programmer (and every programming student) has had some experience. All of us perform at least some testing of our code logic before we are ready to say that we have finished coding. As emphasized in Part 1, the approach to this testing varies greatly by individual, by project, and by organization. Some programmers test very formally, that is, they prepare a plan or design for the situations to be examined and carefully carry out those tests. Others test highly informally, almost as a natural extension of the code-writing process. Programmers who use on-line environments are particularly prone to blend all three activities of logic development (writing the code), debugging (removing errors), and testing (measuring the quality and correctness). They may log onto the terminal, enter a few lines of code, and then execute the code, using some simple data. If that works they proceed to add a few more lines of code. If it doesn't, they change it and execute it again. After several hours they have a complete program and may feel confident that it is correct without any further testing. In effect, the testing was performed in the very small as the logic was developed.

The work environment and development methodology also greatly influence testing practices. Organizations may require logic walk-throughs and code inspections at various stages of logic development. Independent testing of modules and units or quality reviews and audits may be specified. Designers may be required to prepare and specify tests to be conducted or to sign off test results. Test cases may already be available (from prior versions of the program or in a bank of prepared test situations). Time pressures and other work demands may alter testing priorities and force testing plans and strategies to change. All these factors combine to shape the manner in which testing in the small is conducted.

Testing in the Small—Key Objectives

Objectives for testing in the small may be stated as two basic questions that must be answered:

1. Does the logic work properly?
   * Does the code do what was intended?
   * Can the program fail?

2. Is all the necessary logic present?
   - Are any functions missing?
   - Does the module do everything specified?

These two questions drive all of the program testing activity that we conduct. Somehow the programmer must establish (gain confidence) that the logic works properly and does not contain errors or lurking problems. In addition, we must establish that all the logic is present (nothing omitted or left out).

The primary means of answering such questions is by designing a set of tests that may be walked through the logic and then developed and executed. To return to the student testing analogy, it is similar to testing a student's knowledge of multiplication and division through a series of actual exercises, each of which has a correct answer (expected result). When the student does enough problems correctly, we infer that his method of solving the problems (his or her logic) is correct.

Improving Testing in the Small through Motivation and Planning

The first requisite for testing a program effectively is that the programmer must be motivated to *want* to test it. That is, he or she must really want to discover the program's true quality. Testing Principle 6 states that testing must be independent to be effective. Any programmer who tests his or her own work is clearly not independent. Yet, in practice, the large majority of program testing is carried out by the programmer. We might like to assign program testing to a person who didn't write the program (and we will see situations where that is appropriate); however, it is usually impractical. For the extra benefit in terms of confidence and deficiencies discovered, it costs too much in either time or dollars or both. Thus we need ways to help the programmer achieve independence and overcome the natural tendency to avoid careful testing of his or her own work.

I believe that the *best* such mechanism is to require Unit Testing Designs to be completed and maintained as permanent project records. I have already emphasized planning as one key to good testing. Asking programmers to *document* what they will do to test a program ensures that some time is taken from the coding effort and devoted to test planning. This orients the programmer to the testing task and helps greatly to motivate a thorough and systematic test. The test design becomes a document that others (such as the designers or users) may review and helps to organize the testing in the small to ensure that planned testing is actually completed. We will look at a sample later in this chapter.

Gaining the proper testing orientation is mostly a matter of self-discipline. The programmer must take off the builder's hat that has been striving to get the job done and put on the masochistic hat that will tear the software apart and find anything that might possibly be wrong with it. This can't be achieved by sitting at an on-line terminal. The selection of the tests to exercise and the amount of testing required must be planned carefully and without distraction. It does not require a long time (especially in relation to the total effort for code writing and debugging), but it must be *dedicated* time. Once the test design is completed, the programmer must maintain discipline and force himself or herself to carry out all of the testing that he or she earlier decided was necessary. The temptation (when testing is going well) is to drop some of the tests and decide they are not necessary after all.

In my experience, the simple step of asking programmers to supply unit test designs for each program they write does more to improve unit testing than the adoption of any particular testing method or technique. While the techniques are important, the motivation and testing orientation brought on by planning the tests is far more important!

Types of Test Cases

It is helpful to classify potential test cases into several categories. One important classification is based on the origin of the test data. Major types within this classification include *requirements-based cases* (those derived from the specifications or understanding of what the program is supposed to do); *design-based cases* (those derived from the logical system structure); *code-based cases* (those derived from the program logic or the data elements and files used in the program); *randomized cases* (those derived from a randomizing or sampling technique, such as those produced by parameter-driven test data generators); *extracted cases* (those taken from other systems or from live files); and *abnormal* or *extreme cases* (those selected in a deliberate effort to break the system including such items as boundary conditions, limits, and worst-case thinking).

A Classification of Test Cases Based on Source

Type	*Source*
Requirements Based	Specifications
Design Based	Logical System
Code Based	Data Structures and Code
Randomized	Random Generator
Extracted	Existing files or test cases
Extreme	Limits and boundary conditions

Each of these types of test cases is used in both testing in the small and testing in the large. Preparing the unit test design involves deciding which sources of test data are most appropriate and preparing a testing "strategy." In some situations extensive test data are already available, and extracted cases may be the easiest and most effective testing strategy. Most testing in the small involves a blend of all the types of test cases. Requirements and design-based cases play a particularly dominant role, and we will look at methods and techniques for systematically deriving appropriate sets of such cases in the next few sections of this chapter.

Selecting Requirements-Based Test Cases

The most direct source of test cases is the functional or external specification of what the program is supposed to do. The specification defines how the program should behave from an external or macro viewpoint, usually by defining the inputs and outputs and itemizing or enumerating the functions that are performed. This external view naturally suggests various cases to use in testing the program. If the specification says that the program prints three reports, then we should come up with test cases to produce all three. If the specification defines a dozen transactions, then we should test each transaction, and so forth.

Obtaining a good set of requirements-based cases for a program requires planning and systematic coverage of the natural cases. Consider the following specification for an airline reservation inquiry transaction to determine available flights.

Specification for Airline Inquiry

Input	*Processing*	*Output*
Transaction identifying departure and destination cities and travel date	Check flight tables for desired city	Flight display
		or message 1
	If no flight to that city print message 1 No flight	or message 2
Tables of flight information showing flights available and seats remaining		
	If a flight but no seats print message 2 Sold out	
	If a flight with seats display it	

Listed below is a typical transaction (input and output). The input specifies that information on all available flights from Orlando to Altanta is to be displayed for June 14. The output shows the four possible flights and displays the current seat availability.

Airline Inquiry Transaction Examples

Input

ORD   ATL   06   14   Specifies a date of June 14
                           (current year implied)

                           Indicates ATLANTA is
                           destination city

                           Indicates ORLANDO is
                           departure city

Output Display

	FLIGHT			SEATS	
Airline	*Flt. #*	*DEP*	*ARR*	*Coach*	*First*
EA	108	0810	0940	6	9
DE	218	0930	1130	0	2
DE	315	1415	1515	SOLD OUT	
TWA	172	1600	1710	21	13

Natural functional tests for this program include the following major cases:

Major Functional Tests

Case	*Expected Result*
1. Flight available (flight is in the table to the desired city and has open seats)	Display line
2. No flight (city is not in the table)	Message 1 (No flight)
3. No seats (flight is in the table but has no seats)	Message 2 (Sold out)

These cases derive logically from the program specification and exercise each possible major input and output. In that sense they form a *minimal* functional set of tests. Remember, we are trying to measure with our test whether the program is working correctly and does everything called for by the specification. Each initial functional case selected should be examined further to see if it can be accomplished in other ways or represents multiple conditions. Our first case is best split apart into two tests—one for the situation of only one flight available and the other for multiple flights available. The third case might also be split into two cases—one for a single flight with no seats, the other for multiple flights with no seats. After the cases have been reduced to single conditions, the combinations should be examined. In this case it is possible to have no seats available on one flight to a certain city, but some seats available on another flight to that same city. An additional case to test that functional possibility is warranted. The list of possible cases now looks like this:

Expanded Set of Functional Tests

Cases	*Expected Result*
1A Flight available (only flight to the city)	Display one line
1B Flight available (multiple flights to the city)	Display multiple lines
2 No flight	Message 1
3A No seats (only flight to the city)	Message 2
3B No seats (multiple flight, all full)	Message 2
4 Flight available (one flight full, but another open)	Display and Message 2

A final review step is to examine the cases and drop any that are redundant or dominated by other cases. There is little harm in having a few too many cases. On the other hand, it is wrong to use cases that provide little or no additional measurement information. In the expanded tests, an argument can be presented that test case 3B dominates 3A and that test case 4 dominates 1A. Test cases 3A and 1A are discarded to produce a selected set of functional test cases.

Constructing a *functional test matrix* is one way to select a minimal set of functional test cases that "covers" the program functions. The functional test matrix relates program functions to selected test cases or situations.

The sample shows a functional test matrix for the airline flight display program. Entries in the matrix identify the program functions that are exercised by each of the test cases. Completing the matrix ensures that the programmer prepares a list of the program functions and thinks through what will be exercised by each test. This type of systematic planning and organization of test data helps ensure that a thorough functional test set is obtained.

Summary of Steps to Select Requirements-Based Test Cases

• Start with natural cases from the specification and an identification of program function.

• Create a minimal set that exercises all inputs and outputs and "covers" the list of program functions.

• Decompose any compound or multiple condition cases into single conditions.

• Examine combinations of single conditions and add test cases for any plausible functional combinations.

• Reduce the list by deleting any test cases dominated by others already in the set.

• Review systematically and carefully.

The matrix is easily included in the unit test plan or design specification to document the functions being tested and the test coverage. Like the requirements validation matrix discussed in Chapter 5; the functional test matrix offers an excellent vehicle for organizing program test planning information and should be reviewed in any formal reexamination of the program test plan.

Sample Functional Test Matrix

	Test Case Number					
Function	*1A*	*1B*	*2*	*3A*	*3B*	*4*
Enter city and date request	✓	✓	✓	✓	✓	✓
Display flight alternative	✓	✓				✓
Display seat availability	✓	✓				✓
Determine flights available	✓	✓	✓	✓	✓	✓
Determine seats available	✓	✓		✓	✓	✓
Print sold-out message					✓	✓
Print no-flights message			✓			

Selecting Design- and Code-Based Test Cases

The second important source of test cases derives from the program design logic and code structure. The idea behind such test cases is best explained by analogy to electrical circuits or components. If I build an electrical circuit, I can test it functionally by throwing the switch and seeing whether the light goes on. To do that I have to wait until the circuit is completely assembled. Alternately, I can test the circuit as I wire it by checking each junction box individually. Such testing is not based on what the circuit as a whole is supposed to do but rather on the wiring junctions and terminal boxes that are installed (the "structure"). We rely on such testing to find out why a circuit does not work or to test for conditions that are not directly visible, such as loose connections, abnormal voltage drops, and ungrounded boxes.

Testing programs in the small is analogous to testing circuits. In addition to the functional tests, we may also test each logical segment (junction) and develop a set of test cases that covers the design. A low level of design or structurally based testing is the criterion to exercise every statement or every decision of a program. Finding test cases to meet this criterion forces the tester to look at the code, determine which parts have been tested, and construct tests for parts that have not.

Requirements-Based versus Design-Based Testing

Requirements-Based Tests

- Independent of design logic (black box)
- Derive from program specifications
- Can't test "extra features"

Design-Based Tests

- Dependent on design logic (white box)
- Derive from program structure
- Can't test "missing functions"

Note that the electrician who tests wiring structurally may not notice that a wall outlet is "missing". The electrician has to think functionally about where the lamps need to be in a room or note that a wall has no outlet to discover this type of problem. Structural testing considers only the wiring that is present; it cannot test wiring that is missing! Similarly, functional testing cannot discover "extra" features that may have been wired in and that we don't know about. We don't even notice such features unless we look in the wall or inside the box to see what has been done. Looking inside and studying program code to determine how to test it is also called *white-box testing*, whereas testing purely functionally without looking at code may be called *black-box testing*. Pure white box-testing will not exercise or detect problems with functions that have been omitted. Pure black-box testing will not exercise or detect problems with features or functions that are not defined in the specifications.

Design-based cases are selected by studying the software design and identifying areas or features that are not adequately covered by the requirements-based tests. The intent is to supplement the requirements-based tests and cover the design interfaces and paths within the software. Typical examples of design-based cases include exercising alternate ways of accomplishing the same function, exercising alternate or backup dataflows, testing special design features or states, and so forth.

Code-based tests are derived in the same manner but based on the actual software code and data structures. One common code-based criterion is testing so as to cover or execute all statements or all branches. We define a set of test cases that have the property of exercising every statement and every decision at least once as being a *complete code-based coverage test set*. With some programs such complete structural coverage can be achieved with a single test case, while for others it may take several, or perhaps even hundreds. A complete coverage test is analogous to one that tests every wire in a circuit and opens and closes all switches at least once.

Complete Code-Based Coverage

Every statement exercised at least once

Every decision exercised over all outcomes

The criterion for structural code-based testing is simply to test until complete coverage has been attained (or perhaps a quantified percentage short of full coverage, such as 90 percent or 95 percent). This is achievable in a practical sense in most program testing environments and has the great advantage of being able to be verified automatically. The computer can be asked to determine if a particular set of tests cases achieves complete coverage and, if not, which statements and decisions remain untested. (I will discuss software tools for measuring test coverage later in this chapter.)

A variety of methods is available to find and construct a set of test cases that achieves complete coverage. Three such methods have had practical application and deserve comment. The first approach is to start with a set of requirements- and design-based test cases for the program and augment it with any additional structural cases needed to attain complete coverage. If a good functional test plan is developed, the cases will meet or nearly meet the code-based coverage criterion as well. Often only one or two additional test cases need to be developed to gain full coverage. Situations where that is not the case may suggest poor functional understanding. This method is particularly practical when a coverage measurement package is available to determine the extent of test coverage achieved.

A second method is heuristic, based on white-box path analysis. The program logic is charted and an initial path is selected as a starting point. Data for this path are created to build the first test case. These data are then modified to create the next case, and the program chart is marked to show the additional segments exercised. Additional test cases are added until all program segments and decisions have been covered. An example of this approach is shown on the following pages.

The third method for finding a complete code coverage test set is an algorithm based on mathematical graph theory called basis testing. This approach to obtaining structural coverage is important enough to merit its own section and is discussed later in the chapter.

Three Means of Obtaining Complete Code Coverage

1. Start with a good functional set and augment it for any remaining statements or decisions
2. Heuristic, based on path analysis of the program
3. Structured Basis Testing

Testing Extremes and Abnormalities

Another type of case that plays an important role in program testing is that designed to explore abnormalities and extremes. We know that the "best" test cases are those that have the highest probability of finding faults if they are present. Exceptional conditions, extremes, boundary conditions, and abnormal cases all make superb test cases because they represent error-prone areas. Good program test planning treats them as a special category to ensure that some time is spent designing and creating such cases.

No method will derive the abnormal cases for us. Ingenuity, experience, and creativity are all important. Most of the extreme cases involve black-box thinking, but occasionally program or data structures suggest cases as well. Group reviews of proposed cases, as always, are an excellent means of bringing out fresh ideas and unique perspectives. In my classes I often ask individuals to prepare a program test design and then use the class as reviewers. After the exercise, we ask the person who prepared the test design whether he or she would change any part of the plan on the basis of what emerged during the review. In hundreds of such exercises I have never received a negative reply. Quite simply, the old adage that "two heads are better than one" aptly

Obtaining Complete Coverage Test Cases Heuristically

Example Program Code Segment

1. #RIGHT = 0;
2. DO J = 1 TO #QUESTIONS;
3. IF KEY(J) = ANSWER(J) THEN #RIGHT = #RIGHT + 1;
5. END
6. SCORE = (#RIGHT/#QUESTIONS) × 100
7. IF SCORE $\geqslant$ 90 THEN GRADE = A;
9. ELSE IF SCORE $\geqslant$ 80 THEN GRADE = B;
11. ELSE IF SCORE $\geqslant$ 70 THEN GRADE = C;
13. ELSE GRADE = F;

This segment checks answers on a quiz against a key, counts up the number right, computes a numerical score, and then records the letter grade.

Step 1: Draw a flowgraph of the code segment to be tested.

This is the flowgraph for the quiz grading code segment listed above.

NOTE: The construction of flowgraphs will be discussed in detail in the next section.

Obtaining Complete Coverage Test Cases Heuristically

Step 2: Select a test case and mark off the structure exercised.

Assume we select a two-question quiz with one right and one wrong answer to be scored. Such a case will exercise a path that passes through the following sequence of nodes: 1, 2, 3, 4, 5, 2, 3, 5, 2, 6, 7, 9, 11, 13, and 14. This path is shown on the segment flowgraph to the right. It would produce a calculated grade of *F*.

Step 3: Examine structure not yet exercised and add cases as required.

As we examine the flowgraph we perceive that three additional cases are needed to exercise each edge of the graph and obtain complete coverage.

A one-question test with the right answer will exercise statement 7 and the path through statement 8 to 14. A five-question test with four right answers will exercise statement 9 and the path from statement 10 to 14; finally, a ten question test with seven right answers will exercise statement 11 and the path from statement 12 to 14. If we mark off the paths on the flowgraph we will see that the four cases exercise every statement at least once and all decisions over all outcomes. Thus the four cases are a complete coverage test set.

describes the situation. This is especially true when it comes to designing cases for testing extremes and abnormalities.

To illustrate the thinking involved, we present a Triangle Analyzer Example Program Specification. You may find it helpful to read the specification and prepare your own test cases before reviewing the "book solution." Test yourself and then review the solution and contrast it with your analysis of the testing required.

Triangle Analyzer Example Program Specification

Input: Three numbers separated by commas or spaces.

Processing: Determine if three numbers make a valid triangle; if not, print message NOT A TRIANGLE.

If it is a triangle, classify it according to the length of the sides as *scalene* (no sides equal), *isosceles* (two sides equal), or *equilateral* (all sides equal).

If it is a triangle, classify it according to the largest angle as *acute* (less than 90°), *obtuse* (greater than 90°), or *right* (exactly 90°).

Output: One line listing the three numbers provided as input and the classification or the not a triangle message.

Examples: 3,4,5   Scalene   Right
             6,1,6   Isosceles   Acute
             5,1,2   Not a triangle

The first step in developing a black-box test for this program is the selection of requirements-based test cases. Recall, from earlier in this chapter, that the technique of preparing a matrix of functional possibilities is one way to aid systematic coverage. Since there are only two major outputs, each with three possibilities, the use of a matrix of the possible combinations naturally suggests itself. Two of the entries in the matrix are not possible (an equilateral triangle is always acute), and a third raises some question (the problem of entering an irrational number for an isosceles right triangle). Assuming the input will permit us to enter the $\sqrt{2}$ in some fashion, we have seven functional cases plus the one case required to exercise the NOT A TRIANGLE message.

Triangle Analyzer Program—Selection of Functional Cases
Matrix of Possible Output Combinations

	Acute	Obtuse	Right
Scalene	6,5,3	5,6,10	3,4,5,
Isosceles	6,1,6,	7,4,4,	1,2,$\sqrt{2}$
Equilateral	4,4,4	Not possible	Not possible

Functional cases

Input	*Expected Output*
1,2,8	Not a triangle
6,5,3	Scalene acute
5,6,10	Scalene obtuse
3,4,5	Scalene right
6,1,6	Isosceles acute
7,4,4	Isosceles obtuse
1,1,$\sqrt{2}$	Isosceles right
4,4,4	Equilateral acute

Next we wish to augment the functional cases with cases that test for extremes and abnormalities or boundary conditions. Test cases that I consider to be appropriate for this triangle analyzer program include those shown in the Selection of Extreme Cases illustration.

Look over these cases and compare them with your own test design. How do they compare? Would you change your plan? Notice that thinking of boundary cases like 0,0,0 or 1,1,2 and the close to equilateral or close to isosceles cases takes creativity *and* a good understanding of the problem domain. As emphasized in Chapter 1, such work isn't easy, and it usually is *not* rewarding.

Triangle Analyzer Program — Selection of Extreme Cases

Boundary Conditions for Legitimate Triangles

1,1,2	Makes a straight line, not a triangle	
0,0,0	Makes a point, not a triangle	
4,0,3	A zero side, not a triangle	
1,2,3.00001	Close to a triangle but still not a triangle	
9170,9168,3	Very small angle	Scalene, acute
.0001,.0001,.0001	Very small triangle	Equilateral, acute
83127168,74326166, 96652988	Very large triangle	Scalene, obtuse

Boundary Conditions for Sides Classification

3.0000001,3,3	Very close to equilateral	Isosceles, acute
2.999999,4,5	Very close to isosceles	Scalene, acute

Boundary Conditions for Angles Classification

3,4,5.000000001	Near right triangle	Scalene, obtuse
1,1,1.4141414141414	Near right triangle	Isosceles, acute

Input Extremes and Invalid Formats

3,4,5,6	Four sides
646	Three-digit single number
3,,4,5	Two commas
3 4,5	Missing comma
3.14.6,4,5	Two decimal points
4,6	Two sides
5,5,A	Character as a side
6, – 4,6	Negative number as a side
– 3, – 3, – 3	All negative numbers
	Empty input

Testing with Extracted or Randomized Data

The task of creating or constructing test data for each of the tests we design is far from trivial. While most situations may be exercised quite simply (especially when testing in the small), others arise for which the time and effort required to construct the case are a concern. In such situations the proper testing may rely on test data obtained from actual data and extracted for test purposes or on generated data such as that produced by a test data generator software package. Both techniques produce large volumes of data easily, but two problems limit their overall utility. The first is the difficulty in providing expected results for all of the test data that are generated or extracted. The second is the time required to review large volumes of output to try to determine whether actual results match expected results. Despite these limitations, such test cases are an important element in the testing practitioner's tool kit.

Extracted actual data are especially useful in situations where a program is being rewritten or enhanced. Consider a payroll program that is to be changed slightly. A base month of data (payroll files, computed checks, withholding, etc.) may be saved from the old program and used to test the new one. The new program is expected to produce exactly the same checks (plus or minus the known effect of any particular enhancements) and to balance all dollar totals to the penny. Such "parallel" testing is extremely important when planning in the large, and I will discuss it further in the next chapter.

Another common use of extracted test data arises with file-oriented and transaction-driven programs. Extraction programs can be used to select certain fields from existing files and build new test records or test transactions based on their contents. Consider a program change involving the addition of several fields to an existing file. A test file can be built by merging the existing file with a data file containing just the new fields. Test data would be hand created only for the new fields; extracted live data supply the rest.

When suitable live data are not available, test files may still be obtained automatically with a test data generator package. A wide variety of such packages is available. Examples include DATAMACS and PRO/TEST. DATAMACS allows parameter statements to be embedded within a COBOL program. The COBOL record definition statements in the program can be used to specify to the generator how the records should be formatted. PRO/TEST is independent of any programming language and operates as a stand-alone package. It has parameters and commands to facilitate extraction from existing files as well as generation of new data.

An example of how the commands are used to specify a desired test data file is illustrated, using the PRO/TEST Generator.

The example shows the definition of a record to the test data generator. Once this has been done, any number of records may be generated simply by supplying another command card that indicates how many records are desired and what file they are to be placed in.

Many other test generator packages are available. All provide facilities that permit records and files to be defined and generated. Most also have features that permit extraction and checking of files after testing is completed. While extremely useful in testing in the large, the generators may easily be misused in testing programs. A program is *not* better tested because several thousand or even several hundred thousand test records have been processed. Unless the test data generated explores the program extremes and abnormalities, little confidence can be gained from even the most voluminous tests.

Test Generation Example—Using the PRO/TEST Generator

1 - 5	RNGN	10,1000,10	/Sequence number from 10 to 1000 in increments of 10
6 - 20	CONX	'ABC CO', 'ACME ENG'	/Company name, will take each entry in the list until exhausted and then goes back to the beginning
25 - 26	RANN	1,30	/Generate varying number of detail records between 1 and 30
25 - 205	DITO	25,26	/Repeat based on number generated in position 25-26
25 - 26	RNGN		/Put in serial number of detail record
27 - 30	RANP	+ −	/Generate a credit or debit and store in packed format
TOTAL	CALC	TOTAL,PLUS(29,32)	/Add up all credits and debits
21 - 24	USEP	TOTAL,RESET	/Place at the head of the detail record

This example first specifies that a sequence number between 10 and 1000 in increments of 10 be generated and placed in positions 1 to 5. The first record would contain 10, the second 20, and so forth. The next command inserts a constant in positions 6 to 20, using the list of constants provided. The third command generates a random number in the range from 1 to 30. The DITO uses this number to repeat that many detail records, each with a serial number in the first two positions and a random-packed credit or debit amount generated in the next four positions. The TOTAL command adds up all the credits and debits in the record, and the last statement causes this total to be placed back in positions 21 to 24 of the record.

A few hand-constructed cases are often superior in testing effectiveness and certainly consume far less computer time. However, when used wisely the generator tool quickly pays for itself. Volume testing and stress testing of program performance are two areas in which generated data may be especially useful.

Structured Basis Testing

Structured basis testing is a special method for obtaining complete code coverage. The basis testing method is a pure white-box structural technique. Test cases are derived from the code logic and are independent of the functional specification. A set of test cases produced by the method is said to be a *basis test set*. This name comes from the fact that the paths taken by the test cases in the basis test set form a "basis" for the set of all possible paths through the program. That is, *every* path (regardless of how many may exist) may be built up as a "linear combination" of the "path segments" traveled by the basis cases.

The reader is probably familiar with the concept of a basis set from mathematics or physics. Consider a basis set of vectors for a vector space. The *dimension* of the space tells us how many independent vectors are needed in the basis set. Thus, three-dimensional space has *exactly* three basis vectors. There are many sets of three vectors that comprise a basis (the ones we are most accustomed to are the coordinate axes), but all have the property of being able to define any point in the space as some combination of the three basis vectors.

Mathematical graph theory provides the theoretical foundation for extending the idea of a basis set to program structures. Any program structure may be represented by a *graph model* showing decision points and the possible logic paths through the program. Mathematically a graph is an object made up of *nodes* and *directed edges* connecting the modes.

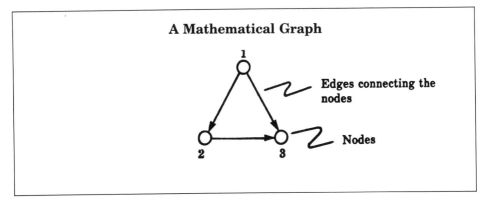

A Mathematical Graph

Edges connecting the nodes

Nodes

To produce a program graph model we need to look only at statements affecting the flow of control through the program. Assignment statements or other sequential statements have a graph model that is a straight line and we need not be concerned with them.

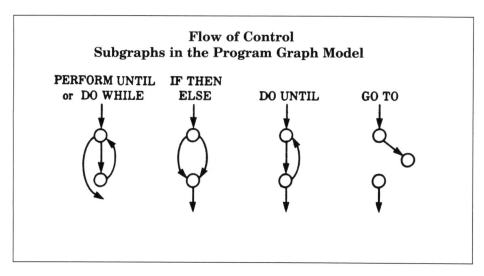

Flow of Control
Subgraphs in the Program Graph Model

Statements that do affect the graph are those where branching can occur. The subgraphs show what the program graph looks like for the most common branching and decision constructs. The DO WHILE construct has the branching decision before the loop, whereas the DO UNTIL makes the test after the loop statements have been executed at least once. Thus the flowgraphs appear as shown. The IF construct creates two paths—one if the condition is true, the other if it is false.

Drawing the Program Flowgraph

Step 1 of the Basis Testing Method

a. Proceed statement by statement.

b. Ignore sequential statements.

c. Add a node for any branching or decision statement.

d. Expand the node by substituting the appropriate subgraph representing it.

The GO TO is just a nonsequential branch to some other node in the program. Straightforward substitution of these subgraphs will convert any program code segment into a graph model of the program flow for that segment.

With a little practice the practitioner should find it easy to produce flowgraphs. Drawing a program flowgraph is the first step of the basis testing method.

Once the program flowgraph has been drawn we call on a theorem from mathematics to calculate how many *independent* circuits exist in the graph. That number establishes how many test cases we need in our basis set. If we can find a test case for each of these independent circuits, then any possible path through the program can be built up as a linear combination of the cases, and we will have obtained our basis set. Fortunately, this can be accomplished straightforwardly, and the method has proved to be a practical and efficient program testing strategy.

The number of independent circuits (and thus the number of test cases we will need) is calculated by using either of the two formulas shown in Step 2.

Determining the Number of Basis Test Cases (Complexity)

Step 2 of the Basis Testing Method

Formula 1:   C   =   # Regions + 1
Formula 2:   C   =   # Edges − # Nodes + 2

The number of independent circuits in the flowgraph is often referred to as the *complexity*, and thus we use C in our formula. The measure has found substantial application as a complexity metric in addition to its role in basis testing. Intuitively, we would expect a measure of complexity to correlate highly with the amount of testing needed. A complex program should require more test cases than a simple one. Applying either of the formulas to a flowgraph is straightforward. Regions are enclosed areas within the graph. A sample calculation using both formulas is illustrated.

Once we have the complexity, we know how many test cases we need to find. If we make sure that each test case we select is independent (represents one of the independent circuits), then we will end up with a set of cases that forms a basis for the set of all possible paths through the program. The simplest method of assuring independence is to add test cases that exercise at least one new edge of the graph. To start, we may select any path, since the first test case by itself must be independent. Tests are then added one at a time by picking up new edges of the graph until the required number is obtained. An example of the process is shown in Step 3.

Note that in this last simplified example the total number of possible paths through the program segment is four. Specifically, the four cases are two positive numbers, two negative numbers, A positive and B negative, and A negative and B positive. Only two cases are needed to obtain complete coverage. Either the first two or the last two meet the criterion of exercising each statement and each outcome of both decision statements. The basis set requires three cases (since the complexity was three) and in this instance any three of the four possible paths form an independent set and could be used as the basis test set. Regardless of which is selected, it can be shown that overall testing effectiveness is essentially the same. Basis testing always provides complete coverage and, in general, is a much stronger criterion.

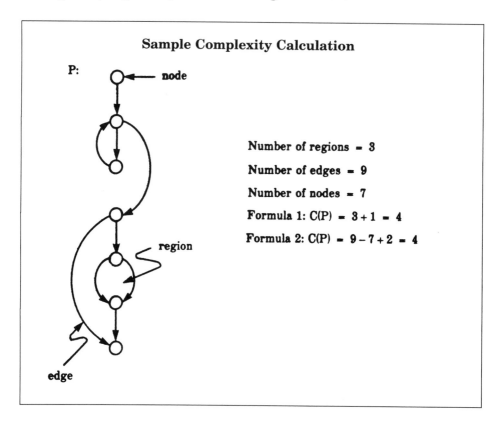

Sample Complexity Calculation

P:

Number of regions = 3

Number of edges = 9

Number of nodes = 7

Formula 1: C(P) = 3 + 1 = 4

Formula 2: C(P) = 9 − 7 + 2 = 4

So far we have used the code structure (flowgraph) to derive a set of test cases that make up a basis for all possible paths through the graph. To actually "test" the cases, we must have *expected results* for each test case and then either execute the cases or walk through them to verify that the code produces those results.

To obtain expected results we go back to the program specification and ask what the program "ought" to do with the derived test data. If this is answered by someone other than the programmer, misunderstandings about program specifications will tend to be discovered and much more effective testing will result. Having different people get involved with test data selection and expected results determination provides much of the value obtained from a completely independent test function.

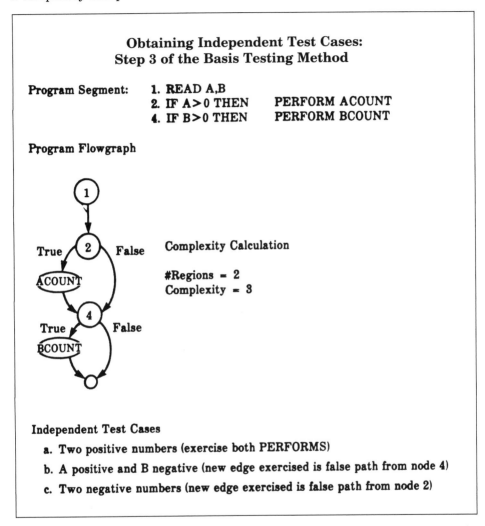

The final step is to use the basis cases that have been derived from the code to test the code. The methodology has answered the what-to-test question and provided the data. All that remains is to execute (or walk through) those data and check actual results with expected results. If the program performs as expected for each of the basis cases, testing is completed successfully. If it does not, we have a discrepancy (either in the program or our understanding of expected results) that must be corrected.

Obtaining Expected Results

Step 4 of the Basis Testing Method

Use the program specifications to determine what the program should do for each basis test case that has been derived.

Executing the Basis Test Cases

Step 5 of the Basis Testing Method

a. Execute each basis test case.

b. Check actual results against expected results.

c. Testing completed when confidence obtained that each case performs satisfactorily.

A diagram of the complete structured basis testing procedure is provided on the opposite page. The procedure is summarized on page 98.

As emphasized earlier, this is a pure white-box method. It is a technique in testing in the small that practitioners should be familiar with. Unfortunately, its current impact is very limited. Few programmers use it and most have not even heard of it!

How effective is basis testing? Experiments and experience with the technique demonstrate that structured basis testing will detect most program control flow errors and a substantial proportion of the errors found by any other method of unit testing. Like all white-box structural methods, it can't reveal omitted functions or discover problems with code that has not been written! It does provide confidence that the code that *has* been written is of reasonable quality. It also has the major advantage of being a true engineering process. Regardless of who performs the method, the number of test cases in the basis set is the same and the level of confidence obtained is essentially identical. Although the cases in the basis set may differ and one may discover one or two errors that another might miss, the broad class of errors discovered and the quality measured by basis testing is unvarying. The point is that everyone who does basis testing (independent of skill level or experience) gets the same result.

Another advantage is that the method is well suited to desk checking and testing of code that is not yet ready for execution. Pseudocode and other high-level or top-down logic can be flowgraphed just as "real" code can.

Once we have the graph model representing the logic, the method can be used to derive a basis set of tests for the pseudocode logic. These tests can then be "executed" by walking through them in a review or as part of a logical desk check. The high-level logic may be formally and systematically tested in this way *before* it is expanded into actual code. Even where top-down development is not the practice the programmer can basis test each segment of code as he or she *codes it on paper*—before it is even keyed or compiled! I shall have more to say about this in a subsequent section on desk checking methods.

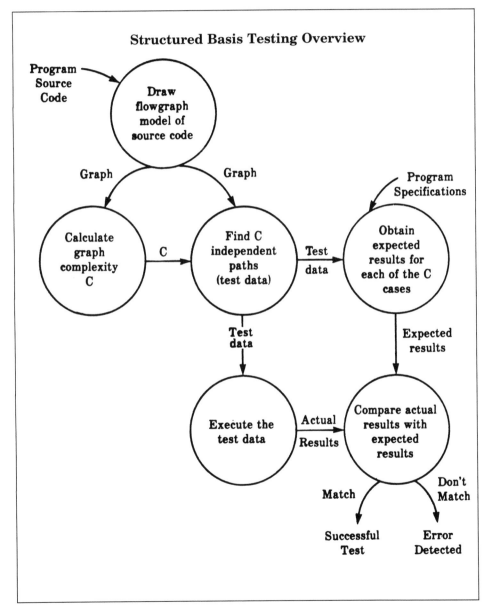

Structured Basis Testing Overview

While the method is easy to teach and learn, it has proved difficult to implement. Given the struggle involved with any new methodology—structured programming is a good example—this should not be too surprising. One major problem my clients have experienced is forgetting that basis testing is a testing, not a debugging, process. Consider what will happen if the method is applied to a segment of code that is full of serious logical faults. The graph model may end up with edges that don't connect, or, if they do, there may be *no* paths through the program (a looping problem, for example). When this happens we can't find a single test case, let alone an independent basis set. This is not a failure of the method. As a test method it helps only to measure quality. The fact that we can't construct the basis set means that the program has problems. The method is not intended to help fix those problems. That is properly a debugging task, and testing cannot resume until the program has

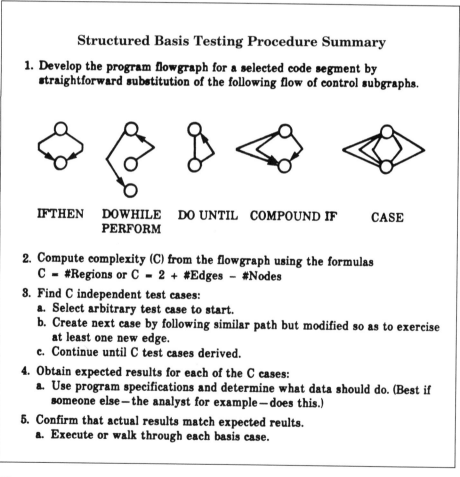

Structured Basis Testing Procedure Summary

1. Develop the program flowgraph for a selected code segment by straightforward substitution of the following flow of control subgraphs.

IFTHEN   DOWHILE   DO UNTIL   COMPOUND IF   CASE
             PERFORM

2. Compute complexity (C) from the flowgraph using the formulas
C = #Regions or C = 2 + #Edges − #Nodes

3. Find C independent test cases:
   a. Select arbitrary test case to start.
   b. Create next case by following similar path but modified so as to exercise at least one new edge.
   c. Continue until C test cases derived.

4. Obtain expected results for each of the C cases:
   a. Use program specifications and determine what data should do. (Best if someone else—the analyst for example—does this.)

5. Confirm that actual results match expected reults.
   a. Execute or walk through each basis case.

been cleaned up. In a paradoxical way, we find that basis testing works best on programs that are almost correct. When the program is awful, all we learn is that it doesn't work. In that case we don't need testing—we need better programming!

The best way to learn the method is to use it in the work setting on actual projects and assignments; there is no substitute for this. The programmer needs several days under the tutelage of someone who understands the method and can provide help as questions and problems arise. Reading *about* the method is not likely to succeed. One has to learn by doing and gain personal confidence that the method will work and is worth the time and effort required to use it.

Basis Testing Effectiveness

Effectiveness

- Stronger than complete code coverage
- Will detect most control faults
- Also catches a broad class of other types of errors
- Excellent vehicle for code review or walk-throughs
- Can be applied to high-level logic or pseudocode

Efficiency

- Well-defined procedure
- Efficient in machine resources and practitioner time
- Generates simple and easy to execute test cases

The hands-on experience and practice period can also deal with any adaptations needed for local environment or language differences. In this introductory description I have not described how to handle the more complex and specialized constructs that may arise. As one example, consider the common case of routines with multiple entry and exit points. The proper graph model treatment can be seen in the illustration below.

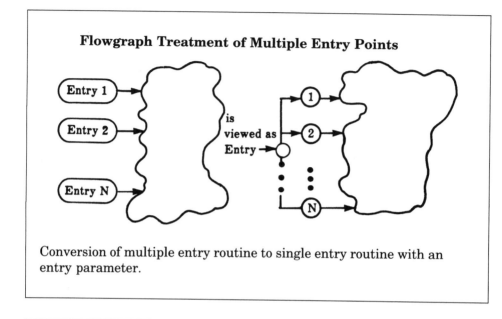

Flowgraph Treatment of Multiple Entry Points

Conversion of multiple entry routine to single entry routine with an entry parameter.

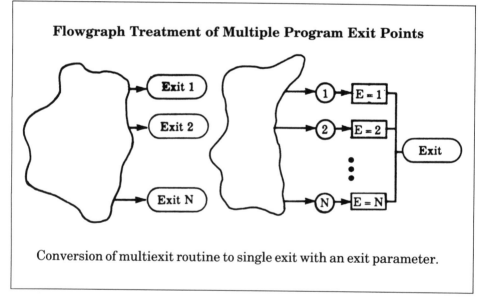

Flowgraph Treatment of Multiple Program Exit Points

Conversion of multiexit routine to single exit with an exit parameter.

Multiple entries are treated as an initial decision with paths to each entry; multiple exists are treated as paths to a single exit. The result is that the basis set will force a test of each entry point and an exit from each exit point, which is the common sense testing action most of us would use anyway. Similar extensions can be made for most language features practitioners employ.

Syntax Testing

Another specialized technique the practitioner may have occasion to use is syntax or grammar-based testing. Just as we systematically explored program control flow structures with basis testing, we seek to explore the data structure with data-driven testing. One special data-driven technique is called *syntax testing*, which was developed as a tool for testing the input data to language processors such as compilers or interpreters. It is applicable to any situation where the data or input has many acceptable forms and we wish to test systematically that only the "proper" forms are accepted and all improper forms rejected. This fits a reasonably broad class of programs, including string recognizers and data validation routines.

To use syntax testing we must first describe the valid or acceptable data in a *formal notation* such as the Backus Naur Form, or BNF for short. An example of BNF notation is illustrated in Step 1 of the Syntax Testing Method.

Step 1 of the Syntax Testing Method

Describing the Syntax in BNF Notation

Assume we wish to define an "Operator" to be either a right parenthesis followed by two to four letters and a plus sign or two right parentheses. A BNF notation for this syntax specification is the following:

OPERATOR	:=	MNEMONIC $+/$))
MNEMONIC	:=	$LETTERS_2^4$
LETTERS	:=	A/B/C/ . . . . . . /X/Y/Z

The / is used to indicate a choice in the specification and is read as OR. Thus the last line tells us that LETTERS is either an A or a B or a C, etc.

Once the syntax is formally defined, we use it to derive "valid" cases by drawing a tree representing the syntax and choosing cases to "cover" the tree in a "systematic" fashion. A minimal set of valid cases can be derived by picking cases that will exercise every nonterminating branch and at least one of the terminating branches in the complete syntax tree.

Step 2 of the Syntax Testing Method

Deriving Valid Syntax Cases

Draw the syntax tree for the BNF syntax.

Select test cases that cover *every* nonterminating edge in the tree (i.e., edges that do not end at a leaf node on the tree).

Select test cases so that *at least one* terminating or leaf node on each branch is covered.

Example:

a. Syntax tree for the previous example is

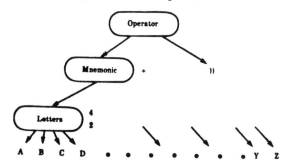

b. Covering nonterminating branches.
Select test case of)DXAB + as one choice.

c. Covering at least one terminating leaf on each branch.
Left side of the tree is already taken care of.
Select test case of)) as the only choice for the right side.

Minimal covering set of valid test cases is)DXAB + and)).

Step 3 of the Syntax Testing Method

Deriving Invalid Syntax Cases

a. Start with the uppermost level in the tree.

b. Introduce one "error" at a time on the selected level.

c. Continue for all "errors" that can occur at that level.

d. Move to the next level and repeat until the entire tree has been traversed.

Example	*Test Case*	*Error Introduced*
Level 1	) +	Missing MNEMONIC
	)XXXZ –	Minus instead of +
	)CDP	Missing + sign
	CCCN +	Missing left parenthesis
	)	Only one left parenthesis
	)))	Three left parentheses
Level 2	)ABCDE +	Five letters
	)X +	One letter
Level 3	)AB2D +	Number instead of letter
	)AB)D +	Delimiter instead of letter
	)A DN +	Space instead of letter

Step 3 is to use the syntax tree to derive "invalid" test cases, that is, cases that we expect the program to reject. This is done by taking one level of the tree at a time and testing for single "errors" on that level. The example continues with Step 3 of the Symtax Testing Method.

We have now derived a set of valid cases and a set of invalid cases. The final step is simply to execute the derived test cases and confirm that our program does indeed accept the valid cases and reject the invalid ones. In the example we have two cases to be accepted and eleven to be rejected.

Step 4 of the Syntax Testing Method

Executing the Syntax Test Cases

a. Confirm that all valid cases are accepted.

b. Confirm that all invalid cases are rejected.

Syntax testing provides a systematic means of defining test cases with complex and rigid data structure definitions. The key to using it is the input specification, which must be formally describable. As stated syntax testing will not handle situations in which the syntax allowed depends on the value of other data elements or the state of the system. The method can be extended to treat such situations by combining certain functional and structural testing notions with the syntax testing cases.

One major benefit of syntax testing comes from the assurance that there are no misunderstandings about what are legal data and what are not. When a formal syntax description is written out, such problems will surface even before the testing begins. This is another example in which the process of designing and creating test cases helps to prevent errors. Ideally, the formal syntax should be used to specify the system in the first place.

Even without a formal input data syntax, the data viewpoint is still useful in deriving appropriate test cases for program testing. A careful review of the program data definitions or data dictionary will identify situations in which individual data elements are used for multiple purposes or where changes in data types and representations occur. These are examples of error-prone situations that may need special test cases to ensure proper operation. Care should also be taken to identify context-dependent data exceptions and extremes (such as division by zero). Test cases that explore the program behavior at or near such exceptions bear particular fruit in discovering errors that may otherwise be overlooked in normal functional or structural testing.

Testing in the Small Tools and Aids

Besides the test data generator packages, there are a number of other tools that support testing in the small with which the practitioner should be familiar. These include program logic analyzers, test coverage measurement aids, test drivers, and test comparators. Many other specialized packages and tools may be useful in particular applications. Some of these are described in the section on tools for testing in the large in the next chapter.

The best way to describe the tools available and give some perspective for the features they offer is by example. Some common tools in use are illustrated in this section. The inclusion of a particular vendor's tools does *not* imply preference or recommendation over competing vendor offerings. In general, there is a wide choice of products with similar capabilities. One of each type is described in the text to provide the reader with some feeling for what is available and to help demonstrate how the tools may be used to improve testing effectiveness. The only criterion for selection was pedagogical.

Program Logic Analyzers

Consider first the set of tools that might be called program logic analyzers. These are any of a rather diverse set of packages that read in programs as input and then analyze them in some fashion to determine their logical structure. Typically, they produce reports intended to help in understanding how the program performs or to aid in making modifications. They also produce documentation charts and printouts intended to serve as a part of the permanent program documentation. Although not originally designed as testing aids, many serve that purpose nicely. One good example of this is the product called SCAN/370, the four basic features of which are listed.

SCAN/370 Basic Features

1. Scans COBOL source code and annotates how each paragraph or section may be entered.
2. Flags the range of each Perform routine and displays alternative ways of reaching it.
3. Lists "dead" code that cannot be logically reached.
4. Produces a hierarchical processing chart showing the logical structure of the program.

Some typical SCAN outputs are offered as examples. The following pages show how SCAN/370 annotates a source listing to identify alternative ways of reaching each code segment. In general, these alternatives are each logically independent test cases that should be exercised in testing the program. An example of an overall structure chart for the program that was analyzed is also provided. Both of these outputs are extremely useful in evaluating the impact of potential changes and in designing testing strategies needed to test them. (Refer to Chapter 9 for more on methods for testing software changes.) The outputs may also highlight program discrepancies directly and are useful in support of program reviews or walk-throughs.

Test Coverage Tools

A second commonly employed tool is any one of the many packages that measure and report on test code coverage. These tools take a source program as input and "instrument" it so that it is able to produce a report showing the statements and branches exercised by a test case during actual program execution. Typically, the reports may be cumulatively prepared over a number of different test cases or runs. This enables the tester to determine which parts

SCAN/370 Source Code Annotation

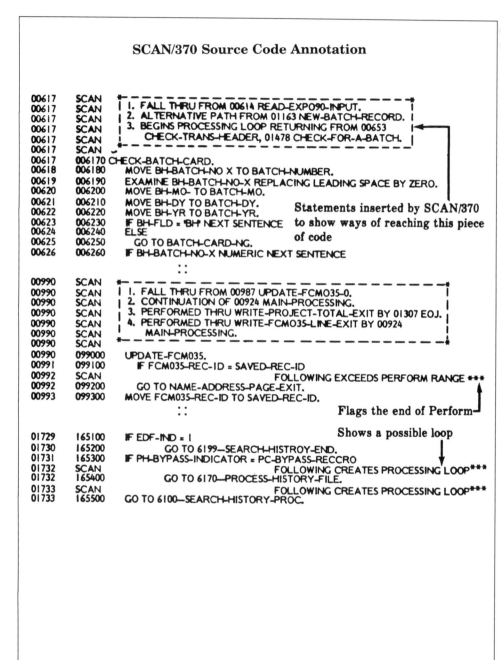

```
00617   SCAN    +---------------------------------------+
00617   SCAN    | 1. FALL THRU FROM 00614 READ-EXPO90-INPUT.        |
00617   SCAN    | 2. ALTERNATIVE PATH FROM 01163 NEW-BATCH-RECORD.  |
00617   SCAN    | 3. BEGINS PROCESSING LOOP RETURNING FROM 00653    |
00617   SCAN    |     CHECK-TRANS-HEADER, 01478 CHECK-FOR-A-BATCH.  |
00617   SCAN    +---------------------------------------+
00617   006170  CHECK-BATCH-CARD.
00618   006180      MOVE BH-BATCH-NO X TO BATCH-NUMBER.
00619   006190      EXAMINE BH-BATCH-NO-X REPLACING LEADING SPACE BY ZERO.
00620   006200      MOVE BH-MO- TO BATCH-MO.
00621   006210      MOVE BH-DY TO BATCH-DY.
00622   006220      MOVE BH-YR TO BATCH-YR.       Statements inserted by SCAN/370
00623   006230      IF BH-FLD = 'BH' NEXT SENTENCE   to show ways of reaching this piece
00624   006240      ELSE                           of code
00625   006250          GO TO BATCH-CARD-NG.
00626   006260      IF BH-BATCH-NO-X NUMERIC NEXT SENTENCE
                        ::
00990   SCAN    +---------------------------------------+
00990   SCAN    | 1. FALL THRU FROM 00987 UPDATE-FCM035-0.          |
00990   SCAN    | 2. CONTINUATION OF 00924 MAIN-PROCESSING.         |
00990   SCAN    | 3. PERFORMED THRU WRITE-PROJECT-TOTAL-EXIT BY 01307 EOJ. |
00990   SCAN    | 4. PERFORMED THRU WRITE-FCM035-LINE-EXIT BY 00924 |
00990   SCAN    |     MAIN-PROCESSING.                              |
00990   SCAN    +---------------------------------------+
00990   099000  UPDATE-FCM035.
00991   099100      IF FCM035-REC-ID = SAVED-REC-ID
00992   SCAN                           FOLLOWING EXCEEDS PERFORM RANGE ***
00992   099200          GO TO NAME-ADDRESS-PAGE-EXIT.
00993   099300      MOVE FCM035-REC-ID TO SAVED-REC-ID.
                        ::                    Flags the end of Perform
                                            Shows a possible loop
01729   165100      IF EDF-IND = 1
01730   165200          GO TO 6199-SEARCH-HISTROY-END.
01731   165300      IF PH-BYPASS-INDICATOR = PC-BYPASS-RECCRO
01732   SCAN                           FOLLOWING CREATES PROCESSING LOOP***
01732   165400          GO TO 6170-PROCESS-HISTORY-FILE.
01733   SCAN                           FOLLOWING CREATES PROCESSING LOOP***
01733   165500      GO TO 6100-SEARCH-HISTORY-PROC.
```

SCAN/370 Hierarchical Chart

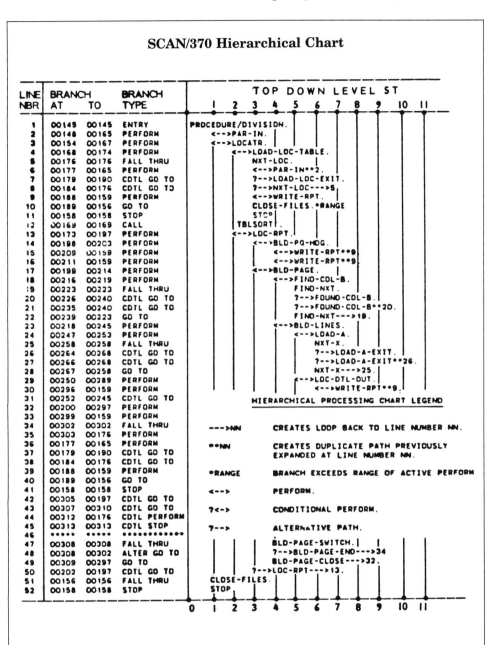

of the program have been exercised in the effort and specifically highlights any portions of the code that have not yet been tested.

An example of this capability is the CHECKOUT package. When CHECK-OUT is used on a test run or a series of test runs, it annotates the source listing to show for each statement the test runs that exercised it and the total number of times it was exercised (both on the last test run and cumulatively over all tests in the series).

Sample CHECKOUT Output

Source Statements Listed Here	Last Used on Test #	Number of Tests That Used This Line	Times This Line Used This Test	Total Times This Line Used All Tests
1.	8	5	65	1041
2	1	1	6	6
3.	*****	NOT TESTED	*********	
4.	*****	NOT TESTED	*********	
5.	8	8	1	8

The example above shows a hypothetical output. If this were a real example, the source code statements would be printed in the space at the left. The sample output is reporting on the cumulative results of eight test runs. The first line of the output indicates that statement 1 was executed during the last test run (number 8); that five of the eight tests exercised this statement; that on the last test this statement was exercised sixty-five times; and that all together the statement has been exercised 1041 times. The statement listing is flagged to show that none of the eight tests exercised statements 3 or 4.

As may be seen, this type of reporting tool documents the test coverage achieved and may be used to ensure that complete coverage has been obtained. The report identifies any code segments not tested during normal program testing. Special test cases for these unexercised segments may then be defined (if it is possible to reach such code) to fulfill the complete coverage criterion.

Another example of a tool to provide test coverage measurement is offered by SOFTOOL. SOFTOOL offers an integrated set of tools in support of either the COBOL or the FORTRAN environments. The emphasis is on the use of instrumentation in conjunction with top-down structured development. Test coverage reports are available at an overall program or system level, at the paragraph level, or at the statement level.

The first part of the SOFTOOL illustration shows a program level report and the second a paragraph level report. The report at the individual source statement level is similar. Each report begins with a summary showing the total number of programs, paragraphs, or statements exercised on the latest test run and over all runs. The summary highlights the amount of different (not previously tested) code that was exercised in the latest test and computes an index of test effectiveness (in the sense of avoiding redundant executions). The index is calculated by dividing the number of executions by the percentage of coverage achieved with these executions. After the summary, the report prints the number of program, paragraph, or statement executions for the last test run and over all test runs. Programs or segments not yet tested may be identified and, as with CHECKOUT, additional tests may then be designed to achieve full coverage. The SOFTOOL reports make excellent test documentation for the entire development activity. I find the tool most useful for reporting on test coverage at the system (or testing in the large) level; however, it is clearly also useful for coverage measurement in the small.

Several other tools, originally designed for other purposes, have been extended to provide test coverage measurement. The capability is available as an option in many compilers and optimizers. A good example is the popular CAPEX optimizer, which was originally offered to support automatic optimization of COBOL programs and provide information for performance tuning. The performance tuning output provided a display of execution time spent in each statement or module. It took little to modify this to include a report of unexecuted paragraphs and statements and thus provide some support for the tester or debugger. This is now a major feature of the product and may offer the practitioner a back-door means of obtaining a test coverage measurement tool. The main disadvantage is that the coverage report is not available cumulatively over a series of test runs.

Test Drivers

A third important tool for testing in the small is the test driver. Test drivers provide a vehicle for testing or exercising programs. Typically, they offer features that provide a "language" for specifying tests to be run and test data to be exercised. The driver acts as an interface between the operating system and the program to be tested. It traps program abends and provides useful information to aid debugging while preventing any system termination or disruption. Most also include features for specifying or simulating routines so that programs may be tested even though they call other routines that have not yet been written. The simulation may simply print a message or cause parameters and results to be passed back to the program under test.

TESTMANAGER offers a good example for illustration. The following example is reprinted, with permission, from the TESTMANAGER product brochure. It shows the testing of a program to calculate currency exchanges. The input to the program is an exchange rates table or file and a conversion request

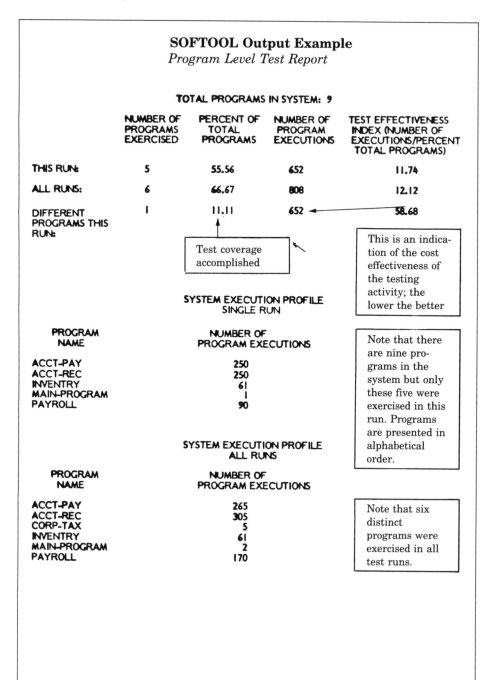

SOFTOOL Output Example
Program Level Test Report

TOTAL PROGRAMS IN SYSTEM: 9

	NUMBER OF PROGRAMS EXERCISED	PERCENT OF TOTAL PROGRAMS	NUMBER OF PROGRAM EXECUTIONS	TEST EFFECTIVENESS INDEX (NUMBER OF EXECUTIONS/PERCENT TOTAL PROGRAMS)
THIS RUN:	5	55.56	652	11.74
ALL RUNS:	6	66.67	808	12.12
DIFFERENT PROGRAMS THIS RUN:	1	11.11	652 ←	58.68

Test coverage accomplished

This is an indication of the cost effectiveness of the testing activity; the lower the better

SYSTEM EXECUTION PROFILE
SINGLE RUN

PROGRAM NAME	NUMBER OF PROGRAM EXECUTIONS
ACCT-PAY	250
ACCT-REC	250
INVENTRY	61
MAIN-PROGRAM	1
PAYROLL	90

Note that there are nine programs in the system but only these five were exercised in this run. Programs are presented in alphabetical order.

SYSTEM EXECUTION PROFILE
ALL RUNS

PROGRAM NAME	NUMBER OF PROGRAM EXECUTIONS
ACCT-PAY	265
ACCT-REC	305
CORP-TAX	5
INVENTRY	61
MAIN-PROGRAM	2
PAYROLL	170

Note that six distinct programs were exercised in all test runs.

SOFTOOL Output Example—Continued
Paragraph Level Test Report

TOTAL PARAGRAPHS IN PROGRAM: 9

	NUMBER OF PARAGRAPHS EXERCISED	PERCENT OF TOTAL PARAGRAPHS	NUMBER OF PARAGRAPH EXECUTIONS	TEST EFFECTIVENESS INDEX (NUMBER OF EXECUTIONS/PERCENT TOTAL PARAGRAPHS)
THIS RUN:	8	88.89	10170	114.41
ALL RUNS:	8	88.89	10410	117.11
DIFFERENT PARAGRAPHS THIS RUN		55.56	10170	183.06

↑

Test coverage accomplished

PROGRAM ID: PAYROLL
PROGRAM EXECUTION PROFILE
SINGLE RUN

PARAGRAPH NAME	NUMBER OF PARAGRAPH EXECUTIONS
BUILD-REPORT-LINE	180
CALCULATE-DOUBLE-TIME	180
CALCULATE-TAXES	180
MAIN-LINE-PARAGRAPH	90
PROCESS-AND-WRITE	90
RETURN-TO-CALLER	90
WRITE-IT	9180
WRITE-REPORT-LINE	180

PROGRAM ID: PAYROLL

PROGRAM EXECUTION PROFILE
ALL RUNS

PARAGRAPH NAME	NUMBER OF PARAGRAPH EXECUTIONS
BUILD-REPORT-LINE	180
CALCULATE-DOUBLE-TIME	180
CALCULATE-TAXES	180
MAIN-LINE-PARAGRAPH	170
PROCESS-AND-WRITE	170
RETURN-TO-CALLER	170
WRITE-IT	9180
WRITE-REPORT-LINE	180

Test Manager Setup Example

• •	ALLOCATE CORE FOR PARAMETER AREAS	⎤
PARAMETER	EXCHANGE-RATE-TABLE CORE FORMAT 56.	
• PARAMETER	CONVERSION-REQUEST CORE FORMAT 28	

PARAMETER   CONVERSION-REQUEST CORE FORMAT 28
        R-FROM-COUNTRY   12
        R-AMOUNT   4   } Set up the
        R-TO-COUNTRY   12.   parameters
•
PARAMETER   CONVERSION-ANSWER CORE 59.
•
PARAMETER   MESSAGE-AREA 40.
•
•   DESCRIBE SIMULATION OF ERRMOD MODULE ⎦
•

SIMULATE.
       MODULE ERRMOD MESSAGE-AREA.   } Specify
       PRINT MESSAGE-AREA.   simulation
END.
•
•   ASSIGN VALUES TO EXCHANGE RATE TABLE
•

EXCHANGE-RATE-TABLE   DECIMAL (4)

62.00	* BELGIUM
2.20	* CANADA
11.00	* DENMARK
1.00	* ENGLAND
8.25	* FINLAND
9.50	* FRANCE
4.00	* GERMANY
4.25	* HOLLAND
1700.00	* ITALY
475.00	* JAPAN
10.50	* NORWAY
9.00	* SWEDEN
3.60	* SWITZERLAND
2.00.	* USA

Initialize input data

•
•   ASSIGN VALUES FOR MODULE TEST.
•

R-FROM-COUNTRY	C 'USA'.
R-AMOUNT	D 5000.00.
R-TO-COUNTRY	C 'ENGLAND'.

TESTMANAGER Execution of Exchange

*   ISSUE TEST COMMAND TO DO MODULE TEST
*
*
TEST EXHANGE   * PASSING AS PARAMETERS
        EXCHANGE-RATE-TABLE
        CONVERSION-REQUEST
        CONVERSION-ANSWER.

PARAMETER LIST CONTENT. ◄——— Addresses passed
001 1F138 001 1F500 001 1EFA0

CALL NUMBER 0001 MADE TO USER MODULE "EXCHANGE".

RETURN TO TMR.

---

consisting of two countries—FROM-COUNTRY and TO-COUNTRY—and the amount involved. The output is the converted amount or an error message passed to the ERRMOD routine if the country is not found in the table.

As the first step we have to set up the input and output parameters and initialize them with test data. Since ERRMOD is not yet written we also will tell TESTMANAGER to simulate it by printing MESSAGE-AREA if it is called. The TESTMANAGER control cards to accomplish this setup are included.

An asterisk at the front of the control statement signifies a comment. The key words are PARAMETER (something to be passed to or from a program) and SIMULATE and END to specify the simulation of the missing routine.

To conduct the first test we give TESTMANAGER the key word TEST followed by the name of the routine to be tested (in this case, EXCHANGE). TESTMANAGER displays the addresses of the parameters passed and indicates when control is passed to EXCHANGE as well as when it returns to TESTMANAGER.

To examine the output, we must tell TESTMANAGER to print the parameter containing the answer (CONVERSION-ANSWER).

The first command requested all the parameters and the answer to be displayed. They are shown both in internal format and as characters for ease of reading and checking.

Expected results may also be defined and initialized in TESTMANAGER. Use of the command PRINT COMPARE will then produce a printout only when the actual results do not match the expected results.

The final illustration is of TESTMANAGER intercepting an interrupt. To create an interrupt condition we alter the EXCHANGE-RATE-TABLE by inserting the word HIGH in it. This forces a data exception and program check when the program tries to refer to the table.

TESTMANAGER reports where the program check occurred and prints a formatted register dump. An attempt is made by TESTMANAGER to reset the interrupt condition and continue if requested.

TESTMANAGER Display of Parameters

PRINT ALL CONVERSION-REQUEST CONVERSION-ANSWER.◀— **Request output**

PARAMETER 'R-FROM-COUNTRY' START IIF500 END IIF50B-E4E2C1404040404040404040
               *USA

PARAMETER 'R-AMOUNT' START IIF5DC END IIF50F-0500000C *....*.

PARAMETER 'R-TO-COUNTRY' START IIF510 END IIF51B-C5D5C7D3C1D5C44040404040
               *ENGLAND

PARAMETER 'CONVERSION-ANSWER' START IIEFAO END IIEFDA.

000000 40404040 F5F0F0F0 4BF0F040 E4E240C4 D6D3D3C1 D9E24040 40404040 407E4040
               * 5000.00 US DOLLARS

000020 404040F2 F5FDF043 F0F040D7 D6E4D5C4 E240E2E3 C5D9D3C9 D5C740
               * 2500.00 POUNDS STERLING

TESTMANAGER Interrupt Example

```
*                    OVERWRITE EXCHANGE RATES
*                    TO FORCE ERROR CONDITION
*
EXCHANGE-RATE-TABLE HIGH.
R-TO-COUNTRY C 'USA'.
TEST
CALL NUMBER 0005 MADE TO USER MODULE 'EXCHANGE'.

PROGRAM CHECK INTERRUPT.
DATA EXCEPTION AT LOCATION DE0730 , INSTRUCTION TYPE SS CONTENT F9304000C040,
ADDRI-IIF16C, ADD32-OE0680,

OP1 CONTENT-FFFFFFFF, OP2 CONTENT-0C, PROGRAM STATUS FF850007EEDE0736.

REGISTERS DUMP.

  R0 000E06F0 R1 000E06F0 R2 00000000 R3 00000038 R4 0011F16C R5 0011EFAD R6 000E0180
  R7 0011EFA0

  R0 0011F138 R9 0011F500 RA 000E00E0 RB 000E06A8 RC 000E0640 RD 000E03A8 RE 000F02FC
  RF 4E0E0A08

TMR HANDLED PROGRAM CHECK NUMBER 001.

THE FOLLOWING HAS BEEN APPLIED.
UP1 ONE OR MORE DIGITS SET ZERO.

SAVE AREA TRACE.

SA 11E160 W01 00000070 HSA 00000000 LSA 000E03A8 RET 001156C0 EPA 050F00E0 R000000000
         R1 000E0098 R2 00000000 R3 00000000 R4 00000000 R5 00000000 R6 00000000
         R7 00000000 R8 00000000 R9 00000000 RA 00000000 RB 00000000 RC 00000000

SA DE03AB W01 00300000 HSA 0011E160 LSA 00000000 RET 5EDE09AC EPA 011156FC P0000E0942
         R1 000E0638 R2 00000000 R3 00000000 R4 000E0260 R5 0011EFA0 R6 000E0160
         R7 0011EFA0 R8 0011F136 R9 0011F500 RA 000EC0E0 RB 000E06A9 RC 000F0640

CONTINUATION NOT REQUESTED.

RETURN TO TMR.
```

Test Comparators

A final set of tools of importance to testing in the small are the test comparators. These specialized packages facilitate comparison between files and outputs and generally support the output verification task. Many offer features for creating "expected result files" by extracting from existing files and/or inserting special data. Two typical tools in the comparator classification are DATABASIC from Consumer Systems and COMPAREX from Serena. The major features and capabilities of these products are listed.

Two Comparator Tools

Databasic

1. Creates miniatures of production data bases for IMS/DL/1.
2. Lets programmers manipulate the test data files.
3. Creates test file subsets that are perfect subsets of the production master.
4. Checks out test results by comparing the test data base to the production master and printing out mismatches.
5. Prints out any data base segment to review test results.

Comparex

1. Processes *any* file, including ISAM, VSAM, TEST (source code, JCL), and DATA (master files, load modules, test cases).
2. Isolates INSERTED, DELETED, AND MODIFIED records.
3. Allows record SELECTION for inclusion/exclusion in the comparison.
4. Permits multiple print formats for differences report.

DATABASIC contains the capabilities of both an extractor tool and a comparator. Miniature data bases may easily be created and manipulated and then compared after test execution. COMPAREX isolates inserted, deleted, and modified records between two files and prints out a formatted difference report. Features are available to specify only selected records or record types in the differences report.

The four major categories of testing tools presented in this section (program logic analyzers, test coverage measurement tools, test drivers, and test comparators) together with the test data generators described in the previous section cover the most important tools *now* in use for testing in the small. As emphasized earlier, many additional specialized tools are available. More are sure to come in the near future. The practitioner interested in maintaining current awareness of potential tools would do well to subscribe to one of the special tool catalogs or information sources that are updated regularly. More information on these sources is provided in Chapter 8.

Testing in the Small—A Recommended Practice

So far in this chapter I have discussed techniques that may be applied to the testing in the small effort. The techniques and tools have been presented individually as part of the portfolio of skills the accomplished testing practitioner should be familiar with. How should the techniques be integrated? What overall testing in the small approach is best? What procedures and practices are recommended?

A key issue affecting the answers to any of these questions is *when* testing effort should best be applied and who should perform it. We tend to think in terms of a model that assumes programming occurs first and testing follows. Such a view ignores the fact (and the requirement) that the programmer must have some means of establishing confidence that the code he or she has just created or jotted down is "good enough" to be keyed and entered into the compiler. For all of us some amount of testing goes on *as* we write code. Individual variations, as usual, are extreme. Some programmers check their codes very extensively at their desks and may be so good at testing "up front" that they have little need for more traditional execution-based testing after the program is compiled. Others scramble codes together and rely almost totally on execution time tests to check them out and get them cleaned up.

Most practitioners have not thought very much about the testing they should do. I believe that up-front testing (like all testing) must be planned and designed. An informal perusal or mental review accomplishes little. A specific review with clear objectives and known or defined expected results accomplishes a great deal. The program test design should address all aspects of program testing and establish an overall or total testing strategy. Many alternatives are possible. The approach I recommend is the following:

Recommended Unit Testing Approach

1. Develop program specifications (a statement of the program's required behavior from a black box point of view).

2. Inventory the requirements-based test objectives and identify requirements-based test cases derived from the program specifications.

3. Review the requirements-based inventory and test cases as a part of the program specifications (detailed design) review.

4. Develop the program design (a specification for how the program is to be built).

5. Inventory the design-based test objectives and identify design-based test cases derived from the program design.

6. Identify extremes and worst-case test scenarios or cases based on the program specifications and the program design.

7. Identify any additional test cases to be obtained from randomized or existing test files to complete the program testing.

8. Document all identified test cases and the overall test set architecture in a draft Test Design Specification.

9. Organize the tests identified into test procedures, and document the test runs and the individual tests using Test Case Specifications and Test Procedure Specifications as needed.

10. Review the completed test design in conjunction with the program design or code review.

11. Code the program and implement the test design.

12. Execute the implemented test set on the compiled program with instrumentation available to record code coverage achieved.

13. Modify and revise the code and the test set as necessary.

14. Re-execute the modified tests until test completion criteria are met.

This approach emphasizes test design *before* software design and code, and will detect and discover many faults and errors in the program specifications and design *before* they become code faults. The program test set is designed and developed in three increments, or phases. At requirements time, the requirements-based test cases are inventoried and designed. At design time, the design-based cases are specified, and, at execution time, any supplemental cases needed to provide code coverage or probe execution-based results are added. Designing the tests in this way allows for them to be used in any program specifications or design and code reviews and maximizes test effectiveness and productivity.

SUMMARY

1. Questions testing in the small must answer:
   - Does the logic work properly?
   - Is all the necessary logic present?
2. Organizing program testing is best achieved by preparing unit testing designs.
3. The test design establishes the testing strategy and defines the source of test cases to be utilized:

Requirements Based	from the specifications
Design Based	from the design structure
Code Based	from the data structure
Extremes	from limits and boundary conditions
Extracted	from existing files
Randomized	from test data generators

4. Different programs require different testing methods.
5. Test planning and design ensures the best blend of the techniques available.
6. Test planning and design provides the opportunity for others to review proposed testing.
7. The functional test matrix is one technique for organizing requirements-based test cases.
8. Structural testing depends on systematic code analysis to exercise the underlying logical structure.
9. Complete coverage means every statement is exercised and all decision outcomes are exercised.
10. Three ways to achieve complete coverage are:
    - Start with black-box test cases and add cases as necessary to exercise any logic remaining untested.
    - Heuristic, based on program logical analysis.
    - Structured basis testing methodology.
11. The structured basis testing method consists of the following steps:
    - Draw a program flowgraph and select a logical piece to be tested.
    - Calculate the complexity C.
    - Derive a basis set of cases containing C independent test cases.

- Obtain expected results for each derived test case.
- Execute or walk through the cases.

12. Structured basis testing is well suited to test pseudocode or top-down logic.

13. Testing extremes depends on careful analysis of limits and boundaries.

14. Extracted and generated data play a limited role in program testing but are important to plan for and use when appropriate.

15. Syntax testing provides a means of deriving test cases that "cover" a complex input specification.

16. Five important categories of tools for testing in the small are:
    - Test data generators
    - Program logic analyzers
    - Test coverage measurement aides
    - Test drivers
    - Test comparators

17. The recommended testing in the small practices is to design program tests in three increments.
    - Requirements-based tests at requirements time
    - Design-based tests at program design time
    - Code-based tests at execution time

18. Code coverage measurement should be utilized to determine the need for supplemental code-based tests.

Chapter 8

Testing Systems—Testing in the Large

In earlier chapters I emphasized the importance of testing each phase of project work as it is carried out. With effective, ongoing testing a project will not *start* testing in the large unless reasonable confidence in the design and in the testing of individual programs has first been obtained. Without such confidence, the problems of testing in the large easily become unmanageable. Trying to test a complex system that has a shaky design and many seriously defective pieces *will not work*! This lesson has been learned over and over again.

One cannot *skip* design and program testing. All that happens when we try is that we learn the system doesn't work. Then we are driven back into cleaning up and correcting the design and the individual programs before we can continue anyway. Many programmers have tried. They are the clients I see. Bogged down in systems testing with the project 95 percent completed, they struggle to make up for inadequate early testing. The best they can hope for is excessively high system testing cost. The worst is project failure.

Despite the lessons we keep relearning, most projects don't begin work on designing and preparing system level tests until late in the design phase or until coding is nearly completed. The reasons are hard to understand, but certainly procrastination and misplaced optimism play important roles. We want to believe that we're doing such a good job that early testing is unnecessary. Since we don't "have" to test in the beginning, we put it off and wait until it is forced on us. Analyst availability plays a part as well. In the early work on a project the analyst's primary concern is software design work and preparing program specifications so programming can start. Only after that does the analyst begin to think seriously about testing, and by then it is too late, coding is already under way, and there is simply not enough time left to properly design and prepare the tests.

Meaning of Testing in the Large

In this chapter we will examine techniques and guidelines for effective testing in the large, which means any testing of *groups* of programs together. Various projects use different names for parts of the overall testing in the large effort. Examples include component testing, functional testing, systems testing, product testing, delivery testing, stress testing, parallel testing, field testing, acceptance testing, and so forth. Most organizations and designers of major projects do prepare some form of plan for this testing in the large effort. The plan establishes the testing approach and usually defines at least three distinct levels of testing to be performed. The most common names for these levels of testing are *integration testing, systems testing,* and *acceptance testing.*

Integration testing centers on getting programs assembled into components or functional pieces, systems testing on functional performance and behavior of the total system, and acceptance testing on the readiness for system installation and production use.

Major Testing in the Large Levels

Integration testing	• Interfacing of programs and modules
	• Assembling system components
	• Program/module interactions
Systems testing	• Functional performance
	• System capabilities
Acceptance testing	• System requirements
	• Implementation readiness

In some projects, a clear distinction between these levels may not exist. For example, in small projects it is common to find only systems testing and acceptance testing (integration is treated as a part of the systems test). In larger projects the three levels may be repeated for different parts of the system (components or builds) and additional testing steps, involving quality assurance and independent testing and validation efforts, may be defined. Here I treat all of this testing under the one broad heading of testing in the large and the planning effort for all of it as the preparation of a key document I call the *Master Test Plan.*

Objectives for Testing in the Large

The first step in any good plan is to establish clear objectives. For testing in the large our key objective is to determine the overall system performance. Two basic questions need to be answered:

What is the system quality?

• What is the system capable of doing?
• What are the limitations?

Will the system support operational use?

• Are major failures unlikely?
• Is quality adequate for use?
• Is there sufficient readiness to use the system?

Answering these questions is essential to support the higher objective of making a good decision about installing a system. All of our testing is but a means to that end. While that should be obvious, I find it is easily forgotten in the heat of system testing. The goal is not to "complete" the testing, but to obtain enough confidence about the product to be able to use it safely!

Specific objectives for testing in the large have to be carefully established and agreed to by all key parties. What level of quality is good enough? How much of the system has to be working before implementation can occur? Which requirements and test cases have to be working? Which parts are less critical and may be deferred? What amount of implementation risk is acceptable?

Guidelines for Achieving Good Testing Objectives

• Start early—the first draft of the acceptance test should be prepared during requirements definition.
• Write down tentative objectives and let people *see* them.
• Prepare a Master Test Plan and have it reviewed by project designers and end users.
• Develop requirements-based and design-based coverage inventories, and use these to derive the design of test cases.
• Be receptive to critiques and willing to modify objectives as the project proceeds.
• Document all agreed-upon objectives in the Master Test Plan.

These questions are a major part of the already very sizable testing in the large planning effort. They are not easy questions to resolve. Most project managers avoid answering them and are forced into making the implementation decision "in extremis." The purpose of the Master Test Plan is to help raise such issues early enough that they may be dealt with effectively.

The key is to document the objectives and make them visible for review and discussion. This is the fundamental role of the Master Test Plan and because of this document's importance to testing in the large I discuss it in much more detail in the next section.

Master Test Plan—The Central Tool for Managing Testing in the Large

I have emphasized the importance of good planning to effective testing. The careful preparation of the Master Test Plan is an *essential* prerequisite to preparing for and managing the testing in the large effort. Unplanned and ad hoc systems testing leads to almost certain disaster. Careful advance planning is no guarantee that all will proceed smoothly, but is a *necessary* step that greatly improves the odds.

The Master Test Plan, or MTP, is a formal document that defines the testing objectives, establishes a coordinating strategy for all testing, and provides the framework for detailed planning of all steps and tasks in the process.

The Master Test Plan—What Is It?

A document (or series of documents) that is outlined during project initiation and is expanded and reviewed during a project to guide and control all testing effort.

The Master Test Plan—Why Have It?

The plan is the primary means by which testing may be directed and controlled

• Raises testing issues

• Defines testing work

• Coordinates testing efforts

• Assigns and obtains resources

The MTP is the primary vehicle for shaping testing strategy as well as documenting the agreed-upon plans. Its contents will vary significantly, depending on the organization and the project. Some companies have broad, established testing policies that apply to all projects. In such cases, the MTP simply refers to the procedures and extends them as necessary. In others, the MTP must be more extensive. Project variables will also affect the contents significantly. A typical table of contents for an MTP has been included.

The Master Test Plan—Typical Table of Contents

Testing Strategy/Approach

- Testing life cycle definition
- Overall testing approach
- Major tools/techniques to be employed
- Definition of components and test pieces or builds
- Procedure to revise/expand and review

Test Design and Implementation Approach

- Overall organization of test cases
- Test objectives and criteria
- Requirements validation matrix
- Test design techniques
- Other test data information

Responsibilities

- Testing Organization
- Resources and schedules
- Tasks and assignments

Testing Deliverables

- Test documents
- Test procedures and supporting software
- Test reports

Procedures

- Test procedures
- Problem reporting and tracking
- Retesting

Controls

- Changes
- Reports and information

A major contribution provided by the Master Test Plan is the definition of the *Testing Life Cycle*. The concept is that at each step of development there are key testing deliverables; the MTP must define those deliverables and establish clearly who is responsible for each one. Earlier, we introduced the testing life cycle and an outline of a typical set of testing deliverables. Each of the deliverables represents a major task or milestone within the overall testing effort. Taken collectively the testing deliverables define the testing work, and documenting it in the MTP provides the vehicle for managing its completion.

Over the last decade the development life cycle has matured and there has emerged a broad consensus among project managers as to what the major deliverables are. The testing life cycle is still in its infancy, and much debate can be expected over the "best" way to define and break up the work. Initiating this debate is one of the main purposes of the MTP document—the starting point in the overall testing strategy. Just as I recommended the analysis of *alternatives* when reviewing designs, I believe several testing strategy alternatives should be outlined and the impact on the testing life cycle displayed. Key individuals should then review these alternatives and help establish the best approach. Once a consensus has been reached, the first draft of the MTP can be issued and used to record the group viewpoint or stimulate further discussion as needed. The emphasis here is on *inducing commitment* from important project players and end users. The testing strategy must be understood and supported. To do that people must get involved in shaping the strategy and come away with some sense of ownership or feeling of personal contribution.

Once the initial draft of the MTP has been published and reviewed, there is an established framework for more detailed test planning. All planning information is available in one place and project participants know where to find it and what to expect. Supplementary information is issued throughout the project as more detailed plans are developed.

These supplements may come out as separate documents that refer back to the coordinating MTP, or they may be provided as updates and extensions. Typically, separate documents will be provided to detail the integration test, systems test, and acceptance test steps of the testing in the large strategy. Separate documents for individual test cases (or groups of cases) called test specifications are also commonly employed, and techniques for constructing these are discussed next.

Putting the Master Test Plan Together

A Strategy for Inducing Commitment

1. Start with a *tentative* testing strategy for discussion.
2. Outline several alternative strategies for comparison.
3. Open Presentation/Discussion
   - Present the alternatives
   - Show testing life cycle implications
   - Stimulate *open* dialogue and comment
4. Analysis of Expected Demands
   - How is each area affected by the tentative strategy?
   - What are the likely implications?
5. *Revise* the tentative strategy on the basis of discussion and analysis.
6. Statement of Commitment
   - From each unit
   - What commitments will they make?
   - How can they help?
   - What help will they require from others?
7. Identify major testing deliverables.
   - What testing work has to be performed?
   - What are the end products?
8. Establish major test responsibilities
   - Use the statements of commitment
   - Assign each deliverable
9. Publish initial Master Test Plan for review.
10. Review formally—test the test plan.

Test Case Specifications and Folios

Specialized techniques for organizing test data for program and unit testing are normally not necessary. The number of cases used to test a program is usually modest—10 to 20 is typical—and the amount of data in each is not extensive. As a result, test cases are usually documented as a part of the unit plan or as a natural extension of the program specifications.

When testing in the large the situation is very different. The problems associated with specifying tests and keeping track of all information related to a given case are burdensome. Careful planning and organization are needed to avoid seriously impacting the quality and/or cost of the testing work. It is not uncommon to have hundreds, or even thousands, of cases and situations. For each we must have detailed procedures and specifications that define the test and tell how it is run as well as the current status. (For example: Have test data been developed? Has the test been run? When was the last time it was run? What were the results?) Tests at the systems level involve many more data, and fully specifying even a single test may require pages of output. Multiplying by hundreds of tests creates a very large data management task that is a critical part of the testing effort. *Test case folios* and *test information systems* are important tools in addressing this need.

The test case folio is simply a folder or a document containing information on a case or related group of cases. It may be created to bring together the tests relating to a specific function or system requirement or any other convenient grouping. Once the folio is organized, *everything* related to the test cases is stored in it.

Test Case Folios—Possible Contents

1. Identification for the test group or test case
2. Testing objectives (what the test accomplishes)
3. Description of the situation being tested
4. Test data (or a reference to where it is or how generated)
5. Expected or required results (what the anticipated result is)
6. Entrance criteria (what has to happen before the test can start)
7. Setup and execution procedures (detail of how test is conducted)
8. Exit criteria (what it takes to sign off the test)
9. Responsibility (who is responsible for the test)
10. Activity log (record of executions or changes)
11. Actual results

All of this information is important. Because items 6 to 11 may appear to be an overkill to some practitioners, they deserve further comment. Entrance and exit criteria spell out what has to happen before a test can start and what has to be confirmed before it can be successfully signed off. For complex test situations, such pre- and post-conditions are far from obvious. Entrance criteria can be used to specify how much of the system must be present (i.e., which modules and functions) or what environment is required (daytime, test system, version, change levels, etc.). Exit criteria define the checking or verifications that must be made after test execution. They may specify certain data base or file conditions, balancing requirements, and so forth.

Setup and execution procedures define *how* the test is to be conducted. This section of the folio can specify session sequences or refer to utility programs and procedures that must be run to conduct the test. The responsibility block defines who is responsible for the case and who is authorized to change any parts of it. Changes occur in test folios much as they do in programs. Data may have to be augmented or modified, test procedures may be changed, entrance and exit criteria altered; even the test objectives and expected results will occasionally undergo change. This has led some organizations to adopt change control procedures or version control on the folios. Thus we have version 5 of test group 38, and so on. The activity log is used to record all changes made in the folio and keep track of all attempted executions. Actual results may be stored in the folio as output listings and recorded in the activity log to maintain a complete audit trail of the results for the case. Many practitioners maintain only the most recent test run output. Practical experience has shown a need to maintain all the listings. One common example occurs when a test is suddenly discovered not to be working and we want to know how far back the problem can be traced. Other similar needs arise during retesting and debugging.

The benefits of using test case folios are substantial and grow with project size and complexity. A case can be made for retaining all of the folio contents and certainly for the use of the folio as a basic organizing tool. Besides helping to organize the testing information, the folios provide a consistent documentation format and help encourage careful planning and design of each case. Some companies have automated the folios and built what might be called a *test data base* or *testing information system*. Such systems provide a facility for entering and storing all the folio information in on-line files. Reports and displays permit easy access to the information as needed during the project. The resources used in testing are also captured and included in the data base so the system can provide broad management reports that show testing status and costs and maintain an ongoing project record.

Unfortunately, such systems are not readily available in the software marketplace. Any such system must interface with existing project control and development tools, a requirement that tends to force heavy customization. Companies that have automated test systems have built their own. One common approach is to start with a data dictionary or a library support system and extend it to support test case information. Software products for this application should become more readily available within the next few years.

Integration Testing

Testing in the large begins when we first combine programs. A group of programs must interact reasonably well before it makes sense (or even becomes possible) to test the group functionally. The objective of integration testing is to test program interfaces and confirm that programs have been linked together correctly. Our concern is not with function or requirements during this early testing in the large; instead, our goal is to ensure that we have a basic *skeleton system* that will serve as our test platform. Fatal errors such as improper calling sequences or mismatched parameters and data must be found and corrected before any cases can produce meaningful output.

Integration Testing Objectives

- Obtain a working skeleton as rapidly as possible.
- Establish confidence that the skeleton parts interface and link correctly.
- Demonstrate that simple test cases and transactions are being handled properly by the system.

Most practitioners have little appreciation for the considerations involved in planning effective integration testing. Some of the considerations that good integration test planning must address are listed below.

Considerations for Integration Test Planning

Which modules should be assembled first?

How many modules should be assembled before integration testing starts?

What order should be used to integrate the modules?
- Top levels working down
- Critical modules first
- Bottom levels working up
- Functional groups

Should there be more than one skeleton?
- How is each skeleton defined?
- Are there distinct build levels

How much testing should be done on each skeleton?
- What tests should be conducted?

These questions have no simple answers. Answering them requires a weighing of trade-offs. Any time we break down the testing task into pieces and levels we add some additional testing work. We do this in the belief that it will save work in the long run. We have learned through practical experience that attempting to test too much at once complicates the testing job and may greatly enlarge debugging and error correction time. The optimum selection of modules to be integrated and tested together cannot be made by consulting any formula—it is inherently dependent on the individual project and must be examined by looking at the pros and cons of different alternatives. Such analysis is what good integration test planning rests upon.

To illustrate, consider just the choice of the *order* of integration. We assume we have already made the decision that a certain group of modules should be tested together as a single skeleton or component.

The question is, Which modules should we start with first? All of the six listed alternatives are choices made in practice.

Some Alternatives for the Order of Module Integration

1. *Top-level modules*—Start with the driver and command or top-level modules and then work down by "plugging in" the additional modules.

2. *Critical modules*—Start with the critical system modules and integrate them, then add the rest of the skeleton around them.

3. *Bottom-level modules*—Start with the individual programs as they complete unit testing and integrate by working up to build bigger and bigger pieces.

4. *Functional modules*—Select a specific function and integrate the modules needed for that function, then proceed to the next function, and so on.

5. *As-available modules*—Take the modules that are ready and fit them together as much as possible.

6. *Complete skeleton*—Integrate all the modules in the skeleton at once and hold off any integration testing until all are interfaced.

Many combinations of these six choices are also possible integration order alternatives. For example, number 1 may be combined with numbers 2, 3, 4, or 5. Once the top level has been integrated, critical components, bottom-up components, functional components, or as-available modules can be put together and then plugged into the top level structure as a unit.

Choosing one of these orders as "best" for a particular project involves looking at the cumulative impact of many factors. The amount of "scaffolding" code that has to be constructed is one such factor. By scaffolding code we mean extra code that has to be written to support the testing process. This includes test driver or stub routines and many special programs that are written to set up test conditions or check testing output. Just as scaffolding on a building is temporary and not part of the final construction, scaffolding code is eventually removed and not a part of the final product.

How much scaffolding code is needed depends greatly on the integration alternative selected. For example, bottom-up integration requires test driver code to exercise low-level routines. Top-down integration requires stub routines to simulate missing modules. The total amount of scaffolding required is significant. In one large project where this was carefully measured, it exceeded 20 percent of the total delivered code! Nothing is quite so frustrating as discovering that a sticky problem is due to faulty scaffolding. Such errors are common because of the ad hoc manner in which most such code is implemented and tested. Scaffolding does impact project success, and integration planning should directly evaluate how different strategies of integration will affect it.

Another factor relates to project schedule. If ceratin modules are behind schedule and starting systems testing execution is a top concern, the integration test team may be forced to work with whatever modules are available. It may be critical to get something up and running, and the choice of that something will determine the integration priorities. Integrating critical or difficult components first may allow system testing to proceed independently on the most difficult parts of the system and thus speed up implementation.

Still another factor is system reliability. Top-down testing exercises high-level modules much more heavily than the low-level ones. Bottom-up testing is just the opposite. If system reliability depends on low-level modules, then bottom-up integration may be preferred. This is another argument for the critical-software-first approach. Such critical modules are usually the ones that influence system reliability most. Integrating them first reduces the risk that they will not be completed on schedule and increases their reliability.

All of these considerations and factors influence our choice of the best integration plan. My personal preference is biased toward small skeletons that are functionally oriented. I look for the *smallest* number of modules that may be combined and still tested effectively. That requires some means of input and output and at least some minimal processing capability or function. This grouping then becomes a skeleton to be integrated and tested as a unit. The methodology might be described in five steps.

Suggested Integration Testing Methodology

1. Select a minimal group of modules that support some basic function and are not too difficult to test as a unit.
2. Link the module group together to form a skeleton and get the basic function running.
3. Test the integration of the skeleton
   - Exercise all input and output parameters of each module.
   - Exercise all modules and calls.
   - Exercise all program options and special utility routines.
4. Stress test the skeleton.
   - Test load
   - Test performance
   - Try to break the skeleton
5. Then integrate the next group of modules.
   - Repeat steps 1 to 4 as necessary to complete the build level

Two major problems plague integration testing in practice. The first is integrating modules that have not been properly unit tested. Just as a single bad apple will quickly rot the entire barrel, it takes only several poorly tested modules to ruin a solid integration testing plan. Some form of quality check or acceptance must be made by the integration test team to ensure that modules are ready to be integrated. The second problem is failing to treat integration testing formally enough. Like all testing, the integration tests must be designed and planned to ensure thorough coverage. All interfaces should be checked, not just a random few. Systematic completion criteria such as exercising all input and output parameters, exercising all calls, etc. need to be established and used to define the integration testing work and determine when it is completed.

Organizations that experience trouble with integration testing can expect to trace their difficulties to one of these two problems. The rush to get systems testing started makes us fall prey to accepting poor unit testing and to integrate with little planning or formal interface testing. Making the effort to test the integration carefully guarantees that we have a properly assembled skeleton and provides the platform needed to conduct our systems testing. It is worth it in terms of the trade-off of cost versus quality in our final product!

Systems Testing

Systems test execution starts when integration testing has been completed. It ends when we have successfully determined what the system capabilities are and corrected enough of the known problems to have confidence that the system is ready for acceptance testing. Systems testing is the major piece of testing in the large. It consumes the bulk of the testing resources and careful planning, and control of its conduct is essential to a successful outcome.

When System Testing Begins and Ends

System test design and test development *begins* in the requirements phase with the design of requirements-based tests

System testing execution *begins* when a minimal system or skeleton has been integrated

System testing *ends* when we have measured system capabilities and corrected enough of the problems to have confidence that we are ready to run the acceptance test

---

The Master Test Plan and test case folios have already been discussed as important tools in planning and organizing the systems test. In a real sense everything I have talked about in the book has been motivated by lessons learned from systems tests that have gone awry. The systems test for a large, complex project is a large and complex task. The emphasis on testing and reviewing each phase of work as it is conducted, on thorough and systematic unit and integration testing, and on the Master Test Plan concept are all aimed at the prime goal of reaching the systems test in such a position that it can be completed relatively easily.

This is the payoff for all the effort we invested earlier! We want to avoid the agony so often experienced in the final throes of project implementation. We want to minimize the painful and labor-intensive process of searching for and correcting major system deficiencies. We want to avoid last-minute changes that go poorly tested. This is our motivation for improved testing processes and what makes an investment in better testing methodology produce such a high return.

The planning for systems testing starts with the requirements-based test cases—those sufficient to demonstrate or cover the system from a black box perspective. It may be well for the reader to return to Chapter 7 and review the earlier discussion of requirements-based test designs. All the same principles and guidelines apply. The only difference is that we are now planning the testing for a group of programs instead of a single one. Some of the functional cases derived for program testing may be reused during systems testing. Others derive from the system requirements specifications.

As each group of cases is designed a test specification should be created for it. The format should specify the information needed to define each case.

Requirements-Based Systems Testing

Purpose: Provide a *systematic* demonstration that all functions are available as specified.

Is user oriented

- No knowledge of internals
- Derived from user manuals or requirements specifications

Key technique is careful planning and inventories of test objectives

- All classes of valid system input must be accepted
- All classes of invalid system input must be rejected
- All functions must be exercised
- All classes of system outputs must be exercised
- Effective states must be entered
- Interfacing systems or procedures must be invoked

Organize and prepare test specifications

- Around requirements
- Around key functions
- Around special test cases
- All test cases to be documented
- All test cases to have predicted results

Look for systematic coverage

- Functional coverage matrix
- Requirements validation matrix
- Transaction flows
- Functional boundaries

Review

- To identify additional tests
- Evaluate effectiveness of current ones

At a minimum this must include the test objective, test data, expected results, and any test procedures or special requirements. As mentioned earlier, entrance and exit criteria and an activity log are also very helpful.

A second major part of the systems test is the tests of *performance capability*. Requirements-based cases concentrate on demonstrating system functional capability. Additional cases are required to measure and explore system performance limits. Common examples include the evaluation of performance parameters such as response time, run requirements, and file sizes. Also included in this category are tests for other quality attributes such as reliability, maintainability, and integrity. Many systems tests do an excellent job of testing functional capability but fail miserably when it comes to measuring the broader aspects of performance and quality. These areas contribute greatly to operational failure and must be carefully tested.

Performance Capability Systems Testing

Purpose: Provide a systematic determination of what the performance capabilities are and demonstrate that performance and overall quality will meet the operational requirements of the system.

Is volume and limit oriented

- Drive the system to its limits
- Determine where it breaks down
- First test to specification, then break and analyze

Key technique is careful planning

- Sources of test data
- Use of simulators and test data generators
- Experiments and models

Organize test specifications

- Around each performance feature or attribute
- Around each quality factor

Review

- To identify additional tests
- Evaluate effectiveness of current ones

One of the performance capability tests has been given the special name of *volume testing*. A volume test is planned with the specific objective of determining how many transactions or how many records can be operationally supported. Functional cases that have already been tested are reintroduced to the system at higher and higher volumes until the system is no longer capable of effective operation. If the test is carefully designed, it determines a range of suitable volumes for the system and measures the "breakpoint." Extracted test data (taken from live files) or generated data (either from a test data generator or replication of already defined cases) avoid the problem of having to hand prepare volume data.

Other special performance tests are gaining more common use. These include tests of system documentation (usability, completeness); system reliability (failure analysis, stress testing, operational testing); and system maintainability (documentation, time to make standard changes). Just as with the functional tests, specifications for each case or case group have to be organized and formal documentation maintained to ensure that we have thought out the test case carefully and understand what it is attempting to measure.

In addition to the requirements-based tests and the performance tests, the system test also emphasizes design-based tests developed to test or break the software design. Most of the tests derived from the design are suitable as system level tests and should be included in the system test set. These tests were designed in parallel with the software design activity and have already been used once to walk through and validate the design specifications. Now, they are implemented and executed as a part of the integration and system test.

When discussing testing in the small I placed emphasis on structural test cases and developed the technique of structured basis testing to provide systematic coverage of the underlying logic. Until recently, these notions had little impact on testing in the large. The reasons were strictly practical limitations. Systems testing is applied to large numbers of programs at once, with many thousands of lines of logic. The test cases are usually constructed without the designer ever looking at the code. Systematically examining the logic to produce additional systems test cases requires too much time to be worth the effort. However, during the last few years new tools and techniques that are changing the picture have come along. I believe these will play increasingly important roles in systems testing in the future.

The concept is the same as in testing in the small. What we would like to do is select a set of test cases that systematically *cover* or explore the system logical structure. While it is generally impractical to spend time analyzing low-level logic to achieve this, there are ways in which structural systems coverage may be achieved.

Design-Based Systems Testing

Purpose: Provide systematic test coverage of the software design structure.

Approaches

1. Include design-based tests developed during the software design.
2. Model high-level system flow and apply structural testing ideas from unit testing to these models.
3. Instrument the system to *measure* the structural coverage obtained by normal systems testing and to identify areas requiring further cases.

One approach is to apply the structural analysis at a high logic level. System or transaction flow diagrams offer a good illustration. It is common practice in on-line systems to define the various transactions with transaction flow diagrams. By transaction, I mean a set of operations that begins with an input and ends with one or more outputs. The transaction flow diagram is a *model* showing the sequence of steps performed in the processing of the transaction. The model illustrates what happens functionally; it does not show the detailed or actual control structure of the program. Nevertheless, we are able to apply structural testing techniques to it just as we did in program testing. A basic set of test cases that will test each process step and exercise all decision outcomes can be derived. We can also use the flow diagram to find achievable (structurally possible) flows that logically should not exist or to develop special cases for the most tortuous possibilities. All of these make excellent transaction cases. Similar types of structural analysis may be applied to system flow diagrams and high-level system design models or logic flows.

Another approach to obtaining structural system coverage is through *instrumentation.* At the simplest level we might establish the criterion that every module in the system is entered by at least one of our selected cases. We could "instrument" the system to record each module entered during testing, check this list against the list of module names, and report any modules missed. Cases would be selected as in any systems test planning effort. These cases are then executed by using the instrumented system to automatically record the extent of coverage. The method may easily be extended to test for more complete structural coverage. All interfaces might be instrumented so as to gauge the effectiveness of the integration test. If instrumentation is inserted at each program decision point, path coverage may be measured and any statements not executed by the set of systems tests determined. Some organizations have established criteria such as 70 percent of all system branches being exercised by the systems test cases. Use of such quantified coverage criteria provides insurance that the systems test has been comprehensive and has actually been performed.

Systems testing should produce a key deliverable called the *test data set*, which is a special set of cases designed to exercise a system over most or all of its capabilities. Its purpose is to support retesting when system changes are made. The cases are normally a subset of those used in the systems test. The logical time to produce the test data set deliverable is during systems testing. All that is required is to "save" the cases we have constructed so that they will be available for reuse as changes to the system occur. Preparing the test data set as a product of systems testing costs little; preparing it at any other time is usually so expensive that we end up not having one at all!

The System Test Data Set

- A special set of test cases designed to exercise a system over most of its capabilities
- Prepared as a product of the systems test
- Used to retest the system after any changes are made to it
- Output compared to show performance not affected

I shall have much more to say about the test data set in the next chapter. The key consideration here is to plan to produce one as a part of each systems test. If a test data set is produced for every system as it is developed, then a complete data base of such test files will be available for all operational systems. Such a test file is a prerequisite to high quality, cost-effective maintenance.

Acceptance Testing

The third major testing in the large level is the acceptance test. The purpose of acceptance testing is to confirm that a system is ready for operational use. The systems test measures and determines what the systems capabilities are. It ends when the *tester* is confident that the system is ready to be used. The acceptance test is performed for or by *someone else* (normally the eventual user) to demonstrate that the confidence is justified.

I favor an acceptance test that is expected to work and is executed smoothly and rapidly (preferably within several days). If the systems test has been thorough, there should be few surprises and virtually no new discrepancies discovered during the acceptance test. This test exists as a final stage of confidence building for the user and as protection against overly risky implementation for the organization.

System Acceptance Test

Purpose: To demonstrate that a system is ready for operational use

Approach

- Focus is on user requirements
- A final stage of confidence building
- User involvement is major
- Is *expected* to be successful

The selection of the tests to include in the acceptance test should be made by the user, but with expert professional help from the test planners. Many approaches are possible. The focus is on major functional and performance requirements. If good requirements testing was done during the requirements definition phase tests will already be defined and associated with each requirement. All the acceptance test planners need do is dust them off and review or augment them as necessary. Most of the acceptance cases can be taken directly from the systems test. The only difference is that the cases will now be run in a quasi-operational environment, perhaps using the actual hardware, software, and user environment that is planned for production. Other common test approaches are to take a typical day's worth of transactions, or a hypothetical month or year of operations, and to demonstrate that all business for the typical day or hypothetical period is properly processed.

Major Sources of Acceptance Test Cases

- Requirements tests
- Subset of the systems test cases
- Typical processing day or period
- Pilot operation

When testing a replacement system, the *parallel run* is a commonly used strategy. The "old" system processes a selected amount of data (day or month, for example) during its routine production run. These data are saved and reentered as input to the "new" system to be processed, again "in parallel." The output is compared and balanced against the parallel run output to confirm proper processing.

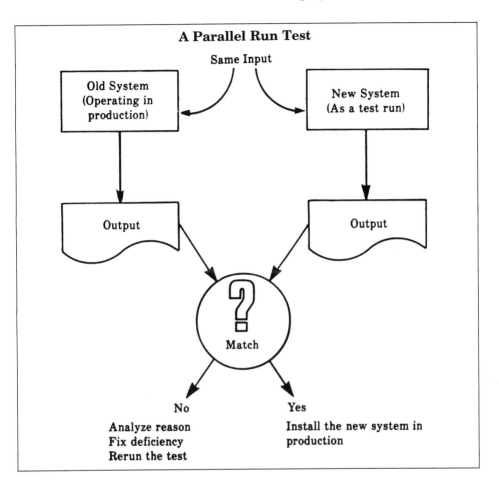

A Parallel Run Test

Another special test that is often included within an overall acceptance test plan is some test for endurance or reliability.

Endurance is defined as the ability of a system to operate continuously. This type of acceptance test tries to establish that a system has sufficient endurance or reliability to permit installation. The main criterion is carefully defining how much degradation can occur—for example, does invoking error recovery or backup count?—and requiring a complete restart whenever that level is reached.

Example of Acceptance Test to Test Endurance

- Test will be run on operational hardware and software.
- Test will contain periods when system is stressed significantly.
- Duration will span the full run cycle. (For continuous systems this should be at least twenty-five hours.)
- All interfaced systems must be in operation throughout the test.
- Test will exercise the system over a full range of inputs, including illegal and unexpected.
- All major functions and interfaces will be exercised during the endurance run.
- Not completing the entire test for any reason requires the full test to be restarted.

Similar formal tests should be defined for each major requirement or performance criterion. Test specifications for each case selected are as important to acceptance testing as for any other testing in the large activity. Special emphasis needs to be given to defining test objectives, and "success" criteria and all the important quality attributes need to be acceptance tested, including reliability, maintainability, and documentation.

Organizations experience several common problems with acceptance testing. The biggest is forgetting that a *perfect* system is not the goal! We all know that every system has deficiencies. We don't want to wait until all of these are corrected before we begin using the system. Rather, the system should be accepted if it is good enough to use. The primary issue is usability and reliability. Will the system support operational use? Thus the acceptance test should be designed to focus on usability and reliability and not get bogged down with a mass of minor discrepancies and problems. If is fine to keep track of such minor problems, but they must not interfere with the broader objective of the test or adversely affect the system's acceptance.

A second major problem occurs when the acceptance test responsibility is placed totally in the user's hands and the user is not equipped to carry it out.

Two Common Pitfalls in Acceptance Testing

- Forgetting the objective—striving for perfection instead of effective operational use
- Testing without planning—informal playing with the system by the end user as a substitute for true acceptance testing

Planning effective testing takes an experienced and knowledgeable professional. Novice users cannot be expected to know the importance of a careful test plan or of carefully documenting expected results for each test case. Their testing takes the form of "informal system exercise." They try some cases to see what happens. If things "look" all right they accept the system; if they don't, they reject it. This is a poor approach to acceptance testing and may be likened to the situation of a teacher deciding on what it takes to pass an exam after the test is over.

Automated Tools and Aids

Software tools and support packages are very important to testing in the large. Knowing what tools are available and how to select and use them impacts the testing in the large plan and can greatly influence effectiveness and cost. The most important tools include instrumenters, comparators, test data generators, file extractors and conversion aids, test data capture and playback systems, simulators, debugging and documentation aids, and test case management or testing information systems.

Important Tools for Testing in the Large

- *Instrumenters*—to measure and report test coverage during execution

- *Comparators*—to compare outputs, files, and source programs

- *Test data generators*—to generate files and test data input

- *Capture playback systems*—to capture on-line test data and play it back

- *Simulators and test beds*—to simulate complex and real-time environments

- *Debugging aids*—to aid in determining what is wrong and getting it repaired

- *Testing information systems*—to maintain test cases and report on testing activities

- *File aids*—to extract test data from existing files for use in testing

- *System charters and documenters*—to provide automatic system documentation

---

I gave examples of many of these tools in the last chapter. (The reader should refer back to Chapter 6 for examples of how instrumenters, comparators, and test data generator packages operate.) While helpful in unit testing situations, the tools are often indispensable for large-scale testing.

Many situations arise when it is necessary to build large test or conversion files quickly. Test data generators serve that need ideally. They also facilitate volume and performance capability testing. Planning for testing in the large should always consider their potential use carefully. Properly employed, they may save enormous amounts of time that is otherwise spent laboriously constructing test data.

A closely related tool is the online capture/playback facility. With a capture playback tool, online transactions and keystrokes for messages from terminals may be "captured" as they are keyed or sent and then later "replayed" or resent to the system under test. An example that has gained popular use is TRAPS—*Test Recording and Playback System*—developed by the Travelers Insurance Company. With TRAPS, online tests can be recorded using a PC as a 3270 terminal. The tool runs on the PC and captures all keystrokes entered as well as the screen responses from the application, and permits saving them in named "playfiles." When the playfile is played back as a test, the tool compares the saved response with the actual response from the application and records and reports on any mismatches that are found. In this way, retesting of on-line tests is automated and becomes self-documenting—both critical aids to conducting productive and effective on line testing.

The instrumenters are equally important. Test coverage may be measured in the large, just as it is in the small. In many ways the measurement of coverage in the large is more informative because other information about the extent of structural testing is not available. The SOFTOOL package described in Chapter 7 has good facilities to support such measurement. The program or system level report shows the programs executed during the last test and over all tests in a given test series. This allows confirmation that the system test set invokes all programs and provides documentation that the tests are actually executed. The same capability is available at the paragraph level and the statement level. If considered as the system is constructed, a self-instrumenting capability is easy to build in. As a simple example, each program or paragraph may be built with a compile time option to write a record to a special file each time it is invoked. Processing this file will give an effective measurement of test coverage without requiring the purchase of any specialized packages. Other similar self-measuring techniques are in common use.

As with test data generators, proper use of comparators can save a great deal of time and improve system testing effectiveness. Planning for their use is the same as that discussed in the last chapter. The decision to use the comparator should be made when the test case is designed. Testing procedures and the definition of expected results can then be constructed with the comparator tool in mind.

Simulators and test beds are two additional tools of significance to testing in the large. Two examples suffice to demonstrate how knowledge and use of the right simulator may totally alter the testing in the large plan. Consider first the problem of testing a large on line system with many thousands of terminals dispersed geographically in a large network. There is no practical way to control input at the dispersed terminals so that, without a simulator, testing must be conducted from a few selected test terminals. Such testing cannot effectively measure response times, yet for volume or stress testing that is the key issue! The solution to the problem is the use of a network simulator.

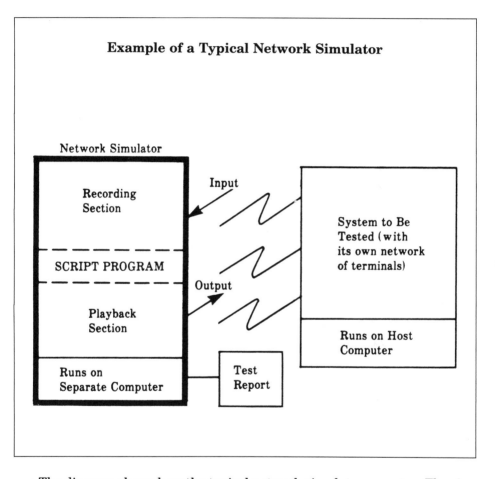

Example of a Typical Network Simulator

Network Simulator

Recording Section

SCRIPT PROGRAM

Playback Section

Runs on Separate Computer

Input

Output

System to Be Tested (with its own network of terminals)

Runs on Host Computer

Test Report

The diagram shows how the typical network simulator operates. The simulator can be connected to an existing network and instructed to record actual network transactions as they occur in real time. In effect this is a legal "wiretap" to provide a permanent record of everything that occurred at every terminal in the system. Once this is recorded, the system may be tested by instructing the simulator to play back the transactions just as they occurred. To the system this looks just like a typical business day, with thousands of on-line terminals sending in their transactions. Even line drops and line failures are replicated just as they occurred in real time. Since the simulator is running on its own computer, the response times in the test system are realistic. By supplying a "script" of special instructions to the simulator we are able to play back the transactions twice or ten times as fast, or select special transactions, define new transactions, and so forth. This allows us to design comprehensive tests and exercise the system being tested at steadily increasing levels until we learn where it breaks or where response time reaches unacceptable levels. Such superb testing capabilities are simply not possible without the use of this type of support tool.

As a second example, consider the problem of testing a system that requires operation in dozens of different hardware and software configurations. This is a case where an advanced test bed system or environment simulator (see figure) is ideal.

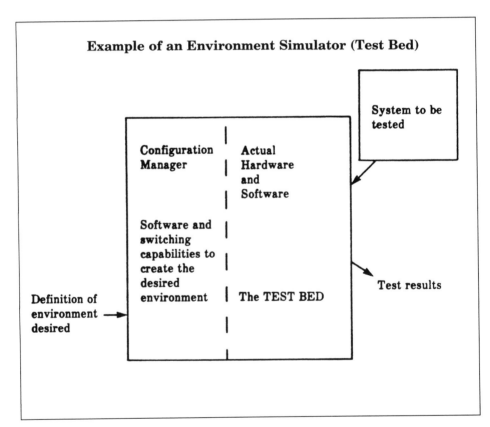

Example of an Environment Simulator (Test Bed)

System to be tested

Configuration Manager | Actual Hardware and Software

Software and switching capabilities to create the desired environment | The TEST BED

Definition of environment desired

Test results

Input to the environment simulator is a description or definition of the particular "test bed" or hardware/software environment desired. The configuration manager "creates" this environment by selecting the appropriate system and making it available for the system to be tested. A test can then be run by using one environment; then the environment can be "changed" and the test run again. Comparators compare the test results and report any discrepancies.

These examples are two of the more common uses of simulators in large-scale testing. Many other powerful simulators are available. These are often industry specific, and testing planners must take special efforts to learn what is available and how it may be used to simplify or improve the effectiveness of their testing.

Debugging aids and system documenters are also important to the testing in the large effort. The many diverse system charting and automated documentation tools help the tester to design tests and understand the overall system. The debugging aids are designed to help discover the underlying problems or causes of discrepancies discovered during testing. Although both the documenters and the debugging aids are, strictly speaking, not testing tools, testing practitioners must be familiar with them and often will have to use them in carrying out their responsibilities.

A final tool of major significance is the testing information system or test data manager. These were discussed earlier in this chapter in the section on test case folios. They offer facilities for maintaining and tracking all data and provide testing status and performance reporting. In general, such systems are not available as off-the-shelf packages. However, DEC's Testmanager tool is one that comes close. Testmanager provides a facility for naming and storing regression test procedures and may be integrated with a coverage instrumenter (PCA) to give execution-time coverage analysis.

Tracking and maintaining familiarity with all the tools mentioned in the last two chapters is not easy. The tools are proliferating rapidly, and many of the best ones are not promoted in the public marketplace. If you are considering tools in your organization, this may be an area in which consulting help is advisable. Many catalogs and directories are available. Reifer, Inc., and SRA are two companies that sell a specialized catalog of software tools, and Software Quality Engineering maintains a catalogue covering just testing tools that are of direct interest to testing practitioners. The National Bureau of Standards is involved in a major project to build and maintain a tool data base. The Datapro and Auerbach manuals are other excellent sources (at least for software that has been successfully marketed to a number of active users). Finally, a number of companies offer a data base search for software products. Sof-Search manages a data base of over forty thousand different software products that permits users to search and receive hard-copy reports within forty-eight hours. All of these sources, together with user groups and professional associations, provide excellent means of staying abreast of what is available.

147

The benefits of selecting the right tools are major. *Good* tools produce significant productivity gains and can strengthen testing effectiveness sharply. They often help in building the testing discipline and tend to have a multiplier effect, brought about through the synergy of people and machines working together effectively. Improper care in selecting the tools and getting them implemented is guaranteed to produce failure and result in another package that lies around gathering dust. There are many such failures. To avoid them you must pick a tool that is easy to use and integrates easily into the existing development and testing methodology within the organization and then you must provide training and help the practitioner to use the tool properly. Without support, even the best tools wither away and fall into disuse. The true total costs of acquiring a package tool are usually greatly underestimated. The cost of selecting a tool, getting it installed, operating it, and supporting it properly over its lifetime is likely to be at least ten times the cost of the license fee. While the fee gets all the attention, it is only a small part of the total cost of acquiring a new tool.

SUMMARY

1. The cornerstone for effective control of testing in the large is the Master Test Plan.

2. The Master Test Plan is the integrating vehicle for all project testing issues.

3. The Master Test Plan should address
   • Strategy and approach
   • Testing life cycle definition
   • Test documents and deliverables
   • Responsibilities
   • Procedures
   • Information and controls
   • Tools and aids

4. The concept of a testing life cycle is that there are key testing *deliverables* to be produced during each stage of software development.

5. The purpose of the Master Test Plan is to shape and define the testing life cycle.

6. The Master Test Plan is an essential document
   • Crucial to prepare carefully
   • Crucial to review
   • Crucial to maintain

7. It must be drafted early in the development process (preferably during requirements definition or early design)

8. Testing in the large generally consists of at least three distinct levels
   • Integration testing
   • Systems testing
   • Acceptance testing

9. Two basic questions must be answered by the testing in the large plan:
   • What is the system quality?
   • Will the system support operational use?

10. Testing in the large cannot make up for ineffective design and unit testing.

11. Test case folios provide an organized means of *documenting* and *maintaining* all test case information and specifications.

12. Test case folios form the basis for an automated data base or testing information system.

13. Integration testing serves to confirm that we have linked a basic system suitable for testing.

14. The approach to integration has a significant impact. It must be carefully planned and evaluated.

15. A suggested integration test approach is to:
    - Select *small* functionally related groups of modules.
    - Get a basic or simple transaction running.
    - Stress-test the integrated modules to confirm a solid test platform.

16. Systems testing execution begins when a minimal skeleton is integrated.

17. Systems testing ends when we feel confident that the system will pass the acceptance test.

18. Systems testing depends on good planning
    - Requirements-based tests
    - Performance capability tests
    - Specialized tests (volume, documentation, etc.)
    - Design and implementation-based tests

19. Systems testing must produce a test data set for subsequent modification testing as a product.

20. Acceptance testing serves to *demonstrate* that a system is ready for operational use.

21. Acceptance testing must be planned and formal.

22. A vital part of the Master Test Plan is the selection and effective use of test tools for all phases of testing in the large.

23. Major tool categories of importance to testing in the large include
    - Instrumenters
    - Comparators
    - Test data generators
    - Simulators and test beds
    - Debugging aids
    - System charting and documentation aids
    - Capture playback systems
    - File aids
    - Test case management systems

24. The total cost of a software tool is many times the license fee or purchase price.

Chapter 9

Testing Software Changes

Testing Changes—An Introduction

In most organizations the majority of time is not spent in new development, but in making changes to existing systems. We know that testing such maintenance changes properly is fundamental if ongoing software quality is to be maintained.

Testing changes is also important to new development. We can seldom enjoy the luxury of testing a static product. Planning for testing in the large has to recognize that testing is performed *while* the system is changing. Fixes and corrections are applied as we move along, and the testing of changes and system retesting is a major concern.

Thus, in both the maintenance and the new development environments, special attention must be given to testing changes. Given that some changes are made, the basic question we must answer is, what has to be retested to provide proper confidence that the system will continue to perform as intended? What amount of testing is required? How should the testing be structured and who should perform it? Despite the importance of these questions, most organizations have given them little study. If testing itself is improvised and poorly structured, testing software changes hasn't even been considered!

Any change, no matter how trivial, involves its own minidevelopment cycle. First, we have to design the changes we are going to make. This requires understanding the system or program logic; understanding the intended new result, and coming up with the changes that have to be made to achieve it. Second, we have to build the changes. This involves actually changing the code and modifying the system to conform to the new design. Finally, we have to implement the changes and install a new system version. This involves replacing the changed modules in the production library, ensuring that operators and users are familiar with any new impacts, updating documentation, and so on.

All these activities must be tested, just as every step of the normal development cycle is tested. The fact that the change might involve only a few statements does not take away the need to test the design (the means of achieving the change), test the changes in the small (the individual modules changed), and test the changes in the large (any overall systems impact). Experience has shown that most such changes are not tested sufficiently.

One set of studies found that the probability of making an incorrect change (one that introduces a new problem that subsequently has to be fixed or corrected) is little more than 50 percent—even for very small numbers (fewer than ten) of statements changed! Much of this is due to overconfidence and ineffective or nonexistent software change testing. We change just a couple of statements and *believe* we have not affected anything adversely. We execute one case that tests the path that was changed and tell ourselves that the change has been tested. Almost no design testing and very little testing in the large is performed. Is it, then, any wonder that we experience so many problems?

Developing careful design-based tests for even the tiny changes is more important than ever because original design concepts and subtleties have been forgotten. Systems testing is necessary to ensure that local changes do not have unanticipated side effects and to confirm that old faults are not causing any new problems. Quite simply, what we need is a mini (and sometimes not so mini) testing life cycle for each software change that is made! We may feel this is difficult and "too expensive" to justify, but that is what the testing practitioner must work to achieve. In this chapter I talk about techniques for achieving this goal and how the extra costs can be controlled or avoided.

Reviewing Change Designs

The most fertile area for improving software change quality is better design-based testing. This condition exists because, sadly, any form of design review on small changes is *nonexistent* in most organizations. Any steps toward more formal, or even more careful, analysis of planned changes is sure to pay off greatly.

All of the material on testing designs presented in Chapter 6 is applicable, but is probably an overkill. We don't need—and could not justify—a full design review every time we are about to make changes to a system. We do need—and *must* find a way to provide—an effective measurement of proposed changes to give ourselves reasonable confidence that they don't mess up something they shouldn't have affected and really do achieve the desired change in a reasonable manner.

The critical questions for change design review become the following:

1. *Does the design for the change provide for all new features and desired requirements?*

   • Has anything been left out?
   • Has the change been applied to every affected part of the system?

2. *Does the design for the change ensure that there are no adverse side effects?*

   • Can anything else be affected?
   • How could this change create a problem?

We are still concerned with whether the design alternative is the best that might have been selected, but usually that is not nearly as important as it is in the early phases of new development. The key questions are the two listed above. Tracking the reason that changes fail shows two common change problems occurring over and over again. The first is unforeseen side affects. The change accomplishes what it was supposed to, but also affects something that was working before. The second problem is partial change completion—a change is applied to most parts of a system, but one or more parts are overlooked. It takes little design testing effort to detect the presence of either problem. The approach I recommend is the following:

Change Reviews

1. Description of change—have the person who is responsible for the change write down a description of it.
2. Modules affected—have the written description include how the programs that are affected were determined and which they are. Sort out:

   • modules requiring change

   • modules that are unchanged, but could be affected.
3. Change test plan—identify how the modification is to be tested.
4. Review the change description and change test plan (either by passing it on to an individual who can read it and sign off or by bringing it before a Change Review Team)

The key steps involve writing down what is being changed and then having the result reviewed by someone else. The time spent need not be extensive; it is the principle involved that makes the difference. Our old friends, planning (in this case a few minutes of thought) and independent evaluation, can once again bring about dramatic testing improvement.

We have found that evaluating changes works best when performed in groups or blocks of related changes. If the environment is such that you can group the proposed changes together, then the best strategy is a formal, simultaneous review by the entire group. Three or four qualified staff (including the end user) should be brought together and all change designs for a single system reviewed by the group.

All of the discussion of formal review techniques in Chapter 4 applies. If the change cannot be grouped easily, passing it by a single *qualified* reviewer works almost as well. In either case, the person preparing the change knows that some review will occur and is forced to spend a few minutes organizing his or her thinking and writing down what is to be changed and how it will be tested. That provides an effective feedback process and greatly reduces the number of errors that are made.

Preparing the Changes

Assuming we have a solid design for the change, the second step is to actually code the changes and check them out to be sure that they are ready to be installed. We must test both in the small (each program that is changed) and in the large (at the system level).

Let us assume a work environment that provides on-line terminal support for programmers and three independent working libraries (disk data sets) in addition to the production library, which contains the current production version of each system. The three work libraries might be named the personal library (the programmer's own work space), the integration library (where tested modules are brought together), and the acceptance library (which contains an exact copy of the production version of the system and is used for system level testing).

Developing changes and testing them effectively involves seven steps as follows:

Testing the Changes

1. *Move module copies to personal work space*—The programmer copies modules that need to be changed from the acceptance library into the personal library.

2. *Code changes made*—The modules are changed as required by the change design. Changes are applied to the module copies in the personal library.

3. *Testing in the small*—Testing in the small is carried out in the programmer's personal library. Whenever possible, this should involve executing existing cases or the test data sets that were used to develop the program.

4. *Move tested modules to the integration library*—Once satisfied that the modules have been changed as required, the programmer requests approval to move them into the integration library. This should require project leader/librarian approval and occur only after the change has been reviewed. Only the project or development leader has access to the integration library.

5. *Integration testing (if applicable)*—If this is a development effort with a separate stage of integration testing, the changed modules are reintegrated into the system and any specific integration tests are executed. In a maintenance environment this step will normally not occur.

6. *Testing in the large*—The changes are tested in the large by temporarily moving the modules from the integration library into the acceptance library. (No permanent change to this library occurs unless the production library is changed.) Test data sets are used to exercise the entire system or selected features as defined by the Change Test Plan. (Any defects found produce formal problem reports.)

7. *Installation*—Once all testing in the large is completed and sign-off for change installation is obtained, the new modules are moved into the production and acceptance libraries and deleted from the integration library. A copy of the production library before it is changed is maintained in the retired library in case the old production version has to be restored.

This methodology ensures that proper change control is maintained. Without strong controls over the code and documentation being changed, testing the changes properly becomes hopeless. It does not deal with the special situation of emergency maintenance, when a fix must be applied to the production system as soon as possible. With emergency maintenance our primary goal must be to restore system operation—thorough change testing has to be deferred a little as a practical expedient.

Testing Emergency Maintenance

1. *Fix developed and tested in personal library*—As before, the proposed change is prepared and tested in the small in the personal library.

2. *Fix tested against acceptance library*—The fix is temporarily applied to the acceptance library (remember, the programmer has no way to change the library permanently) and *limited* testing in the large is performed. If a test data set is available it should be run.

3. *Fix applied to production on emergency basis*—Operations inserts the fix by operating from an auxiliary library.

4. *Testing the completed change the following day*—The next day the changed module is moved into the integration library and the change testing methodology is followed. Once it has passed acceptance testing and been moved into production, the auxiliary library may be deleted.

An auxiliary library is required for emergency maintenance to avoid changing the "real" production system without proper testing and sign-off. Operations continue using a JCL (Job Control Language) override to the auxiliary library until this has been done. If a fix is allowed to be applied directly to production, the acceptance and production libraries are no longer exact duplicates, and problems may occur with the retired library as well. This gets compounded and creates major change control problems when multiple emergency maintenance is going on at the same time.

The Change Libraries diagram on page 157 shows how the libraries described above may be used to control the testing of changes. Other approaches to organizing the change testing will work equally well. What is important is to have a *standard* procedure to ensure that effective testing is completed *before* any changes are moved into production.

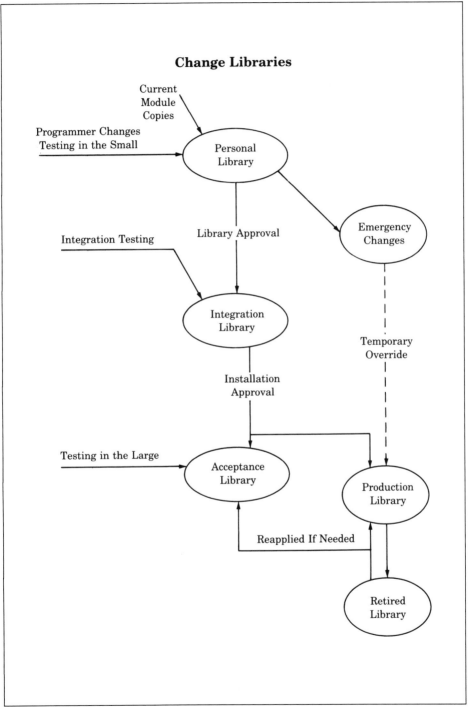

Change Libraries

Testing the Changes in the Large

After changes have been tested in the programmers' personal libraries and released for testing in the large, the decision must be made as to how much systems and regression testing is required. If possible, the entire test data set should be rerun. If this is viewed as impractical or too expensive, the Retest Planning Matrix is one tool that may be useful for planning the change testing needed. I recommend preparing this matrix as a routine part of the testing in the large planning. Once completed, it is useful for guiding retesting during development and for determining the testing required for later maintenance changes.

Looking at the sample retest planning matrix, you see that the matrix relates test cases (folios, test procedures, or just individual cases) to system programs and modules. A check entry indicates that the case is to be retested when the module is changed. A question mark signals that retesting will be required in some cases and not in others—that is, we must examine the change to determine whether the test is necessary. No entry means that the test is not required. In the example, we have twenty modules and eighty-five test procedures. The completed row tells us that case number 3 is to be rerun whenever modules 2, 9, 15, 16, or 20 are changed. The completed column tells us that if we make a change in module 2, we have to rerun test cases 2, 3, 8, 84, and 85 and possibly tests 7 and 9.

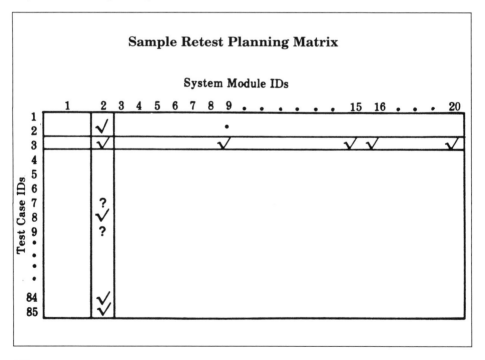

Completing a retest planning matrix during initial development takes very little time. The planning matrix may be reviewed by system users and will help show the level of retesting expected whenever changes are made. Only minor continuing effort is required to keep the matrix current. Whenever modules are changed, the matrix should be reviewed to assure that it still indicates an appropriate retesting plant. If new cases or modules are added, then new rows or columns are simply added to the existing matrix. The matrix may also be generated automatically by instrumenting each module so as to invoke a utility that indicates which modules are executed by which test procedures.

The retest planning matrix helps us to *decide* what should be retested. The data needed to execute the selected cases will be available *if* we have maintained it since the initial development of the system. If not, the cost of recreating it quickly becomes prohibitive. It is impractical to have to start from scratch and prepare tests for small changes. Constructing new test data every time a change is made takes too long. To test changes effectively we *must save the test data for reuse!*

One Critical Key to Testing Changes Effectively

Save and maintain test data for reuse whenever changes are applied.

It should be emphasized that running the complete system test set (full regression run of all test cases) is necessary in high-risk situations to ensure that all functions and system capabilities continue to perform as required after a change has been made. Even assuming a "perfect" change, it is possible for systems to fail because of "old" faults already existing in the system. Short of retesting all functions, there is no way to prevent such faults from causing a major failure or unacceptable system behavior!

When the cost or time required for full regression is prohibitive, it is helpful to group or "batch" the changes to be tested. Testing in the large for a group of related changes takes no more effort than testing any one individually. Batching fixes and corrections minimizes retesting effort and justifies more comprehensive testing. Maintenance organized so that changes are batched and only applied at regular intervals is called *scheduled maintenance*. Schedules are established for each system (usually quarterly or semiannually). Changes are held and applied all at once at the designated interval. This permits a single design review of all the proposed changes, avoids having to change the same code multiple times, and allows a thorough systems and acceptance test to be carried out before the changes are made effective. It greatly improves change quality and saves a lot of money at the same time. Of course, if too many changes are grouped, then debugging becomes complicated by added difficulty in quickly isolating the source of the problem.

A Second Key to Testing Changes Effectively

Batch changes together for testing whenever possible!

Testing Installation Readiness

The final step in testing software changes involves accepting the change and being certain that the installation is ready for it. Collecting failure data shows that this is another highly defect-prone area. If we have tested the change design and code properly, we will have done the bulk of the work and satisfied ourselves that the change does what it is supposed to and will not have adverse side effects. Now we must determine that we are prepared operationally.

Installation Readiness Testing

1. *Completion of installation checklist*—A checklist form should be available to ensure that all required parties are cognizant of *any* planned changes. The form should describe the change to be made and specifically describe any functional or operational impact.

2. *Approval signatures*—The checklist form is routed to designated persons who are responsible for approving changes. Documentation completeness is verified, operations signs off that all operational procedures have been readied, and the user signs off that all user training is complete. Quality assurance should spot-check these steps and audit to ensure that the procedures are followed thoroughly.

3. *Change is installed*—The approved change is entered in the production system and announced to affected persons.

The key element is control over the process and consistent change testing and retesting procedures to make sure that every base is covered. It is easy for a correct change to cause a significant failure because people did not know about it or were improperly prepared for it. Effective testing must prevent this from happening.

SUMMARY

1. Changes must be designed, built, and implemented, and testing each step is necessary to have proper confidence that the change will work as expected.

2. Careful review of change design is crucial.
   - Is the design complete?
   - Does it upset anything that is working?
   - How will it be tested?

3. Testing each module in the small is crucial.
   - Every module changed must be carefully tested.
   - Techniques are the same as testing newly coded modules.

4. Testing in the large is crucial.
   - Careful planning is required to determine the tests needed.
   - A Retest Planning Matrix helps coordinate this planning.
   - Full regression retesting should be used whenever possible.

5. Control over any changes to the system is essential.
   - Changes applied to personal libraries
   - Moved to integration libraries when ready
   - Tested against production duplicate (acceptance library)
   - No changes occur to production until tested properly
   - Emergency maintenance done with auxiliary library

6. Maintain and test data sets and use them for retesting.

7. Batch changes together for testing and review.

8. Test installation readiness thoroughly before making the change effective.

Chapter 10

Testing Software Packages

Purchasing software packages and systems written by others is something every organization is likely to do with increasing frequency. The explosion in available software, the steady improvement in the quality of such packages, and the ever-increasing cost of new development make outside software acquisition appear more and more attractive. (At this writing there are more than fifty thousand packages available for medium- to large-scale systems. No one really knows how many are available for small micros and minis.)

What are the testing implications? How do we go about measuring the quality of the possible choices and determining that the packages are ready for use? Are testing techniques and principles the same for in-house development and maintenance? If not, what is different and how should we adjust our testing methodology?

Testing Packages—An Introduction

What happens to the testing life cycle when we buy a software package? In comparison with the traditional development life cycle, we can observe several major differences.

Package Testing Life Cycle Implications

1. User does not participate in requirements/design development and validation process.
2. User understands less about the design and details of how the system performs.
3. User cannot perform testing in the small (considered impractical in terms of time and money).
4. Code-based testing is usually not possible (source code is often not provided).

Major testing of the package is done by the developer as the package is built and maintained. As users, we don't control this testing (often we know virtually nothing about it) and cannot, even if we had the will and the money to spend, repeat it for ourselves. Even when the source code is supplied, we cannot afford to go back and conduct a thorough design test or test individual modules in the small over again.

Our objectives have changed. The most important measurements we have to make are those that determine whether the package will fulfill our own requirements and provide reasonable confidence that problems and potential failures have been minimized. These objectives are very different from those the developer uses to guide his or her testing. The developer's testing is concentrated on determining whether the package performs as advertised (documented). Our task is much tougher: we must test the developer's testing (make sure it performs as advertised); then we must make sure that the package does what we want it to do (check to see that it meets our requirements); and finally, we must test to be sure we are ready to put it into operation (make sure everyone knows what to do and how to use it, that it interfaces with other systems, and so on). Thus the following three critical questions guide the testing that must be performed.

Testing Packages—The Critical Questions

1. Does the package perform as advertised?
2. Does the package fulfill our requirements?
3. Are we ready to install it?

Planning for a testing life cycle that provides answers to these three questions is what good package testing is all about. It is false to *assume* that the testing work is reduced when a package has been purchased. Consider again our student analogy. When a new student transfers near the end of the year, the teacher is faced with a difficult testing problem. He or she does not know what material the student has been working with and knows nothing about the student's natural strengths and weaknesses. Simple tests that might be highly reliable measures for students who have been in the class all year (and tested as the material was learned) are easily seen to be inadequate measures for the new student. More, rather than less, testing effort may be required to measure comprehension and skill level properly. With a software package we face the same difficulty. Not having been intimately involved with the design and development, we find ourselves having to take a great deal of time just to find out how the package is supposed to work. (Remember: Understanding the specifications is a prerequisite to effective test planning.) Additional time and effort must be spent testing whether the package will work in our environment. It is common to see a package perform beautifully in one company and fail miserably in the next. The difference is not because the package stopped working! Rather, it is due to how the package is used and what the company does with the information. Testing whether the package really serves the business need and that people know how to use it properly are major aspects of package testing and take a great deal of time to carry out. In short, planning for package testing is just as important as it is for development testing! I recommend that a Master Test Plan (MTP) be used for *every* package acquisition and that this plan be reviewed and validated as carefully—if not more so—than is done in the normal testing life cycle.

Planning for Package Testing

A Master Test Plan should be used to coordinate all testing on every package acquisition.

The MTP for a package should address these three critical questions separately. Techniques and guidelines for approaching each question are considered in following sections.

Testing Package Specifications

Testing to measure whether a package performs as advertised may be the least important of the three questions we must answer. Nevertheless, it must be given attention. Some of the approaches that may be taken to do this include the following:

Methods of Testing Package Functions

1. Exercise developer-supplied test data (test data set).
2. Survey the existing customer base.
3. Evaluate the developer test and quality assurance methodology.
4. Independently test critical functions/features.

One straightforward approach is simply to obtain and run the vendor-supplied test data. Test data come with most commercial packages. If the test data set is a good one, it will exercise most of the functions and features and include an expected output file. Testing consists of executing the supplied data and confirming that critical results match those in the expected output file. All this shows is that the package is performing for you in the same way it did for those who put together the test set. It provides confidence that the package performs as advertised only if we verify that the expected outputs are "right" and that the tests provide comprehensive coverage (at least for the features we are most concerned about). I recommend analyzing the supplied test set as follows:

Evaluating a Vendor-Supplied Test Set

1. Start at a random spot in the user manual and pick out ten features/options/or capabilities.
2. Complete an evaluation matrix for each of the ten features described (see example below).
3. Score the completed evaluation matrix.
4. Evaluate the score. Scores less than 75 generally indicate poor vendor test sets that offer little assurance. Scores over 90 reflect a special effort by the vendor to supply thorough testing data.

The key to this approach is the evaluation matrix. The specific format is not critical; but I have found that an evaluation matrix similar to the following works well.

An Evaluation Matrix for a Vendor Supplied Test Set

Feature Number	Is Test Case Available?	Is Test Case a Good Test?	Proper Output?	Score
1	YES	YES	YES	10
2	YES	YES	YES	10
3	NO	—	—	0
4	NO	—	—	0
5	YES	YES	YES	10
6	YES,2	YES	YES	10
7	YES	NO	Missing header	4
8	NO	—	—	0
9	YES	YES	YES	10
10	YES	YES	YES	10
			Total Score	64

Completing the matrix requires answering three questions for each of the ten features selected. First, is there a test case that exercises the selected feature? (In the sample there was not for features 3, 4, and 8. Feature 6 had two tests.) Second, if there is a test case, does it exercise the feature effectively? In other words, is it a "good" test of the particular feature? (In the sample the test for feature 7 was judged ineffective. Entries for features 3, 4, and 8 are not applicable since no test case is present.) Finally, the third question we ask is whether the output "properly" reflects the way the system "says" it is supposed to perform. In other words, does the feature perform as described when the test is run. (In the sample, all outputs were judged correct, except for feature 7, which was partially incomplete due to a missing header.)

To score the completed matrix, assign 10 points for any feature that has a good test that produces correct output (yes to all three questions) and 0 points to a feature without a test case (no to question 1). Others should receive a score somewhere between 0 and 10. In the sample, a value of 4 was assigned to feature 7, based on an overall judgment of the effectiveness of the case. The total score is then obtained by simply adding the scores for each of the ten features.

Executing developer-supplied test data is an excellent tool for learning how a system works. The process of getting the system to produce controlle' output and being able to see what happens as various inputs are introduced is extremely helpful to the user and analyst. It is easy to do and provides at least some minimal confidence about the system. If the test data set is available it should certainly be exercised. Coupled with a systematic evaluation of the test set effectiveness (such as that obtained through the evaluation matrix), this will answer whether the package performs as advertised.

A second approach to determining whether the package performs as advertised is to test the critical functions and features independently. These are identified and test cases are constructed for them just as in normal testing in the large. The package is then tested *before* any local modifications are applied. All the guidelines and techniques of formal testing in the large discussed in Chapter 8 apply.

Two other approaches involve indirect testing. Users of the package may be contacted and visited to discuss their experiences with the software. Alternatively, the vendor's testing and quality assurance methodology may be examined to "test" how well the vendor tests and controls his or her products.

In practice, a combination of the approaches is employed. A visit to the vendor development site, visits to several selected customers, a sample of independent tests, and the successful execution of a validated test data set taken together provide high insurance to the purchaser that the package will perform as advertised.

Testing Requirements

This is the most difficult and most important question to be answered. Some attempt is made to answer it before the package is ever purchased. Hopefully, we will not buy something unless we have fairly strong confidence that it will fulfill our requirements! The problem is that we often don't know enough to evaluate the decision properly. We assume that, because others have successfully used the package, it will work for us. When new software is developed it is *preceded* with a lot of emphasis on requirements in order to determine and decide what is to be built. When software is purchased this requirements step is often skipped.

A package that looks attractive is presented to us, and we make the decision to acquire it. That is the reality many of us experience. As testers, we have a doubly difficult job: we not only must test the package, but we also have to make sure we know the requirements.

Package Requirements Must Be Defined

It is difficult to test whether a package meets your requirements unless you *know* what your requirements are!

Determining and testing requirements for a package acquisition is no different from testing requirements in the initial stage of new development.

The critical questions (Are any requirements missing? and Do we need all those now listed?) are the same. The testing technique—formal review with an emphasis on determining how to test—is the same. The only difference is that with a package, once we design a requirements test, we can immediately go ahead and test whether the package can handle it. We don't have to wait while the software is designed and built; it is already available for us to exercise!

Testing Requirements with Packages

- Establish the requirements and test objectives
- Design and develop the requirements-based tests
- Prepare and implement test procedures
- Execute the tests

As much as possible of this testing needs to be done *before* the decision is made to purchase. As with all requirements testing, a major benefit arises from listing the requirements and determining how we are going to test them. Making this the first step in a package acquisition ensures that the organization has thought out what it needs to buy and provides the framework for the entire selection decision.

My preference is to prepare a Requirements Checklist that potential vendors are required to complete. The checklist lists the features and capabilities established as requirements.

The Requirements Checklist illustrated on page 170 shows a portion of a checklist prepared for an insurance company that was acquiring a new software system to process insurance claims; it was included as part of a formal request for proposal (RFP) issued to vendors. All vendors submitting proposals were required to complete the checklist, responding yes or no to whether their packages supported the features described. The third column was used if the vendor wished to add explanatory comments, such as when a feature was partially supported or planned for future release, and so on. As responses were received this provided an easy means of comparative analysis and was used later as a test planning guide for the key requirements to be tested and confirmed before implementation.

It does require effort to prepare and complete such a checklist. I set aside several weeks with our clients for this task and set up a special task force of *key* people from all major areas impacted by the new system. Individuals on the task force were charged with the responsibility of pulling together their own requirements and reviewing and validating everyone else's. This requires the best talent in the organization and a short burst of very intense hard word. There are other ways of getting good requirements (see Chapter 5), but I have

Sample Requirements Checklist

1. Reports: Yes No Comment

Weekly report of outstanding claims by policy number. (Show age of claim [30–60–90–over 90 days].)

Weekly report of outstanding claim by claim number. (Age of claim as above.)

Paid bank draft register (weekly).

Unpaid bank draft register (weekly).

Monthly claims closed (payment or rejection).

Monthly claims paid. (Include voids and cancellations to give net month to date and net year to date payments.)

Alpha list all policyholders (monthly).

Numerical list all policyholders (monthly).

Weekly report showing any policy activity and changes, including net additional premiums.

Annual 1099 IRS forms for doctors.

2. Controls:

Ability of supervisor to review and control large claims.

Ability of supervisor to review and control rejections.

3. Inquiry via On-Line Terminal:

Display a policy.

Display all claims history (paid, rejected, and outstanding) for a policy.

Display payment history for a policy, including adjustments.

found that this has worked best for us. Investing the effort is worth every penny! It provides the natural framework for both the package selection decision and the requirements testing that follows.

Testing Installation Readiness

The third critical question to be answered is to establish confidence that the organization is *ready* to use the new package. This involves testing all changed code, the package interfaces to existing systems and files, the conversion plans, user training and documentation, procedures, forms, and, in general, anything associated with the proper organization of the new system.

Experience in tracking defects and failures that occur with software package installations shows that the most common problems are procedural mistakes and incompatibility with existing systems. Procedure errors (like using the package incorrectly, supplying improper input, selecting improper option combinations, failing to execute a required action) reflect improper training and preparation. They are much more of a problem in acquiring a package than in new development. Any organization buying a package will spend much less time reviewing and working with it than would be the case if they had developed a new system from scratch. The resulting overall level of understanding and comprehension by both the Data Processing Department and the user areas is low, and this causes the procedural errors. It is also the major cause of the increased number of interface and incompatibility problems with existing systems. Customized changes and modifications to existing systems are required with almost all package implementations. These changes have to be made by people who don't fully understand the new package and easily make errors in deciding how to hook up or modify the code as required.

Testing for these errors and problems involves a combination of the testing in the large techniques already discussed. A partial integration test to verify each of the new package interfaces, a minisystems test emphasizing total system flow and interaction, and a comprehensive acceptance test emphasizing operating procedures and work flow are all required to properly answer the readiness question.

Recap—Package Testing Methodology

Testing a commercial package properly requires a great deal of effort (time and cost) *not* appreciably different from that of the effort required for testing an in-house development!

A Suggested Package Testing Methodology

Before vendor selection is made:
1. Prepare requirements checklist.
2. Prepare overview Master Test Plan to document major testing objectives and strategy.
3. Review requirements list and Master Test Plan draft.
4. Release requirements checklist to potential vendors.
5. Score completed requirements checklists.
6. Contact selected users.
7. Conduct on-site visits to top contenders.
8. Select and negotiate the contract.

After package is received:
1. Evaluate vendor-supplied test set by completing an evaluation matrix.
2. Revise and update the Master Test Plan.
3. Execute the vendor test set on the unmodified package.
4. Test local modifications (requires design, unit, integration, and systems tests of the changes).
5. Rerun the vendor test set on the modified system.
6. Extend the test set by adding tests for local requirements (use requirements checklist).
7. Run the extended test set.
8. Acceptance test the total system.

For a complex package, anything short of this will *not* provide adequate confidence that a new package can be effectively implemented. The cost is significant. I have seen the testing cost exceed the package price on several projects. Twenty-five percent of the price is a reasonable expectation. Failing to budget at least that amount is an invitation to major problems. Even when the package is known to be of high quality and virtually defect free (i.e., the package performs as advertised), this amount is necessary to answer the other two questions.

SUMMARY

1. The testing life cycle for a purchased package is altered significantly.
2. The amount of testing needed for a package is not substantially reduced when compared with new development.
3. Testing a package in the small is impractical.
4. Structural testing approaches are usually not available (either because code is not provided or time required makes it impractical).
5. Testing on a package must address three questions:
   - Does the package perform as advertised?
   - Does the package fulfill requirements?
   - Are we ready to install it?
6. A Master Test Plan should be used to coordinate all testing conducted.
7. A vendor-supplied test set should be tested with a test set evaluation matrix for a selected sample of features.
8. Determining that a package performs as advertised can be done by test set execution or independent testing and, indirectly, by on-site visits and reviews of vendor test procedures.
9. A Requirement Checklist is a useful tool for evaluating alternative packages and organizing the testing.
10. Common package failures are caused by procedural errors and interface errors. Both are due to poor understanding about how the package works.
11. The key to proper testing of packages is understanding requirements and planning the testing as a formal, structured activity.

Part 3

Managing the Testing Function

Introduction

Testing, like any other function, must be aggressively managed to be successful. The technical aspects of effective testing are just a part of the total picture. In this final part of the book, we look at the role management plays and outline what is expected from management in order for testing to be successful.

Chapter 11 explores the role of management of the testing function, and the evolution of testing specialists and the testing function. Chapter 12 discusses how the testing function should be organized and justified. Chapter 13 looks at controls and the measurement of testing effectiveness. Finally, Chapter 14 discusses the overall task of implementing changes to the testing process and establishing an effective testing life cycle.

The responsibility of management to initiate testing improvements and see that testing is effective is clear. A lot is expected from today's manager—software manager and test manager alike. Without active management support, understanding, and action, what is achieved will fall far short of what should be.

Chapter 11

The Role of Management

What should the manager do to manage the testing function effectively? What does the practitioner expect and require from his or her manager? How can management best go about organizing, implementing, and maintaining effective testing procedures?

Most students of management agree that many different management approaches and styles work. The "best" approach is largely a matter of individual preference, with the critical success factors being personality and behavioral style—how the individual influences people. However, beyond the basic people issues there are duties and responsibilities that any manager must fulfill to manage testing properly. Exploring these duties and the role of management in testing is the focus of this chapter.

So far we have considered testing from a largely *technical* viewpoint. Little emphasis has been given to management issues and responsibilities. What do we know about the management role in any enterprise? Management's job, simply stated, is to obtain results through the work of others. Much has been studied about why some managers are able to achieve so much and others so little. The basic responsibilities do not change. Almost all management activity may be grouped into one of three broad spheres of influence.

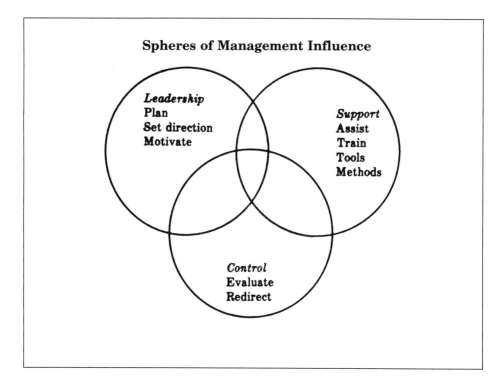

Spheres of Management Influence

Leadership
Plan
Set direction
Motivate

Support
Assist
Train
Tools
Methods

Control
Evaluate
Redirect

The *leadership sphere* involves pointing the way and motivating individuals to seek common goals. It includes setting objectives, expectations, and plans. The *control sphere* involves ensuring that the organization stays on the intended track. It includes monitoring, follow-up, reporting, evaluating, and redirecting. The *support sphere* involves facilitating the workers' performances. It includes training, work methods, tools, and general assistance.

Everything a manager does can be categorized in one of these spheres of responsibility. Generally, a balanced program of action must be undertaken in all three spheres to effect any significant or lasting organizational change. As a simple example, it is clearly insufficient to try to implement a new testing technique (or any other technique, for that matter) by providing only training and technical support and then standing back and waiting for the new method to sweep magically through the shop. Without exception, active leadership and effective controls must be present, along with the support to achieve the sought-after improvements. The concept of a balanced program of action in all three spheres says that management has important leadership and control responsibilities (in addition to merely hiring talented professionals and assisting them in every way possible) that *must* be met if effective testing practices are to be established and maintained.

The Five M's

Testing is of special importance to every manager because it is the process by which product quality is made visible and tangible. The purpose of testing is to measure quality. It is impossible to manage something you can't see or evaluate. Ergo, effective testing is a prerequisite to effective quality management. Quality systems are something that all managers care about. Good quality management means, first and foremost, a recognition of management's quality responsibilities. Providing for an effective testing process and properly measuring product quality on an ongoing basis is something each manager should view as a personal responsibility.

Understanding that testing responsibilities are an inherent part of each manager's job is an important step. Testing is not just a technical issue to be passed off to a practitioner. Testing is not a responsibility that can be fulfilled through interest or desire or encouragement. Direct management action is necessary and expected!

How does the manager approach these personal accountabilities and responsibilities for testing? Actions are needed in each of the three management spheres.

Managing the Testing Function: The Five M's

Leadership Sphere
   Planning
   Setting objectives   *Management*
   Creating a climate
   Incentive   *Motivation*
Support Sphere
   Methods
   Technical assistance   *Methodology*
   Procedures/standards
   Automated aids
   Test time   *Mechanization*
   Test environment
Control Sphere
   Tracking
   Reporting   *Measurement*
   Follow-up

The five M's of *M*anagement and *M*otivation in the leadership sphere, *M*ethodology and *M*echanization in the support sphere, and *M*easurement in the control sphere describe the major responsibility areas for all managers. Whenever I have the opportunity to meet with an organization's management team, I pose a set of questions relating to managing testing.

Questions for Managers Who Claim to be Managing Testing

Management	• Do *your plans* address testing?
	• Do *you* know *who* is responsible?
	• Have *you* published *your* testing policy?
Motivation	• Do *you* provide incentive for people to do quality work?
	• Do *you* encourage people to take advantage of training opportunities in testing methods?
Methodology	• Are *your* testing methods proceduralized and are people trained in their use?
	• Are *you* aware of new testing techniques and are *you* working to introduce them?
Mechanization	• Do *you* provide sufficient hardware and equipment to support testing?
	• Have *you* provided appropriate software testing tools and aids?
	• Do *you* evaluate automated testing aids on an ongoing basis?
Measurement	• Do *you* track errors, faults, and failures?
	• Do *you* know what testing costs?
	• Do *you* quantitatively measure testing performance?

Each manager should take this thirteen-question assessment of performance in the five M's. The emphasis in each question is on the *you*. Answer as honestly as you can whether each point is something *you* do—not what someone else does. A score of 10 or more clear yes answers indicates that you are seriously working to meet your personal accountability. For any question you answer negatively you should ask yourself one additional question: What are *you* doing about it?

Each of these questions addresses personal responsibilities that require action from individual managers for the organization's testing practices to be assured of good health. If you are not responding now, why not, and what are you going to do about it?

The Evolution of the Testing Specialist

In the 1950s we considered everyone in the computing profession to be "programmers." The programmer designed applications, coded logic, operated the system, and provided his or her own support environment. It was not until the early 1960s that the first group of specialists emerged. By this time operating systems had become quite complex and "systems programmers" were being hired for the special job of supporting and maintaining them. A few years later another specialist emerged: the "systems analyst." Users complained that the programmers who were building systems for them were too technically oriented, and many projects failed because of poorly understood requirements. As a result, the analyst was specialized and became responsible for user coordination, requirement definition, and system design. In the past few years we have begun to see a further specialization of the analyst role. "User analysts" or "user coordinators" have been given the responsibility of working directly with users to shape and define priorities. The user analyst typically works for the user and coordinates or oversees all project work. The flow of work moves from the user analyst to the system designer or system analyst to the programmer. Each has become a specialist.

Some companies have developed, in parallel with the development of the analysts, "quality assurance specialists" and "EDP auditors." Quality assurance (QA) has become a specialty in response to the demand for better quality and the need for more effective testing. This need has also helped to justify user analysts. Analyst responsibilities in test planning, design and execution have been steadily increasing to the point where the individual does testing work almost full time. The same is true for many auditors and QA specialists. While it is not broadly recognized yet, I see this group breeding a new specialist, someone we might call the *testing specialist* or *testing manager*.

The primary job of the testing specialist is to ensure that quality is *measured* carefully. Such specialists are not concerned about building systems or fixing deficiencies—they are freed from those concerns to concentrate on making sure that effective testing is performed.

The presence of a testing specialist in a project organization is one means of meeting the principle of independence. Knowing quality will be effectively measured serves to *prevent* many errors from ever occurring and acts as a positive force toward quality work. Measuring quality independently ensures that the impact of poor quality (if it is a factor) is kept small.

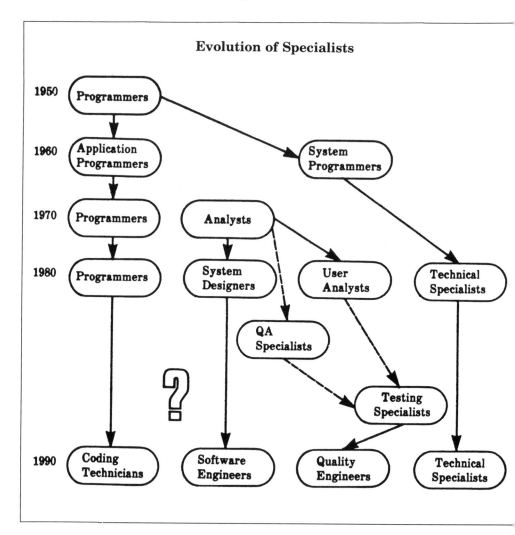

Evolution of Specialists

Is a specialist for testing justified? Consider such established specialties as the data base administrator, the systems programmer, and the capacity planning specialist. What do these have in common that brought about their evolution and acceptance as justified specialists? Three items seem to stand out. We consider something a legitimate specialty if it requires highly specialized *technical knowledge* and extensive *work experience* for good performance. *Impact* is also important. If the impact of poor system performance is minor, then the organization cannot justify dedicating a specialized resource. It is only when there is a large impact (like a key computer system becoming unusable) that employing the specialist becomes justified or even demanded. The case for a testing specialist meets these three criteria. The specialist must have technical knowledge and experience to solve the problems associated with severe impact on systems. Most organizations can no longer live with ineffective testing. Their demands will create the professional testing specialist of tomorrow.

What Does a Testing Specialist Do?

- Ensures that testing is performed
- Ensures that testing is documented
- Ensures that testing techniques are established and developed

Testing Specialist Responsibilities

- Prepare testing plans and designs
- Organize testing activities
- Develop test specifications and procedures
- Develop test cases
- Prepare testing documentation
- Utilize testing tools and aids
- Review designs and specifications
- Test programs and systems
- Test maintenance changes
- Oversee acceptance tests

These responsibilities are crucial to the success of any project. I recommend the use of testing specialists on any project that requires six months or more for completion. This does not *relieve* the manager of his or her individual responsibilities, but it goes a long way toward meeting them.

The Five C's

Finding a qualified testing specialist, if you decide you want one, is not easy. It is rare that any practitioner has the opportunity to spend a long time in testing work, and training programs for advanced testing skills and perspectives are almost nonexistent. This forces us to select people with limited experience in testing and to have them prove themselves under fire. I use five C's as criteria in such a selection. It is far from a guarantee for successful performance, but each of the five criteria is important.

Key Skills Needed in a Testing Specialist

The Five C's

Controlled—Organized individual, systematic planning

Competent—Technical awareness of testing tools and techniques

Critical—Inner determination to discover problems

Comprehensive—Total attention to detail

Considerate—Ability to relate to others and resolve conflicts

Hiring a testing specialist is a significant leadership action; it signals the manager's interest in better testing and establishes clear accountabilities. Since the specialist will track errors and costs and provide feedback to the manager, adding him or her to the staff is an important element in the control sphere. In my experience, it is an excellent first step toward achieving a balanced improvement program.

SUMMARY

1. Every manager is personally responsible for measuring the quality of his or her own work, that is, testing it properly.

2. Management duties fall into three broad spheres of influence: *leadership, support,* and *control.* Actions are needed in each sphere to manage any activity effectively.

3. Testing specialists are evolving as full-time members of software projects.

4. The primary job of the testing specialist is to ensure tests are designed and executed in a timely and productive manner.

5. Testing specialists are recommended as key team members in any significant size project or where risks are high.

Chapter 12

Organizing for Testing

Organizing through Policy

Much of the job of organizing the testing function involves setting the climate for good testing and communicating that it is important. This means establishing policy on testing and the level of testing that is expected in all work performed. An important step toward achieving anything is to communicate an expectation of what you want to accomplish and to assign responsibility.

For many the concept of policy is difficult to grasp. It includes objectives, purposes, goals, and directions and may be written or unwritten, formal or informal. All organizations use policy, to some extent, as a tool for guiding their employees. However, few organizations have done much in the area of testing policies. Many organizations have documented *procedures*, which define how work is to be accomplished (the steps involved, etc.), but few have formalized the expectations. Management has not generally defined what testing is designed to accomplish, or what is expected.

Developing a good testing policy is difficult and time-consuming. A team of key managers and staff (of the organization or of a project) must be brought together and begin by assessing where the organization stands. After a team has established where it is, it can begin to define and shape policy to meet the organization's goals. (This requires good understanding of state-of-the-art testing practices.) Such a team, which might be called a testing policy task force, must prepare a policy framework and establish an ongoing policy development mechanism for overall testing practice in the organization.

Testing Policy Task Force

(A Steering and Approval Body)

Makeup

- Selected managers
- Selected professional staff
- Key user manager
- Quality assurance or audit group manager (if applicable)
- Outside consultants

Key Questions to Address

- What testing methods and standards are appropriate?
- Where and how should the testing responsibility be controlled?
- What type of organization will be most effective?
- How will testing policy be maintained?

The task force's primary role is to establish a framework that all key personnel support. Part of the framework deals with ongoing change. The task force should define how the policy may be changed and the procedures to use to submit ideas and suggestions as a part of its change. If that is done, the initial policy can be viewed as a starting skeleton with the *expectation* that it will be refined and extended over time. It is much easier (and better in the long run) to obtain agreement on high-level testing strategy issues than to become entangled in lower-level—largely procedural—issues.

Successful policy implementation requires *visible* management commitment and effort. Some organizations have permanent ongoing policy or standards committees. Others may appoint a special manager to be responsible. In any case, there must be an *ongoing* effort to ensure that the policy remains viable and is understood by all the affected staff.

I routinely survey my classes about the testing policies in use within their organizations. The following responses came from practitioners who worked in an organization that had established good testing policy. They clearly demonstrate to me why having a testing policy—even a great one—is *not* enough.

Question: Does your organization have an established testing policy or testing standards? If yes, describe it.

Answers: "Yes, but it is only used in the software test department, not in my department."

"No." (Over a fifth of the answers)

"I don't know." (Almost a fifth of the answers)

"An attempt is in progress to document the policy, but the caliber of people here makes it unnecessary."

"I am aware that they exist, but I am not familiar with them."

"Testing policy is well established for salable products, but it is not applied to internal efforts."

"Yes, but I have been here only six weeks, so I am not familiar with them."

These responses indicate that the organization needed to do much more to help the staff understand its stated policies. Over half of those answering didn't know about the policy or thought it didn't apply to their work.

The absence of written testing policy does not mean that no policy exists. Management always sets policies indirectly through its actions or inactions. For example, a poorly tested system implemented to meet an important deadline signals that schedules or budget are more important than system quality. Such signals, whether they reflect true priorities or not, are quickly perceived by professional staffs and established as de facto policies. Signaling firmly to all that testing is an important concern is one of the major benefits obtained through the policy setting effort.

Appendix B contains an example of a testing policy. It may be well for the reader to refer to this appendix and read through the sample. Policy statements are highly particularized, and while your own would obviously look very different, the sample should provide helpful insight. The sample policy establishes testing as an important concern within the context of an overall quality improvement effort. It outlines major objectives, emphasizes areas for testing improvement, and serves notice that testing is a priority. As policy, the document shapes the expectations of both managers and practitioners. As a plan, the document provides direction and a cohesive approach for accomplishing change.

The Test Organization

One of the major policy issues is the testing organization itself. Listed below are major alternatives to be considered.

Alternative Approaches to Test Organization

1. No formal testing organization (testing is viewed as a part of each unit's responsibility)

2. Component of quality assurance (separate quality assurance function exists and is given certain testing responsibilities)

3. Testing review committee (permanent committee to review test plans and oversee testing practices)

4. Project testing specialists (each project is assigned a testing specialist)

5. Software test support function (integral line function responsible for testing work)

6. Product assurance function (independent organization to test customer products)

The use of the term *test organization* means a *dedicated* resource or resources set aside to perform testing activities. Alternative 1, no formal test organization, is actually the most common practice. Designers produce systems, programmers code them, and users accept them, with all performing their own level of testing as the project warrants. No one is concerned with testing *full time* on an *ongoing* basis. Alternatives 2 and 3 are the next most common. Creation of quality assurance (QA) functions became very popular during the late 1960s, and many organizations, especially larger ones, have made significant investments in such organizations. The responsibilities of the various QA units vary widely, but all have at least some influence on testing practices. Most QA groups participate in reviews and issue reports after each formal review. They are deeply involved in standards (development and adherence), and a few actually perform independent testing. Alternatives 5 and 6 involve functional units dedicated *only* to testing activity.

Selecting one of the alternatives or a combination is not an easy decision. What is "right" depends largely on the specific project and development environment. Certainly the existence of an established QA function or independent test team is a key influence. However, there are no clear-cut answers. Important considerations involve looking at past testing practices and the basic organization culture. The industry, the nature of the business application, and the impact of testing failures also play important roles. Cost is another important factor. Any choice involving dedicated resources means special budget and position approvals. Alternative 6 implies *added* independent testing—beyond whatever other testing is performed. This may easily add 20 percent or more to the total cost of a project. The other alternatives do not necessarily imply more work—just that the work is specialized and assigned to a dedicated unit. Some may even save work through economy of scale and efficiency. Thus the cost benefit, which must be weighed and evaluated, is difficult to assess rigorously.

It is clear that some formal test organization is necessary. Without a formal organization testing practices and tools must be set up for every project. Once a project starts it is too late to effect major change. The test organization has to be in place and ready to serve all projects on a continuing basis.

Why Is a Test Organization Necessary?

- Building systems without one has not worked well.
- Effective measurement is essential to product quality control.
- Coordinating testing requires full-time, dedicated effort.

We want a test organization to provide management with independent quality information and to help the organization achieve measurable improvements in software quality. It is not unreasonable to expect it also to provide a *net* reduction in development work load. My best experiences with test organizations have been with alternatives 4 and 5, the project testing specialist and the software test support function. In each case dedicated testing is applied to the entire project—from start to finish—and in each case the testing resources work in direct support of the development resources. This fosters close cooperation and avoids unnecessary redundant testing. I view project test specialists as the best choice for organizations that are primarily project management oriented and are used to the constant formation and re-formation of dedicated work groups. I recommend the test support function approach for all other organizations. I have had poor experience embedding this function in a larger related element such as quality assurance or technical support. The measurement function seems to get lost in such units. A dedicated function headed by a specialized manager concerned only with testing is much more effective.

The Testing Manager

The qualifications and responsibilities of a testing manager are of special interest to me. My colleagues and I have developed an intensive week-long workshop with the specific goal of helping to qualify project test specialists and testing managers. The following outlines some responsibilities we feel should be assigned to the testing manager who heads a test support function.

The Testing Manager's Responsibilities

A First Look at Responsibilities

Test Organization and Policy
- Shaping the organization's testing policies
- Guiding development to facilitate testing

Test and Evaluation Master Plan
- An agreement on what, how, and when the product will be tested

Test Preparation and Readiness
- Planning for and procuring test tools and aids
- Developing the test data base
- Preparing test specifications

Test Control and Conduct
- Ensuring that testing is performed as planned
- Controlling changes
- Reviewing and auditing procedures and testing work

Test Tracking and Costing
- Maintaining test performance records
- Tracking problems
- Tracking the costs of testing
- Providing organization feedback to prevent future errors

Test Documentation and Records
- Recording the test results, test data, review logs, and so forth
- Certifying the testing performed
- Defining what has not been tested

We view the testing manager as having a major coordinating role, overseeing all testing processes and activity. The many relationships the testing manager must maintain and influence are illustrated.

The testing manager, with responsibility for defining and shaping all testing and quality measurement, becomes the focal point for testing in the organization. Working through the test support function the test manager coordinates and supports users, system designers, developers, testers, and all other groups involved with testing.

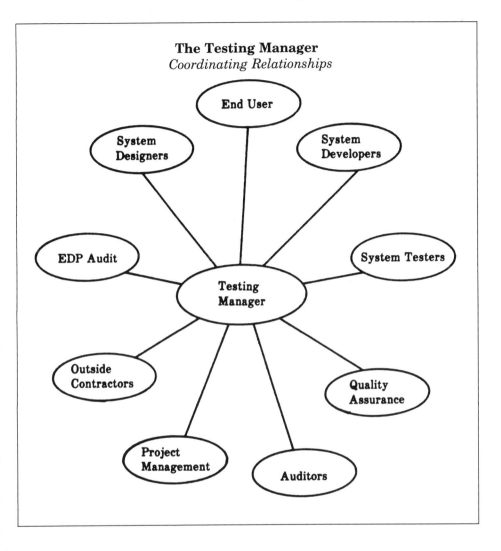

The Testing Manager
Coordinating Relationships

- End User
- System Designers
- System Developers
- EDP Audit
- Testing Manager
- System Testers
- Outside Contractors
- Quality Assurance
- Project Management
- Auditors

Planning and selecting the test organization must be done carefully. Any organizational change brings with it a certain amount of disruption and uncertainty. Managers can easily abuse organizational change. The easy step of reorganizing seldom solves the real underlying problems—and often creates serious new ones. This almost 2200-year-old quote may help us to remember how long the problems surrounding organizational change have been recognized.

On Organization

"We trained hard . . . but it seemed that every time we were beginning to form up into teams we would be reorganized . . . I was to learn later in life that we meet any new situation by reorganizing, and a wonderful method it can be for creating the illusion of progress while producing confusion, inefficiency, and demoralization."

Petronius Arbiter 210 B.C.

Organizing through Standards and Procedures

After developing test policy and defining testing responsibilities, the next step in organizing the testing function is the preparation of testing procedures and work standards.

The topic of standards is a current "hot button." Most organizations seem to have almost constant initiatives under way to develop or revise one standard or another. A great deal of energy and effort are consumed in arriving at the standards that are adopted. Frequently this involves multi-departmental standards committees made up of numbers of professionals with different backgrounds and viewpoints. Feelings about which method is best are not uniform, and bitter debate and conflict often surface. The choices made end up frustrating certain individuals and are an important factor in many career decisions. Compounding these problems is the tendency for standards, once adopted, to become rigid and difficult to modify or adapt. Complaints from practitioners about standards they consider too confining and counterproductive abound in many organizations, even those with active standards revision programs.

In light of all the agony they bring, one has to ask if the standards and procedures initiatives are really worth the effort that is put into them. Clearly, the motivation for the effort lies in the desire to improve quality and/or productivity. The implicit assumption is that work done according to the *standard* procedure is in the best interest of the organization. Most standards and procedures focus on *how* various steps in the development process are to be accomplished, rather than *what* the criteria or end results of acceptable quality work might be. As applied to testing it means that the emphasis is on deciding which testing method or tool to use rather than standardizing the level of testing or the measures of testing effectiveness. Much more is to be gained by starting the standards effort with the *what*.

The idea of working on standards for testing effectiveness instead of standard testing procedures is so deceptively simple that it often catches people by surprise. One outgrowth of such a standard is the adoption of a policy that any test procedure is acceptable as long as it achieves the desired result. Such a standard serves as a liberating force versus the constraining effect of the typical how-to standard. The professional may now consider accomplishing work with *any* method, provided he or she can clearly demonstrate that the *result* meets the effectiveness standard and productivity is at least acceptable. Once established, the testing effectiveness standard serves as an umbrella for the entire standards effort. Unless a particular technique can be demonstrated to improve testing (as measured by the effectiveness standard) there is little justification for imposing it as a work method standard. Even if there were, it might not be necessary to standardize it as a technique because the effectiveness standard alone will suffice to measure and bring about the desired behavior!

Starting with a *What* Standard

What standards are more powerful than *how* standards.

What standards may be used to decide how work should be performed.

The first testing procedure developed should be for measuring testing effectiveness.

Just a few years ago there were limited numbers of testing procedures and standards available for use as samples. That is now changing rapidly. Organizations are developing their testing procedures, and models are available in many industries. National standards activity has also been significant in the testing and quality assurance areas, especially during the past five years. The Software Engineering Standards Subcommittee of the IEEE Computer Society has been particularly active. They have published several standards in the testing area that have been approved by the American National Standards Institute (ANSI) and at this writing are developing many others that directly impact or influence testing practices.

ANSI-Approved Standards That Have an Impact on Testing

1. *Standard for Software Quality Assurance Plans*—Outlines minimum requirements for the preparation and content of a Software Quality Assurance Plan for the development of *critical* software (i.e., where failure could impact safety or cause large financial or social losses). Specifies the development of a plan containing the following sections: Purpose; Reference Documents; Management; Documentation, Standards, Practices, and Conventions; Reviews and Audits; Configuration Management; Problem Reporting and Corrective Action; Tools, Techniques, and Methodologies; Code Control; Media

Control; Supplier Control; and Records Collection, Maintenance, and Retention. Minimum documentation requires a Software Requirements Specification, a Software Design Description, a Software Verification Plan, and a Software Verification Report. Minimum reviews specified include a Software Requirements Review, a Preliminary Design Review, a Critical Design Review, a Software Verification Review, a Functional Audit, a Physical Audit, In-Process Audits, and Managerial Reviews to confirm and assess execution of the Software Quality Assurance Plan.

2. *Standard for Software Test Documentation*—Describes and gives examples of a set of basic software test documents covering test planning, test specification, and test reporting. The Test Plan is defined as an overall document providing direction for all testing activity. Test specification is covered by three documents. A Test Design Specification refines the test approach and identifies the features to be covered by the design and its associated tests. A Test Case Specification documents the actual values used for input along with the anticipated outputs. A Test Procedures Specification identifies all steps required to exercise the specified test cases. Test reporting is covered by four documents. A Test Item Transmittal identifies test items transmitted for testing, a Test Incident Report describes any event that occurs during the test execution that requires further investigation. A Test Log records what occurs during test execution. Finally, the Test Summary Report provides an overall report on the testing performed and its results.

3. *Standard for Software Unit Testing Process*—Specifies a unit testing process consisting of the standardized steps of *planning* the general approach; *determining* features to be tested; *refining* the plan; *designing* the tests; *implementing* the tests; *executing* the tests; *checking* for termination; and *evaluating* the results. The process refers to the Test Documentation standard and requires the completion of two documents to support unit testing—namely, the Test Design Specification and the Test Summary Report.

The approved standards may be purchased from the IEEE Computer Society, 10662 Los Vaqueros Circle, Los Alamitos, CA 90720. Practitioners interested in any of the efforts under development should contact the Software Engineering Standards Subcommittee of the IEEE Computer Society.

Any of these standards are excellent starting documents for the organization that is developing testing policies and procedures. Other good sources include vendors of software and testing tools, special interest groups, and various consulting firms.

Justifying the Testing Organization

Any testing expenditure must be justified by comparing the benefit (in terms of quality measurement and failure prevention or earlier detection) with the cost. How much should be spent on testing? How much should be set aside for dedicated testing resources? What levels are reasonable? When are testing costs too high? When are they too low?

To answer these questions you should start by finding out how much you are spending now. Most organizations don't know. They *think* they know because the project control system reports expenses for each project phase. Such systems detail expenses, often by individual task, for each phase of the development life cycle. However, the cost of the test phase is *not* the cost of testing for the project! Some testing work is carried out in other phases (design testing, unit testing, etc.) and a lot of work is performed during the systems test that is not testing (for example, documentation, debugging, deficiency analysis and removal, conversion, and training).

I have worked with many clients to "measure" what testing *actually* costs. Careful analysis usually reveals a figure between 15 percent and 25 percent of the total project cost. Many practitioners believe that the costs are much higher—I frequently see references citing that as much as 50 percent of the cost of a project is devoted to testing! This comes from mistakenly treating all project expenditure after programming as a testing cost. While it is true, for many projects, that a good way to estimate final total cost is to take actual expense through the programming phase and double it, it is *not* true that most of the cost after programming is the result of testing! In my experience, conversion, training, and debugging are at least as costly in total as is the true testing!

Determining testing costs is a crucial first step to planning any improvement initiative and justifying the investment. An *estimate* of the dollars being spent to test and measure quality, as well as the cost of rework or corrections, is fundamental. Most organizations spend too much time worrying about how to calculate these costs in detail. Crude estimates are fine at the beginning. Estimate conservatively so that the "actual" cost is a larger figure than the one you are working with. Your numbers will be big enough to justify the steps you want to take. There is no need to inflate them and run the risk of having someone challenge your argument.

As a percentage of total development, direct testing costs will approach 25 percent. Indirect testing costs, or the costs of poor testing, are usually at least twice the direct costs and may be spectacularly higher. The total cost of testing in most organizations is sufficiently large to catch the attention of almost any manager. All it takes is the effort and initiative to go out and estimate it!

Once the costs of poor testing have been estimated, justification problems seem to vanish. A sizable testing organization can usually be funded with just

---

Measuring the Costs of Testing

Direct Testing Costs	*Indirect Costs of Poor Testing*
Reviews	Rewriting programs
Program testing	Recovery
Systems testing	Corrective action costs
Acceptance testing	Rekeying data
Test planning and design	Failures
Computer time	Analysis meetings
Test resources	Debugging
(terminals, staff, etc.)	Retesting

---

a percentage of the total. Having the initial estimate also provides a baseline for measuring results and *demonstrating* effectiveness. Management should expect to see a return on the testing improvement investment. The benefits can be tracked and the results become visible!

There are no rules for how much testing costs "should" be. As long as the investment in testing shows a positive return—in reduced costs of correction and failures—it is justified, and, in fact, *adds* to the bottom line. When failure costs have been reduced so that they are no longer significant, then we might say we are spending too much on testing. Short of that, *no* expense is too much.

SUMMARY

1. Policy is the communication of management intent.

2. Implementing good testing policy requires
    *   knowing where the organization stands
    *   knowing what the state of the art is
    *   establishing goals, directions, and intent

3. Some issues to address with testing policy include
    *   which testing methods and standards are appropriate
    *   what the testing organization should look like
    *   who is responsible

4. Successful policy implementation requires visible management commitment and effort.

5. Successful policy implementation requires an ongoing education and awareness effort.

6. A test organization is a dedicated group of resources devoted to testing.

7. The "right" test organization depends on many variables:
    *   existing organizational structures
    *   past habits and culture
    *   testing maturity
    *   project environment

8. Techniques for organizing testing include:
    *   test organizations or functions
    *   testing managers or coordinators
    *   testing policy
    *   testing standards and procedures

9. *What* standards usually outperform *how-to* standards.

10. Measuring the cost of testing is an important step toward justifying any testing initiative.

11. The cost of testing includes direct measurement costs *plus* indirect failure and correction costs.

12. The justification for more direct testing dollars is the reduction of indirect testing dollars.

Chapter 13

Controlling the Testing Function

Testing the Testing

The central theme of this book is *measurement*. Testing is viewed as a critical support function because it provides necessary measurement information. Without this information, management is unable to assess progress or properly evaluate problems.

As testing provides one basis for project control, it is doubly critical to control testing effectively. We must have an ongoing means of "testing the testing." Testing the testing provides information that serves as feedback for controlling the testing function to ensure that it is performing properly.

Some of the key means of testing and measuring testing effectiveness are listed in the following table.

Key Elements for Effective Testing Control

1. Tracking errors, faults, and failures
2. Analyzing trends
3. Tracking testing costs
4. Tracking testing status
5. Test documentation

Each of the elements is described in subsequent sections. Recognizing that there are important control sphere responsibilities that management must fulfill is the initial step. Any good manager knows the importance of strong controls within each area of responsibility. Insistence of good measurement flows naturally once that recognition is achieved.

Tracking Errors, Faults, and Failures

The first element in controlling the testing function is to effectively track errors, faults, and failures. This involves reliably capturing information on problems detected during testing or system operation and then analyzing and summarizing that information so that trends and significant events are recognized.

The ANSI Standard for Software Test Documentation (see previous chapter) specifies two documents related to capturing discrepancy information found during testing. The standard describes a Test Log containing a chronological record of relevant details about each test performed. This includes a description of any test conducted and a recording of the results (error messages generated, aborts, requests for operator action, etc.). Discrepancies, including what happened before and after any unexpected events, are described. Also specified in the standard is a Test Incident Report to further document any event that requires investigation or correction. The Test Incident Report summarizes the discrepancy noted and refers back to the appropriate test specification and Test Log entry. It includes the expected and actual results, the environment, anomalies, attempts to repeat, and the names of the testers and observers. Related activities and observations that may help to isolate and correct the problem are also included. Both a sample Test Log and a sample Test Incident Report prepared in accordance with the ANSI standard are shown.

Sample Test Incident Report

1. *Incident Identifier:*   TR 22–83   October 1, 1983
2. *Summary:* Test procedure TP13–83 failed to produce any output. References: Test Log TL–3–83, test specification TF71
3. *Incident Description:*   October 1, 1983   5:30 p.m.

   During routine system testing of the Accident & Health System V5, Greg Cates submitted test folio TF71 as a part of Test Procedure TP 13–83. Normal system termination occurred, but no printer output file was produced. (See run output listing.)

   Test was reattempted with same results. Perhaps the job library procedure is defective.
4. *Impact:* Test procedure halted until correction provided.

Sample Test Log

1. *Test Log Identifier:* TL-3-83

2. *Description:* Version 5 of the Accident and Health System is being tested by the Test Support Group. The log records the execution of the System Test Plan for that system, specifically, Test Procedures TP10-83 to TP14-83. The tests are being submitted to batch processing through a CRT by the Test Support Group staff.

3. *Activities and Event Entries:*

October 1, 1983		Incidents
0830	Andy Hetzel commenced TP10-83	
0850	Data generation for test folio TF111 complete	
0852	Submitted TF111 run	
0854	Submitted TF42 run	
0854	Stopped testing	
0930	Andy Hetzel recommenced testing TP11-83	
0935	Utility procedure UP8 executed	
0935	TF111 output returned and confirmed	
0935	Submitted TF43 run	
0950	Began TP12-83	
0955	TF42 output returned and confirmed	
0955	Test procedure TP10-83 completed	
0955	Stopped testing	

October 2, 1983		
0840	Greg Cates picked up TP11-83 and TP12-83	
0840	TP43 and TF2 output confirmed	
0850	Test procedures TP11-83 and TP12-83 completed	
0850	Test procedure TP13-83 commenced	
0850	Placed test data base on file UTEST	
0915	Confirmed procedure setup	
0915	TF71 run submitted	
0915	TF102 run submitted	
0940	TF71 output missing	TR22-83
0940	Investigated problem, completed incident report TR22-83 and resubmitted to retry	

Sample Problem Tracking Form

Completed by	Date	Program ID	Test ID	Production	#

Means of Initial Problem Detection

☐ a. Program Abend (Code ____)   ☐ d. Hand Processing
☐ b. Incorrect Output Found by User   ☐ e. Personal Communication
☐ c. Incorrect Output Found by Prog.   ☐ f. Changed Specifications

Effort in Diagnosing the Problem (Do not include effort spent in initial detection)

a. Computer Runs _____   Total Elapsed Computer Time ____ Mins.
b. Working Time ____ Hrs.   Total Elapsed Time _____ Days
c. Outside Help Required (Check all that were needed)
   User Services ____   Technology ____   IBM Manuals ____   Associates ____

Summary Problem Description

_____
_____
_____
_____

- -

Completed by	Date

Change Required to Program—Reasons

☐ a. New Application Requirement   ☐ f. System Hardware Change
☐ b. Specification Incorrect   ☐ g. Program Bug Missing Function
☐ c. Specification Misinterpreted   ☐ h. Program Bug Incorrect Function
☐ d. Specification Incomplete   ☐ i. Program Bug Data and I/O
☐ e. System Software Change   ☐ j. Program Bug Flow of Control
                                                            or Interface

Change in Program Not Required—Reasons

☐ a. System Software Problem   ☐ d. Error Is Not Repeatable
☐ b. System Hardware Problem   ☐ e. There Was No Error
☐ c. Error Was in the Test

Size and Difficulty of Correction

a. Computer Runs _____   Total Elapsed Computer Time ____ Mins.
b. Working Time ____ Hrs.   Total Elapsed Time _____ Days
c. Source Lines Changed ____   Added ____   Deleted ____
d. Nature of Change
   Documentation ____ Hours ____; Table of Constant ____; Job Control ____;
   Program Fix ____;

Summary of Correction Made

_____
_____

Comments — Use Reverse Side of Sheet

Most organizations have a deficiency notice or trouble report form that is available for recording problems. Many of these forms are quite formal and include specific information designed to facilitate problem analysis. One example is the Sample Problem Tracking Form.

This form has two main sections. The top half is used to record the incident. It includes spaces in which to record how the problem was detected and the effort (both hours and computer time) spent on diagnosing what was wrong plus a section for a summary of the problems noted. The bottom half is used to report on the correction and ensure that it is made. The effort required for correction and a classification by type of problem are captured here.

Many other styles of tracking forms are used. Most support the intent of the Test Incident Report documentation standard. The key is to have an ongoing and formal means of capturing defect information, both during testing and after system implementation. Establishing the times the incident reports must be completed and confirming that they are filled out whenever required are important. Also important are the analysis and summarization of the incident data.

Problem Analysis

Incidents must be analyzed to answer several basic questions and support the tracking and feedback effort.

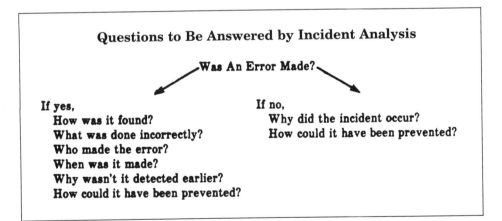

Management should expect to receive reports showing trend data based on the tracking effort at least monthly. I have found the sample frequency and trend graphs illustrated most useful.

The first graph displays a summary trend of the total incident frequency. The incidents found during testing should peak on the basis of testing activity. It is hoped that the number of operational incidents will decrease over the

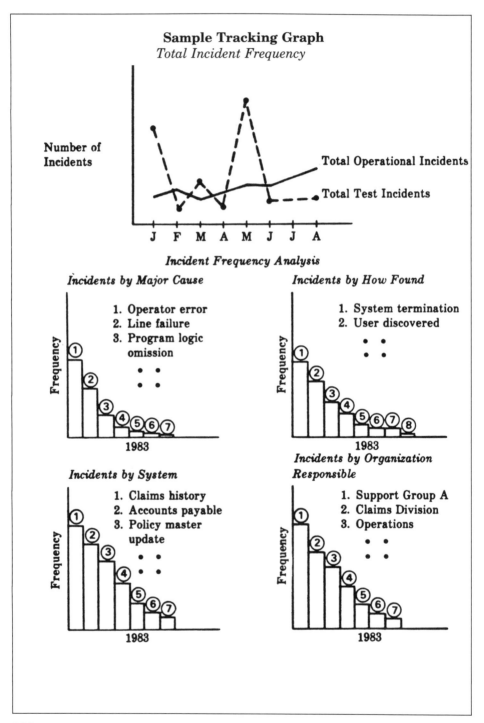

Sample Tracking Graph
Total Incident Frequency

Number of Incidents

Total Operational Incidents

Total Test Incidents

J F M A M J J A

Incident Frequency Analysis

Incidents by Major Cause

Frequency

1. Operator error
2. Line failure
3. Program logic omission

1983

Incidents by How Found

Frequency

1. System termination
2. User discovered

1983

Incidents by System

Frequency

1. Claims history
2. Accounts payable
3. Policy master update

1983

Incidents by Organization Responsible

Frequency

1. Support Group A
2. Claims Division
3. Operations

1983

long term. The other plots provide a more detailed picture of what causes the incidents. All eight should be prepared and charted separately for operational and testing incidents. They provide monthly histograms and trend graphs of the most frequent causes; most common means of detection; most error-prone systems; and errors by organizational unit or responsibility. Careful monthly study of each of these (assuming they are reliably produced!) will go a long way toward helping managers and practitioners see trends and obtain proper feedback from the tracking effort.

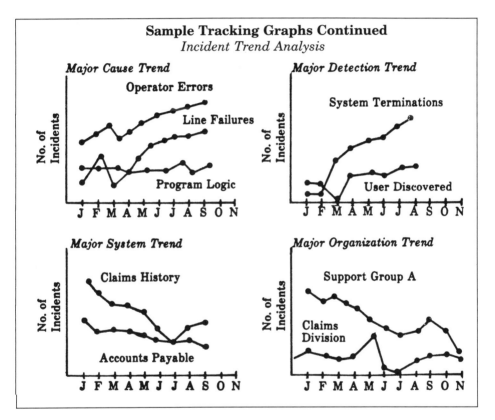

Sample Tracking Graphs Continued
Incident Trend Analysis

Tracking Error, Fault, and Failure Cost

In addition to tracking and analyzing error frequencies, we must also track impact and costs. Certain errors and failures have major impact and cost many thousands of dollars to correct or recover. Others have little impact and cause only minor inconveniences. When analyzing testing performance, we are fundamentally concerned with the ability to detect and prevent failures. Simple frequency counts may not show the trends properly. Tracking costs overcomes this and assures measurement of direct impact.

Assigning costs to every incident is not necessary. Good trend information is obtained if just the larger impact errors are tracked. My rule of thumb is that any failure that has an estimated impact in excess of $500 should be analyzed and have a carefully assigned cost. In practice this will eliminate 80 percent or more of the incident reports and make cost tracking manageable.

Once the costs have been evaluated for the individual errors, trend graphs should again be prepared on a regular basis. I have included some graphs I find useful.

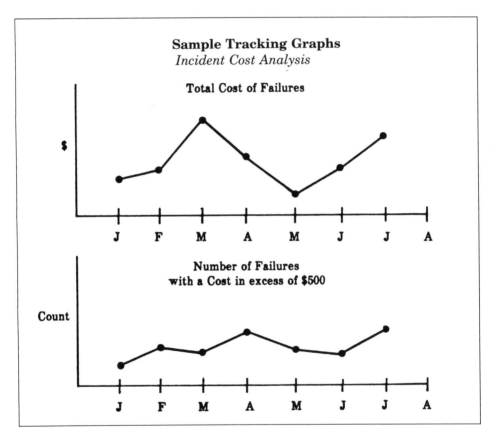

Sample Tracking Graphs
Incident Cost Analysis

Total Cost of Failures

**Number of Failures
with a Cost in excess of $500**

The first Incident Cost Analysis graph displays the cost trend in terms of the total count and cost for all failures in excess of $500. The second shows three plots to help analyze the major factors influencing the cost of failure. Typically, a small number of systems, causes, or organizations are responsible for a large percentage of the total failures. Targeting improvements to these specific problem areas can bring about dramatic savings.

As in tracking frequencies, the key to successful control is reliable reporting and graphing to display trends and identify significant changes.

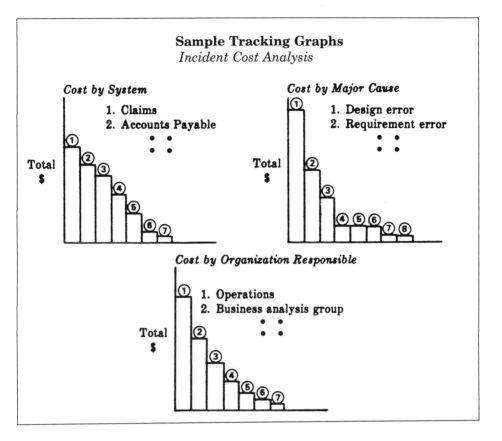

Sample Tracking Graphs
Incident Cost Analysis

Tracking Testing Status

Another important control element is tracking the status of testing work. As with any aspect of project management, status tracking is greatly aided by good planning. A carefully laid out test plan that defines the testing work in detail will serve as a reporting baseline and foster good status reporting.

Tracking Testing Status

1. *Starts* with knowledge of what is to be done and the results expected.
2. *Requires* knowledge of results achieved and barriers.
3. Depends on flow of information and *measurement* of progress.
4. Provides the basis for analysis and redirection.

The frustrations with trying to measure progress properly during testing in the large are real. Case studies abound in which projects have reported over 90 percent-plus completion and still require over a year to finish. There are even many that reach the mythical 90 percent complete stage but never get completed. Our methods and practices for measuring testing progress are very poor. For many organizations, answers to questions concerning the completeness of testing are purely subjective. This is what testing status reporting must overcome. All the following are information needs.

Testing Status Information Needs

1. Status of test design work
2. Status of test case specification work
3. Available test cases
4. What has been tested
5. What has not been tested
6. Which versions are tested with what tests
7. How much testing remains

Measuring progress and maintaining status control over testing mean that it is necessary to know how much testing must be done before a module or component is completed as well as how much has been done to date. Without test plans and specifications, there is no baseline of the work to be done and there can be no effective status reporting. This is yet another important reason for insisting on test plans. (Although we should certainly have more than enough motivation already!)

In larger projects useful status information can be obtained from cumulative plots of faults found versus testing effort or time as shown in the two sample plots above.

It can be observed empirically that the plots take on a characteristic exponential shape and that as the shape develops it becomes possible to use it to roughly gauge the testing time or effort remaining or the total number of errors remaining in the system.

Such plots are more useful if a reasonable estimate of the projected total faults to be found can be established. Estimates of one half percent to one percent of the total anticipated lines of code in a system have been used with some success and provide an initial guess if no better estimate is available. The number of faults corrected is also a helpful addition when plotted on the same graph. It will show if debugging is becoming a serious obstacle to testing progress and provide a further indication of true status.

The dotted line in the Faults Estimated and Corrected graph shows an

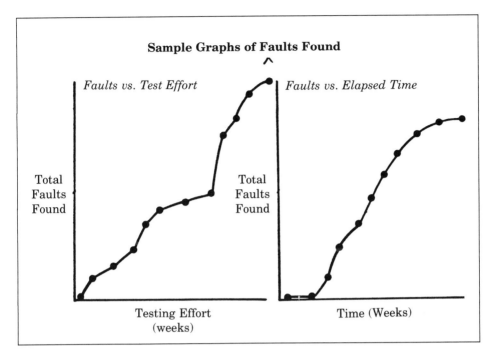

Sample Graphs of Faults Found

Faults vs. Test Effort

Total
Faults
Found

Testing Effort
(weeks)

Faults vs. Elapsed Time

Total
Faults
Found

Time (Weeks)

attempt to predict testing performance, and provides an estimate of progress toward completion. If log data are plotted, straight-line projections may be used and fits estimated for the exponential curves more easily. (It has been noted that plotting the count of incident reports, or, in general, any measure that is highly correlated with faults, gives essentially equivalent results to the plots of faults themselves.)

These curves, while useful, suffer because they do not relate to well-defined criteria for test completion. Having plotted the graphs we are still left with a subjective judgment of how much testing we must perform before we are through. When we have a test design—even a fairly poor one!—the design defines the testing work to be completed and supplies the criteria for stopping. Assuming that we have a number of test cases defined as a part of the test design, we are able to display status directly by graphing the test case results.

As an example, let us assume we are conducting a systems test for a package made up of four major components or subsystems: A, B, C, and D. Test case specifications have been developed for each of the system components, and a set of overall system test cases has also been designed as a part of the System Test Plan and Specifications. The set of cases for each component is selected to exercise the functions in the subsystem thoroughly. The system cases verify overall system functions as well as the interfaces among various components. Assume further that this collection of planned cases represents

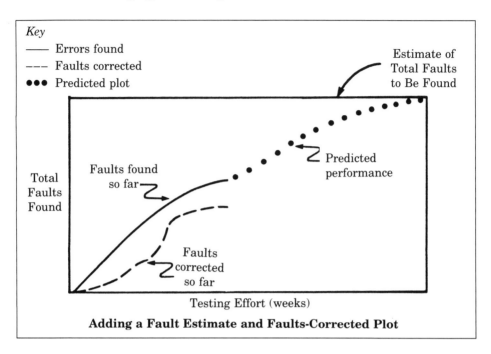

Adding a Fault Estimate and Faults-Corrected Plot

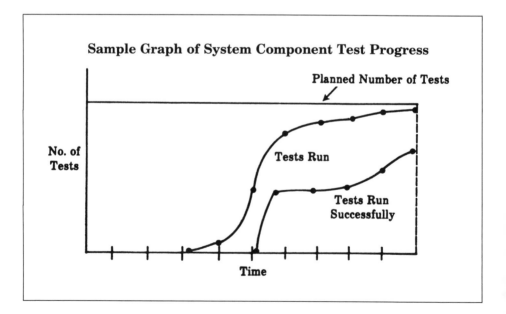

the total testing work to be performed. Then we may very nicely track status toward completion by plotting the percentage of test cases that are run and run successfully.

The System Component Test Progress graph shows what a typical status plot might look like. The total number of planned tests is first drawn in to identify the amount of testing work to be accomplished. Then, during the testing (perhaps daily or at least weekly), we plot the number of tests run and the number that are successful. The curves produced are extremely useful and raise many good questions about testing status. In the sample the number of tests run has leveled off during the last few reporting periods. Why? Does this suggest that the test cases are not ready to run? Is it because some part of the component is not available? Answering such questions helps greatly to determine the true status. Projecting the tests run successfully curve to the line showing the number of tests to be run gives a useful estimate of the testing time remaining.

In practice, the number of tests planned changes during the testing process. Additional tests are defined and others dropped so that the line moves up and down. Such movement by itself is a useful status indicator. Test cases added suggest either a "growing" subsystem scope or poor original test planning.

Test cases dropped may signal the withdrawal of originally planned function or reduced testing effectiveness. In the example of an expanded Test Progress graph, the number of tests planned has changed twice, moving up once and then moving down. This graph also shows the addition of the third

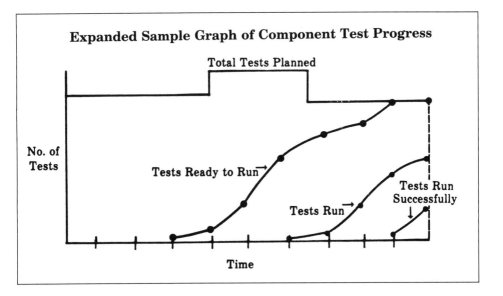

Expanded Sample Graph of Component Test Progress

curve to display the number of tests that are ready to run. Plotting the tests ready to run permits tracking the status of the test case preparation work.

The difference between tests run and tests run successfully is most pertinent to the measurement of progress. Failure of a case to run may mean that the function being tested failed, that the specifications were inappropriate, that some other interdependent function failed, that the case itself failed, or any of a number of other things. Backup and supplementary reports are useful here to indicate special causes and identify areas needing study. The shapes of the curves have proved empirically to be very useful. The shapes shown in the sample curves are similar to cumulative distribution curves in statistics and show up consistently. It is relatively slow—and painful!—to get the first few tests run; thereafter, once some tests are working, the majority will get through quite quickly, while the final few usually bog down and may be even more painful to get working than the initial ones. This behavior leads to the characteristic S-shaped cumulative distribution curve. Knowledge of the expected shape can help us use the curves to predict test completion more accurately.

If we change the vertical scale to show the percentage of tests completed (instead of the number), the tests planned line is always straight at 100 percent, and it becomes possible to display more than one component or subsystem on a single graph. This is desirable for obtaining an overall measure of system testing progress.

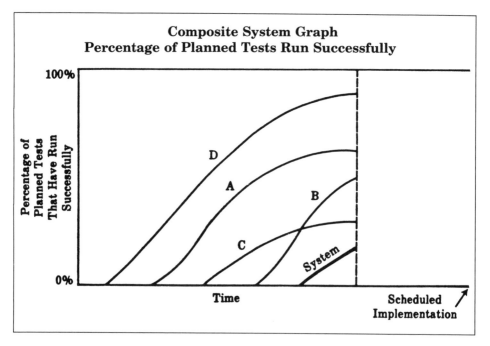

Looking at the Composite System Graph, we can observe that subsystems D and B are doing well. Subsystem A is in trouble. Its testing was moving smoothly until a few weeks ago. Then perhaps a major change was required and the curve flattened out with further testing delayed until the change was completed. Subsystem C shows a different problem. Testing is making uniformly slow progress, perhaps because of poor coding and the need to fix bugs at each test. This combined graph thus gives the manager an impressive tool for measuring testing (and project) progress. If the scheduled implementation date were as shown, it is highly unlikely that all planned tests could be completed. Strong management action would be warranted, to consider changing the implementation date and/or adding resources to the testing and debugging efforts.

Another approach to status tracking is based on the structural testing concepts discussed in earlier chapters. The idea is to plot the degree of system coverage achieved by testing. Any reasonable coverage measure may be used. The simplest is just a plot of the modules, or paragraphs, executed with successful system test cases.

The plot indicates the breadth of the testing being performed. Any reasonable system test will, at a minimum, exercise every module. The plot displays progress toward that goal.

If an instrumentation tool is available (see Chapter 7) the module coverage plot may be produced automatically as the testing proceeds. Other more detailed coverage plots are also possible. I have included several examples. The three sample plots in the illustration show the number of statements, the

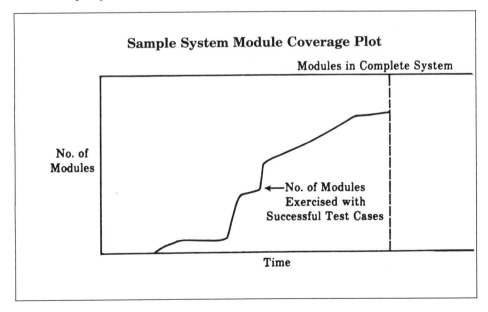

Sample System Module Coverage Plot

Modules in Complete System

No. of Modules

←No. of Modules Exercised with Successful Test Cases

Time

Sample Test Coverage Plots Using Instrumentation

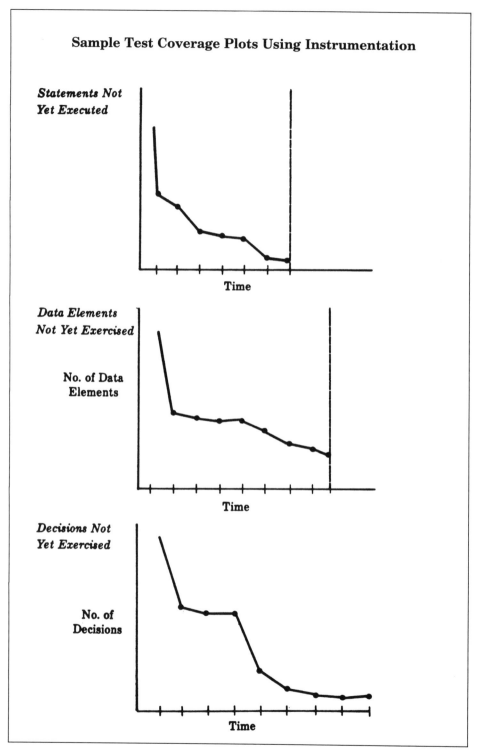

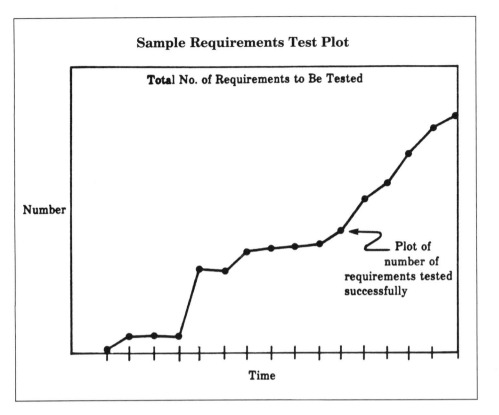

number of data elements, and the number of decisions in the total system that have *not* yet been exercised by any of the successful system test cases. We usually do not expect to achieve 100 percent. The plots show the coverage achieved. Combined with objective criteria (such as at least 90 percent of the decisions and 95 percent of all data elements exercised), they can be very effective in tracking test activity and effectiveness.

One final plot I have found to be very helpful is a graph of the requirements or functions that have been successfully tested.

Assuming the requirements to be tested have been identified, this plot is easy to prepare and displays the testing progress in terms of *delivered* capabilities. If a requirements validation matrix has been developed (see Chapter 5) the cases are already identified for testing each requirement. The number of requirements for completing testing are plotted weekly. Typically, the graph moves up in spurts as a group of related requirements is signed off. For more detail the requirements may be grouped by major function and subplots maintained.

All of the graphs described in this chapter are easy to prepare and maintain. My experience has been that only an hour or two a week is required *once the reporting mechanism is in place!* The hard part is initiating a *reliable* flow of status information. That requires planning and coordination from the very beginning of the project and is yet another reason for my emphasis on a comprehensive Master Test Plan.

The graphs are, of course, only a part of the story. Supplementary reports that break down the reasons for changes in the plots and careful analysis of the plots on an ongoing basis are also essential. The chart trends form the basis for extrapolation and prediction. They depend on a manager's ability to obtain accurate and truthful reporting. For this reason, the graphs should be prominently displayed for all project personnel to review. Presence of the charts helps to signal interest in testing and generates helpful discussion, or even armchair analysis! Most importantly, it adds insurance that the measurement system is performing effectively and that judgments about testing status are based on sound information.

Test Documentation as a Control Tool

Still another critical aspect of proper control over the testing activity is testing documentation. The development life cycle is often characterized by the documents produced during each phase of work. In the same manner, the testing life cycle may be defined, and controlled, by the documents produced during each of the testing activities.

Test documentation has been largely ignored in most installations. Only recently has the notion of a written test plan become commonplace and accepted as a routine project deliverable. Standards for writing the plan or for recording and reporting test results or test status are uneven. In many organizations test documentation is simply not produced. In others, the documentation is haphazard and left to the discretion of the practitioner. The situation is similar to the state of program documentation twenty-five years ago. Everyone recognizes the need, but few do anything about it until a disaster or calamity forces us to stop procrastinating. Auditors know by now to check for program documentation, and most of us have adopted program documentation standards and are forced to live by them, whether we want to or not. The auditors haven't quite figured out that test documentation is just as important. As with program documentation, the change will be painful, but it is certain to come. Within a few years most organizations will adopt standards for test documentation and insist that all projects follow them. The reason is simple: without test documentation we cannot effectively manage the testing activity!

Does your organization have a defined testing life cycle? If it does, what is it? These questions are best answered by looking at the documents that are *required* in support of the testing work.

The sample document plan defines a testing life cycle that begins with a Master Test Plan coordinating all of the testing activity. Design testing and

Sample Testing Documentation Plan

Document	Purpose	Who Writes?	Who Reviews?	Who Approves?	When Due?
Master Test Plan	Overall direction	Test Coordinator	Requirements Review	Project Manager	Completion of requirements phase
Design Validation Report	Report on design testing	Lead Designer	Design Review	Testing Manager	Completion of design phase
Unit Test Plan	Plan program testing	Programmer	Analyst	Programmer	Prior to program coding
Integration Test Plan	Plan for system integration	Test Coordinator	Design Review	Testing Manager	Completion of detailed design
Systems Test Plan	Plan for system testing	Test Coordinator	Design Review	Testing Manager	Completion of detailed design
Acceptance Test Plan	Plan for acceptance testing	Test Coordinator	Preliminary Design Review	Testing Manager	Completion of preliminary design
Test Case Specifications	Specify test cases	Tester	Test Coordinator	Testing Manager	Prior to start of test
Test Procedures	Specify test procedures	Tester	Test Coordinator	Testing Manager	Prior to start of test
Test Log	Log test activities	Tester	Test Coordinator	Test Coordinator	Daily as testing proceeds
Test Trouble Report	Report deficiencies	Tester	Test Coordinator	Test Coordinator	After each deficiency is found
Test Certification	Certify system readiness	Test Manager	NA	Project Management	Prior to operation
Test Evalution Report	Report test effectiveness	Test Manager	Postimplementation Review	Project Management	6 months after operation

validation are formally reported, and unit test plans are specified for program testing. Integration, systems, and acceptance test plans are individually documented. Cases are specified by test case specifications and test procedures. Tests conducted are logged in a test log and any problems found are captured in the trouble report. Finally, a formal test certification is required before operational use and six months after implementation test effectiveness is evaluated. The sample plan contains columns for recording the names of those who are responsible for preparing and approving each document and the time the document must be completed. It provides a quick overview of the entire testing process in the organization.

What specific documents should be required in the testing life cycle? I personally view this as a decision to be made within each organization. Variables such as the nature of the applications, the size and scope of projects, and compatibility with existing project methodologies affect the decision significantly. The IEEE Computer Society Software Engineering Standards Committee has addressed the area of test documentation and produced a set of standards that has been adopted by the American National Standards Institute (ANSI). The ANSI standard defines eight basic test documents. (Standards were described in Chapter 12; the reader may wish to refer back to that section.) The eight documents are listed for ease of reference.

ANSI Standard Software Test Documentation

1. Test Plan	Defines the approach and plan for the testing work
2. Test Design Specification	Refines the test approach and identifies tests
3. Test Case Specification	Specifies a test case identified by a test design specification
4. Test Procedures Specification	Details the steps to carry out a set of test cases
5. Test Item Transmittal	Identifies test items being transmitted for testing
6. Test Log	Records the testing performed
7. Test Incident Report	Documents problems or discrepancies requiring investigation
8. Test Summary Report	Summarizes the testing results associated with one or more test design specifications

---

The first four documents define the testing to be performed in increasing levels of detail. The last three record the testing results. The standard specifies the form and content for each of the eight documents. The standard does not define the specific documents that must be used. As long as the format for any document selected is adhered to, the organization may state that it is following the standard.

The ANSI standard has already had a significant impact on the development of test documentation standards. Any organization involved in putting together such standards should get a copy of the standard and consider it as a potential model. The appendix of the standard shows completed example documents which are of great help in understanding the standard and should be useful for the practitioner as models.

The Sample Testing Documentation Plan and the ANSI standard are two examples of integrated sets of testing documents. Variants or extensions may easily be created. A number of organizations have adopted special forms for use in documenting parts of the testing activity. These augment the basic documents and make it easier for the practitioners to provide the required information. Organizations involved in setting up their own test documentation plans should try to obtain samples from as many other companies as possible. The forms may often be used without change or with very little modification.

The important step is to define which documents will be required and to establish a routine so that the documents "control" the work flow. At a minimum there must be a test plan, a test design, a record of test results, and a record of problems or discrepancies. These documents establish the test work that is supposed to be done; record the testing that is actually done; and capture any problems discovered so that they are sure to be corrected. They also form the backbone of an effective system for controlling the testing work. Test progress may be tracked, at least crudely, with the completion of the documents. It also becomes possible to examine the test plan or the record of the testing performed to determine why certain problems were missed; evaluate the costs of the testing performed; and compare and measure testing effectiveness. All together these provide us with effective basic control of the testing activity.

SUMMARY

1. Controlling the testing function requires that we test the testing work that is performed.

2. Key elements of an effective control program include
   - tracking of error, fault, and failure data
   - tracking of testing costs
   - tracking of testing status
   - test documentation

3. Tracking failures requires
   - a system to capture data as failures are discovered
   - ongoing analysis and reporting of trends

4. Graphs are an excellent analysis tool for establishing
   - error and failure frequencies
   - error and failure trends
   - error and failure costs
   - errors versus test effort or time
   - tests run versus tests planned
   - system coverage completion
   - requirements coverage completion

5. Tracking testing status depends on
   - a definition or plan for the work to be performed
   - reliable information on what has been performed

6. A key control tool is the Testing Documentation Plan.

7. Many different testing documents are prepared as testing work proceeds. Some commonly used examples include:

   - Master Test Plan
   - Design Test Plan
   - Unit Test Plans
   - Integration Test Plan
   - Systems Test Plan
   - Acceptance Test Plan
   - Test Certifications
   - Test Case Specifications
   - Test Procedures Specifications
   - Test Activity Logs
   - Test Deficiency Reports
   - Test Results Reports
   - Test Evaluation Reports
   - Test Design Specifications

8. Eight Documents have been approved as ANSI standard test documentation.

   - Test Plan
   - Test Design Specification
   - Test Case Specification
   - Test Procedures Specification
   - Test Item Transmittal
   - Test Log
   - Test Incident Report
   - Test Summary Report

9. Critical control elements are
   - a test plan (to define test work to be done)
   - a record of testing (to compare against the plan and determine cost and effort expended)
   - a record of test results (to evaluate test effectiveness and determine the costs of failure)

Chapter 14

Putting the Pieces Together

Establishing the Testing Life Cycle

Making significant and lasting changes is hard. Most organizations already have highly structured project methodologies that detail development life-cycle phases and milestones and specify the forms and documents required to complete each step of the work. An effective testing life cycle must be imposed on "top" of the existing work flow before significant testing improvement can be assured.

The goal is to bring these two together in such a way that testing flows naturally out of the development work. The trick is to establish the testing techniques without adding a burden to the development cycle! Efforts that significantly lengthen the development cycle will be resisted and will probably fail.

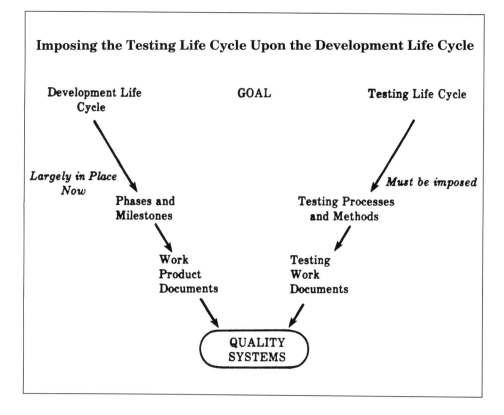

Imposing the Testing Life Cycle Upon the Development Life Cycle

Development Life Cycle GOAL Testing Life Cycle

Largely in Place Now *Must be imposed*

Phases and Milestones Testing Processes and Methods

Work Product Documents Testing Work Documents

QUALITY SYSTEMS

Initiating Testing Improvements

Planning any program of testing improvement requires dismissing two misconceptions or myths that stand in the way of meaningful progress. The first is that testing is a technical problem; some managers who believe that delude themselves by concluding they can make all their testing problems go away by hiring better people or providing training. The second misconception is that any real improvements in testing require more money or slow down productivity.

Statements like, "That's nice and we need to do something about it, but we can't afford it" or "I can't do anything that lowers productivity" are ways of expressing the common belief that better testing costs more money. Yet most organizations are wasting so much money on poor testing that they could implement new techniques and *reduce* testing costs simultaneously, without even counting the enormous savings from reduced errors or failures!

Plans for improvement must take these myths into account and include strategies for overcoming them. If managers don't understand the role they must play in leading the testing improvement effort, "training" sessions designed to foster that understanding are necessary. If money or time are serious concerns, the plan should detail the costs and relate them to realistic and measurable savings targets. Such considerations are as important in the plan as the choice of particular techniques and methodologies and should be given equal—if not unequal—attention.

My advice is to start with a special thrust aimed at better and earlier test design or improved coordination between levels of testing. Testing improvements in these areas yield the highest dividends and almost everyone needs help there. Where to turn next depends on the situation. Likely priorities include the Master Test Plan, the development of testing policy and the testing life cycle, and improvements in error tracking and analysis. The Testing Practices Survey in Appendix A may also provide ideas or a checklist for your practices. Only after these areas have reached a fairly mature stage should major changes in testing in the small or testing in the large be attempted across an organization. This caution does not preclude the individual practitioner or the small project team from adopting any of the techniques. That is really the way major change is accomplished anyway. It takes a courageous and innovative leader to try new techniques and show others that they work; that they are something more than just ideas in a book; and that the organization's interest is served by using them.

Are you one of the innovators? Will you improve your own testing practices? Will you help show the way to your organization? Putting the pieces together takes people who will pick them up and see that they get put down in the right place.

Testing is the *centerpiece* in an organization's entire quality initiative. A strong testing program is an essential prerequisite for any effective quality management effort. Quality can and must be managed if it is to be consistently attained. The place to start is with measurement! Objectives and requirements make little sense before you know what you have, and control is meaningless unless you know something is wrong. Thus, improvement must start with better measurement!

Throughout the book I have emphasized the importance of test planning —the Master Test Plan—and the ongoing nature of the testing activity—the testing life cycle. The central theme is that quality measurement can be structured, disciplined, and managed. Good testing is presented as a way of thinking and behaving. Practical and experience-proven techniques have been described over the entire spectrum of the testing life cycle. Some effort has been made to describe both the *how* and the *why* of the various techniques. The *why* focuses on motivation—where concepts and the ideas come from and why they are important now. The *how* encompasses practical terms that explain the methodologies so they can be easily understood and quickly put to use.

Choose your techniques from the smorgasborg I mentioned in Chapter 7. Many plates and dishes have been placed on the table, and almost all of them look delicious. What are you going to eat? If you take too much you may come away with a stomachache or at least having gained a couple of unwanted pounds. If you mix the dishes poorly they may easily lose their individual effectiveness. The techniques and initiatives you select for use in your own organization must also be well balanced, and too much at once can cause far worse ills than a stomachache!

Well, close the doors and let's get going!

SUMMARY

1. Quality control involves
   - Defining what the requirements are (quality is)
   - Measuring quality
   - Acting on the results (feedback)
2. Testing is the centerpiece.
   - The purpose of testing is to measure quality.
   - Good testing is a prerequisite to quality control.
3. Common testing misconceptions
   - Testing is a technical problem.
   - Better testing means more money or slower development.
4. Achieving significant testing improvements depends on
   - Successfully imposing a new testing life cycle on top of the development life cycle
   - Selecting the "right" set of techniques and methodologies
   - A few—maybe just one—key innovators willing to show the way!

APPENDIX

This appendix contains the following items:

Appendix A—Testing Practices Survey

A survey of industry testing practices completed at the 4th International Software Testing Conference held in Washington, D.C. June 14–16, 1987.

Appendix B—Sample Testing Policy

A sample draft of a high level quality management and testing improvement standard.

Appendix C—Quality Measurement Checklist

A self appraisal checklist intended to help an organization assess and identify software quality management needs and priorities.

Testing References Bibliography

An annotated bibliography of the testing literature.

Appendix A

Software Test Practices Survey

Introduction

This survey was aimed at helping to understand industry software testing practices and trends. It was completed by attendees at the 4th International Conference on Software Testing held in Washington, D.C. June 14–16, 1987. Part I of the survey asked for background information from the respondents (job title, age, sex, salary, work experience, education, etc.) to establish a typical profile. Part II listed various testing practices and asked respondents to indicate whether or not each was normal practice in their organization. A series of question at the end of the survey looked at trends and compared testing practices today with several years ago.

Respondents

The first part of the survey asked for information regarding respondents background, education, job title and salary. Table 1 summarizes the results and provides a perspective on the typical respondent.

As the table reflects, respondents are experienced and well-educated. Over 90% have college degrees and almost half have advanced degrees. One third were female, average age was 37, years of testing experience was five and average salary was just under $44,000 per year.

TYPICAL PROFILE OF SURVEY RESPONDENTS			
RESPONSIBILITY		**AGE**	
Testing and QA Managers	31%	Under 25	7%
Software Analysts and Specialists	27%	25 – 35	44%
Testing and QA Specialists	19%	35 – 45	31%
Software Managers	16%	45 – 55	16%
Other (Consultant, Scientist, etc.)	7%	55 – 65	2%

SALARY		**EDUCATION**		**SEX**	
Under $25,000	3%	PhD	6%	Male	65%
$25,000–$35,000	25%	MS/MA/MBA	38%	Female	35%
$35,000–$45,000	25%	BS/BA	48%		
$45,000–$55,000	28%	Other	8%		
$55,000–$65,000	15%				
Over $65,000	4%				

SOFTWARE EXPERIENCE		**TESTING EXPERIENCE**	
Under 2 years	10%	Under 2 years	37%
3 to 5 years	27%	3 to 5 years	30%
6 to 10 years	37%	6 to 10 years	21%
11 to 15 years	16%	11 to 15 years	7%
Over 15 years	10%	Over 15 years	5%

TABLE 1

Half of the attendees had job responsibilities that were testing or quality assurance related and another 43% were in various software job responsibilities. Almost half of the respondents were managers (job titles of manager, supervisor, director, officer, etc.) with one third being Test or Quality Assurance managers.

Practices

Part II of the survey consisted of a list of test practices for which the respondent was asked to answer YES if the practice reflected normal or common usage in their organization; NO if the practice was not normally employed; or SOME-TIMES if the practice was used on some projects but not others. Table 2 highlights the results from this part of the questionnaire.

	%	%

ANALYSIS OF INDUSTRY TEST PRACTICE USAGE

Test Practice	% Yes	% Sometimes
Record of *defects* found during testing is maintained	73	16
Designated person is responsible for the *test process*	65	13
Test plan describing objectives/approach is required	61	29
Testing is a *systematic* and *organized* activity	61	30
Full-time testers perform system testing	62	19
Testing is *separated from development*	60	20
Test are *required* to be *rerun* when software changes	51	35
Tests are *saved* and maintained for future use	51	28
Test specifications and designs are *documented*	48	36
Test procedure is *documented* in the *standards* manual	45	15
A *log of tests run* is maintained	42	35
A *record of the time spent* on testing is maintained	40	30
Test documents are formally peer-*reviewed*	31	29
Full-time testers perform integration testing	24	24
The *cost of testing* is measured and *tracked*	24	19
Test training is *provided* periodically	22	26
Test results are formally peer *reviewed*	20	31
Users are *heavily involved* in test activities	8	39
Tests are developed *before coding*	8	29
A *measurement of code coverage* achieved is required	5	16

TABLE 2

The most commonly reported practice was recording of defects found during testing (73% of the respondents considered this a normal practice in their organization). The least common practice was measuring code coverage achieved during testing (only five percent viewed this as a normal practice).

The testing practices reported in the survey results are more sophisticated than those in general industry. Respondents to this survey were all attendees at the International Test Conference and that created a bias. Many of the individual respondents are the leading testing advocates within their organizations and would naturally represent the best testing practices within their organizations. One specific result indicative of this bias was that 60% of the respondents indicated that testing was separated from development in their organization. Across industry at large, this percentage is actually less than one third. The explanation is simply that companies where testing is separated from development were much more likely to be represented at the Test Conference.

Several other observations regarding the practices usage should be made. Only eight percent of the respondents regularly develop tests before coding. The concept of test design and development before code is a key aspect of all Software Quality Engineering test courses. We view it as a critical practice if a high level of effectiveness and productivity are to be achieved and yet it is clear that industry has a long way to go before the practice becomes the norm or even fairly frequently employed.

A second observation was to point out something of an inconsistency. A high percentage of the respondents felt that the testing in their organization was a systematic and organized activity (91% answered either YES or SOMETIMES to this practice). However, less than half report that their test practices are documented in the standards manuals, only half regularly save their tests for reuse and rerunnning after software changes, and an extremely small five percent provide regular measurements of code coverage. Such practices are more indicative of the unsystematic, ad hoc approaches that have characterized testing practices in the past than something that could be characterized as systematic.

Trends

The last group of questions on the survey measured changes in testing practices during the past several years. As shown in Table 3, over two thirds of the respondents believed that their overall testing effectiveness was improved today compared with several years ago, and almost half felt it was a *lot* better. However, the time being spent to perform testing is *increasing* and the level of automation is not going up as fast as it might. Over half of the respondents felt that more time was now required for testing and almost a third felt it was a *lot* more. (It is significant that a quarter of the respondents chose to answer DON'T KNOW. A significant number of companies are not tracking the time spent on testing and are not able to compare time being spent today with that of a few years ago.)

COMPARISON OF TESTING TODAY WITH SEVERAL YEARS AGO

Effectiveness

A Lot Better	47%
A Little Better	20%
About the Same	26%
Down	7%

Time Required

A Lot More	30%
A Little More	24%
About the Same	14%
Down	7%
Don't Know	25%

Use of Automation

Up Significantly	41%
About the Same	55%
Don't Know	4%

TABLE 3

Two questions asked respondents if they had changed testing practices during the past year and whether further changes were planned for the coming year. Response to these questions indicated that the rate of change and improvement in testing is accelerating. Over half (53%) indicated that significant improvements and changes were made last year and well over half (61%) indicated that specific significant changes were planned for the next year. Many of the plans related to expected tool acquisitions and improvements in test automation. While this year's survey showed over half of the respondents feeling that automation was not much improved from several years ago, it would appear that is now changing rapidly.

Summary

This survey demonstrates that many companies are acting to improve testing practices and that significant gains in putting effective test methods in place have been realized over the past several years. It further indicates that a period of fairly intense and continued assimilation and improvement lies ahead. For those companies not actively implementing better testing, the reality may well be dropping further behind when compared to a steadily moving industry standard. In other words, standing still means falling further behind! However, the improvements are not coming without cost. Companies are increasing the time spent on testing and spending more money on implementing methodologies and training. It remains to be seen whether improvements in automation and productivity techniques can offset this trend and reduce the cost of software testing in the future.

Appendix B

Sample Testing Policy

1. Introduction and Purpose

This sample draft describes Corporation X's policy of commitment to the development of quality information systems and outlines the broad "quality system" that is used to ensure that quality work is obtained. Where applicable, the policy refers to other more detailed procedures that define specific methodologies in support of the quality system.

2. Quality Management

Systems Division management staff (directors, managers, supervisors and team leaders) have the following direct responsibilities:

- Develop and retain a working understanding of quality management concepts and state of the art tools, techniques, and methodologies.
- Establish a working environment that emphasizes the importance of quality work.
- Recognize quality work and reward professionals for quality performance.
- Introduce tools, techniques, and methodologies to support consistent high quality and high productivity work.

• Develop information to measure quality performance and provide feedback and results to the professional staff.

The intent is to recognize that quality is important; to strive to constantly improve quality; and to manage the entire process. This involves ongoing responsibility for objectives and goals, working out plans to achieve them and to measure the results.

3. Quality System

The collective effort to achieve quality in our work can be looked upon as the "quality system," which consists of three critical components:
• *Leadership*—This involves setting the climate and expectation for quality work. It requires management to show leadership, to set goals, and to expect and demand high quality performance.
• *Support*—This involves providing the tools, techniques, training, and procedures needed to assure that quality is delivered.
• *Control*—This involves measuring results and tracking the information needed to assure that quality is delivered.

Quality management requires the active involvement of all managers in *each* of these three spheres.

4. The Meaning of Quality

Quality in an information system relates to many attributes and factors. There are exterior qualities like usability, reliability, and correctness; interior qualities like efficiency and testability; and qualities relating to future needs, such as flexibility, maintainability, and reusability. The overall quality of any system is a composite of all these factors, weighted appropriately to the particular requirements and needs.

5. The Cost of Quality

The cost of quality falls into three broad categories—prevention, appraisal, and failure. Prevention costs involve investments aimed at getting work done right the first time and preventing quality problems from ever coming up. (Examples include training, new techniques and tools, methodologies, and the like.) Appraisal costs involve all of the testing and checkout efforts to measure whether needed quality has been achieved. Failure costs are those incurred by the need to fix and recover from the quality problems that do arise. Our aim is to measure these collective quality costs on an ongoing basis. Fundamentally, we believe that well-thought-out investments in prevention will be repaid many times over by significant decreases in the costs of appraisal and failure.

6. Objectives

Our objectives for the next one- to three-year period are the following:

- Establish an effective quality management program and create a quality work environment.
- Significantly improve the effectiveness of the testing and quality appraisal work. (Demonstrate higher quality and better checked-out systems.)
- Achieve significant increases in productivity and efficiency in testing activities—minimum 10 percent.
- Improve the user perception and develop a reputation for quality emphasis in all work performed.
- Develop and use quality standards to achieve a balanced tradeoff between the quality required and the effort needed to achieve it. (Avoid overemphasis and overcontrol.)
- Measure and track the quality improvement efforts.

7. The Quality Standard

Procedure (name) contains a methodology for establishing and developing a minimum *quality standard*. Setting the standard involves defining the quality factors and their importance and choosing objective measures to determine if they have been achieved.

Project teams are assigned the following responsibilities relative to the quality standard:

- Determine and establish a quality standard for their project.
- Provide the mechanism to measure achievement of the quality standard.
- Demonstrate that their work meets the standard before accepting it as completed.

8. The Meaning of Testing

All work we do to appraise and determine whether our systems perform as intended can be thought of as testing. This includes reviews, audits, walkthroughs, unit testing, system testing, acceptance testing, test case development, maintenance, and so forth.

A special focus on testing is a natural outgrowth of any quality management initiative, since testing activities play a major role in our quality system (they make up almost the total control sphere) and use a lot of resources (time and hardware). Given the expense and the impact, special emphasis in this area is needed.

9. Testing Objectives

Testing as routinely performed is an instructional and undisciplined activity. Many professionals have not had training in how to test effectively and have little understanding of what they are trying to accomplish. Our broad aim is to establish an effective *process* for the testing work we do and to significantly improve both the resulting effectiveness and efficiency. Specific subobjectives include the following:

- Develop a solid understanding of testing principles, methods, and techniques within the staff.
- Achieve understanding that what we are trying to do is to find the *easiest* way to assure ourselves that the quality standard has been met.
- Introduce new techniques to improve the productivity and effectiveness of the testing process.
- Manage the testing process more effectively and provide feedback for further improvement.
- Adopt and establish a testing discipline so that the *right* amount of testing gets performed (neither too much nor too little).

10. Testing Strategies

After review by the management team a number of strategies were identified as having the highest payoff in terms of improving our testing and achieving the objectives set forth. Our intent is to emphasize these strategies as the major focus of the improvement effort.

- *Specification and Design Validation*—Any successful testing process depends on the existence of good requirements and specifications for what is intended. Assuring that the specifications and design meet the quality standard is a central strategy and strengthening our reviews and walkthroughs to emphasize testability (i.e., early definition of system test data and acceptance criteria) will be a major emphasis.

- *Structured Module Testing*—Techniques for unit testing of modules have been developed that provide a basis for determining how much testing is required and produce the test cases needed in a straightforward and structured manner. These techniques have a theoretical foundation and have proven themselves both in terms of effectiveness and efficiency. Our aim is to introduce them as the normal practice for unit module testing.

- *Top-Down Testing*—The choice of the order for integrating modules and checking out subsystems has a big impact on the system testing process. Our aim is for a methodology that tests and checks out a high level system first and then adds modules in an organized top-down manner.

- *Test Case Library*—Test case development begins with tests defined as the requirements and specifications are validated. Other tests are developed over the project life. Our aim is to develop a test case library to house and control all test data effectively. This would include performance test data, functional test data, and the unit module structured tests. It would be updated as changes to the system took place and might be thought of as an extension or subset of the data dictionary for the system.

- *Test Planning and Reporting*—A comprehensive test plan that defines the testing goals, strategy, approach, and organization will be expected as a regular practice. The plan will also spell out how the results can be captured and tracked, and will provide a means for feeding back quality information to individual team members and to management.

- *Test Facility and Support*—The online and batch systems to support our testing work have clear limitations. Our aim is to significantly improve the test environment and examine new support software that will help us work more effectively.

Separate procedures for each of these six key strategy areas are being developed and will become available in the procedures manual as they are completed. For each area a detailed improvement plan has been laid out. Any staff interested is welcome to review these and help us refine them as we move along. We also welcome the identification of other strategy areas that should be pursued.

11. Summary

Quality is important to our organization. It will be emphasized in every aspect of our work and be expected from staff and management alike. It is *not* something we see being given to a quality assurance group or a separate organization, but, rather, the fundamental pride and determination to do the job the best way possible every time we do it. Our quality organization is ourselves and each is responsible to the whole.

Appendix C

Quality Measurement Diagnostic Checklist

A Self-Appraisal

The checklist contained in this appendix has been developed and used successfully to help an organization identify improvement needs and priorities. Although this self-appraisal normally requires two or three days to be carefully completed, scored, and evaluated, some organizations have completed it in a single day. This checklist provides an objective perspective on how an organization is doing; it helps to diagnose quality or testing concerns that should be given more attention.

To complete the appraisal a team of managers and practitioners should be assembled and made responsible for the project. We recommend obtaining independent ratings from at least four or five different organizational perspectives: DP managers, user management, the professional staff, a QA group or independent test group (if present), and outside auditors or consultants. Other groupings may work equally effectively. You may also wish, informally, to self-score the appraisal.

To evaluate the checklist the team should meet and go through the following procedure:

Part I. Overall Perspective

Sum up each section score for each independent rating group participating and enter all scores under Summary Scores for Part I.

1. Look at the average section ratings in the summary scores table. Are there any that differ by more than 5 points? If so, the team should try to determine why the performance in one section is so much better or worse than in others. Is this based on organizational issues, past emphasis, or what? Does this reflect proper prioritization?

2. Next, look to see if any section scored by any rating group is less than 20. If so, what is the reason? Was it scored fairly? A score this low represents an area in which the need for significant improvement must be addressed.

3. Finally, look at the group averages (rightmost column). Are there any that differ by more than 5 points? If so, try to ascertain why there would be such significant difference in how one group judges an area. Are these legitimate differences in perspective and can they be used to target greater communication and understanding needs?

Part II. Major Project Perspective

Select a recently completed major project, have the team score Part II of the appraisal, and complete the summary score sheet at the end of the checklist.

1. Look at the individual component scores at the bottom of the score sheet. Are there any that are negative? If so, this is a priority area requiring special attention. Scores below 10 to 15 in any area indicate cause for concern; a negative value is a major problem.

2. Next, review the phase scores in the same manner. Are any significantly lower than the average for all phases? Are any below a score of 10?

3. Do the highest and lowest scored components and phases match the team's prior judgement as to the strong and weak areas within your organization's system development life cycle? If so, use the scores to select the component or phase needing the most improvement and have the team develop a set of recommendations.

The author has established norms for each part of the checklist. These tend to be somewhat sensitive to the size and nature of the DP organization and the particular industry served and for that reason are not published in the book. Individuals interested in obtaining comparative reports by industry or organization size should contact the author. Any experience in using the checklist or suggested changes to it are most welcome.

Quality Measurement Diagnostic Checklist, Part I

I. Overall Perspective

To be completed by full evaluation team. Each question is graded on a scale of 0 to 5, from least to most effective.

A. Quality policy and definition

1. Has a quality emphasis been clearly established as management policy? □

2. Do managers and supervisors understand what is expected of them in terms of quality work? □

3. Are annual quality objectives included in the organization's plans? □

4. Are quality objectives regularly set for each project? □

5. Do professionals understand what is expected of them in terms of quality work? □

6. Has the organization established a clear definition or understanding of what is meant by quality? □

7. Do users or customers understand what software quality entails and the policy the organization has set to achieve it? □

8. Are responsibilities for quality in the organization clearly assigned? □

I-A Total □

B. Quality Measurement and Reporting

1. Is software quality evaluated and judged on a regular basis? □

2. Review management reports for the most recent month. Were quality issues included in these reports appropriately? □

3. Review project reports for the most recent month. Were quality issues included in these reports appropriately? □

4. Is "good engineering" (structure, efficiency, ease of maintenance, etc.) a part of the quality reporting? □

5. Is "high adaptability" (flexibility, ease of change and extension, reusability in new environments) a part of the quality reporting? □

6. Is the "cost of quality" tracked and regularly reported? □

7. Are individual professionals evaluated on the basis of quality performance? □

8. Are records maintained on quality failures and errors? □

I-B Total ☐

C. Quality Control and Assurance

1. Are implementation of projects prevented when their quality is below standard? □

2. Are individual managers held accountable for quality work? □

3. Are individual professionals held accountable for quality work? □

4. Is quality independently attested to by a group other than the users or the project team? □

5. Are good techniques and ideas to promote quality fed back to the professional staff? □

6. Are problems and quality concerns fed back to the professional staff? □

7. Is there a group or an individual assigned to plan ways of improving quality in the organization? □

8. Is organizational action taken when the organizational quality objectives are not met? □

I-C Total ☐

D. Quality Techniques and Support

1. Are technical methods and approaches reasonably current and at the state of the art? □

2. Are support tools and software reasonably current and at the state of the art? □

3. Are reviews held regularly and seen as effective? □

4. Is training and development in quality issues and methods regularly conducted and adequately addressed? □

5. Are testing and quality evaluation procedures and policies clearly defined and understood? □

6. Are quality-deterioration prevention techniques and methodologies clearly defined and understood? ☐

7. Are project life cycle techniques and methodologies clearly defined and understood? ☐

8. Are documentation procedures and methodologies clearly defined and understood? ☐

I-D Total ☐

Summary Scores on Overall Perspective Evaluation

Rating Group	IA	IB	IC	ID	Group Average
DP Managers	—	—	—	—	☐
User Managers	—	—	—	—	☐
Professional Staff	—	—	—	—	☐
QA Group (if present)	—	—	—	—	☐
Outside Consultant (if used)	—	—	—	—	☐
Section Average	☐	☐	☐	☐	☐

Quality Measurement Diagnostic Checklist, Part II

II. Selected Major Project Perspective

Select a recently completed (or nearly completed) major project and grade each
question as either a *yes, mostly yes, mostly no, or no.*

A. Requirements

Definition   Y   MY   MN   N
1. Was a requirements document produced?
2. Was a definition of "success" included?
3. Was a definition of "failure" included?
4. Were the requirements at a high enough level?
5. Were the requirements at a low enough level?
6. Were the requirements clearly structured?
7. Was there an index?
8. Were quality requirements included?
9. Was feasibility clearly established?
10. Was an effective change mechanism set up?
11. Was the change mechanism effectively used?

Total ☐ ☐ ☐ ☐

Completeness
1. Were the requirements reviewed for completeness?
2. Were they reviewed by the right people?
3. Did they turn out to be complete?

Total ☐ ☐ ☐ ☐

Simplicity and Understandability
1. Were the requirements understandable?
2. Was the test included with the requirement?
3. Were the requirements reviewed for simplicity?
4. Was overcomplexity avoided?
5. Did the requirements overly specify the design?

Total ☐ ☐ ☐ ☐

II-A Total ☐ ☐ ☐ ☐

B. Specifications

Definition   Y   MY   MN   N
1. Was a clear definition for the specifications provided?
2. Was the structure for the specifications reviewed?
3. Were the specifications at a high enough level?
4. Were the specifications at a low enough level?
5. Was there an index?
6. Were quality specifications included?
7. Was effective mechanism for changes set up?
8. Was the change mechanism effectively used?

Total ☐ ☐ ☐ ☐

Completeness and Consistency
1. Were the specifications reviewed for completeness?
2. Were they reviewed by the right people?
3. Did they turn out to be complete?
4. Did they turn out to be consistent?
5. Were they reviewed for consistency?
6. Were the specifications tested to ensure they met the requirements?
7. Was performance specified adequately?

Total ☐ ☐ ☐ ☐

Simplicity and Understandability
1. Were the specifications understandable?
2. Did the specifications include the tests?
3. Were unclear specifications identified?
4. Was simplicity emphasized effectively?
5. Were the inputs and outputs clearly spelled out?
6. Was the reason for each specification included?

Total ☐ ☐ ☐ ☐

II-B Total ☐ ☐ ☐ ☐

C. **Design**

Definition

	Y	MY	MN	N
1. Was a design document produced?	—	—	—	—
2. Did this document outline key choices and alternatives?	—	—	—	—
3. Were key choices broadly debated and evaluated?	—	—	—	—
4. Were competing ideas encouraged?	—	—	—	—
5. Was an overall architect assigned?	—	—	—	—
6. Were design objectives clear?	—	—	—	—
7. Was feasibility clearly established?	—	—	—	—
8. Was an effective change mechanism set up?	—	—	—	—
9. Was the change mechanism effectively used?	—	—	—	—
Total	☐	☐	☐	☐

Completeness and Consistency

	Y	MY	MN	N
1. Was the design reviewed effectively?	—	—	—	—
2. Was it reviewed by the right people?	—	—	—	—
3. Did the design turn out to be complete?	—	—	—	—
4. Did the design turn out to be consistent?	—	—	—	—
5. Was the design tested to ensure it met the specifications?	—	—	—	—
6. Were risk areas identified easily?	—	—	—	—
7. Was performance reviewed and tested easily?	—	—	—	—
Total	☐	☐	☐	☐

Simplicity and Understanding

	Y	MY	MN	N
1. Was the design understandable?	—	—	—	—
2. Was the design structured into clear and distinct levels?	—	—	—	—
3. Was simplicity emphasized effectively?	—	—	—	—
4. Were the inputs and outputs of each design level described clearly?	—	—	—	—
5. Does each module have a distinct purpose?	—	—	—	—
6. Were the inputs and outputs of each module described clearly?	—	—	—	—
7. Was a system design overview and flow schematic included?	—	—	—	—
8. Were the reasons for each of the major design choices documented?	—	—	—	—
9. Are the major data elements described clearly?	—	—	—	—
10. Are the reasons for the major data elements documented?	—	—	—	—

	Y	MY	MN	N
11. Did the right people understand the design?	—	—	—	—
12. Were the implications of the design understood?	—	—	—	—
13. Were the alternatives understood?	—	—	—	—
14. Was the system test plan developed and reviewed during the design phase?	—	—	—	—

Total ☐ ☐ ☐ ☐

Technical Depth

	Y	MY	MN	N
1. Did design methodologies follow the principles of structured analysis and design?	—	—	—	—
2. Was data defined and described in a data dictionary?	—	—	—	—
3. Did design utilize technology properly?	—	—	—	—
4. Data and files structured using the principles of database systems?	—	—	—	—
5. Consideration for reusability explored?	—	—	—	—
6. Design built on preceding design work for similar applications?	—	—	—	—

Total ☐ ☐ ☐ ☐

II-C Total ☐ ☐ ☐ ☐

D. Development

Definition

	Y	MY	MN	N
1. Was development plan and philosophy established?	—	—	—	—
2. Were the various alternatives defined and evaluated?	—	—	—	—
3. Was the development environment documented?	—	—	—	—
4. Was the language choice carefully thought through?	—	—	—	—
5. Were development objectives clear?	—	—	—	—
6. Was an effective control mechanism set up?	—	—	—	—
7. Did the control mechanism work?	—	—	—	—
8. Was an effective change mechanism set up?	—	—	—	—
9. Did the change mechanism work?	—	—	—	—
10. Was the development plan effective?	—	—	—	—
11. Was testing defined and planned early?	—	—	—	—

	Y	MY	MN	N
12. Was the development plan reviewed effectively?	—	—	—	—
13. Was quality defined and documented?	—	—	—	—

Total ☐ ☐ ☐ ☐

Simplicity and Understanding

1. Were responsibilities clearly assigned? — — — —
2. Was simplicity emphasized effectively? — — — —
3. Did each programmer understand the overall system? — — — —
4. Did the testers understand the overall system? — — — —
5. Did the end users understand the development plan? — — — —
6. Did the end users understand the test plan? — — — —
7. Was the development environment properly understood? — — — —

Total ☐ ☐ ☐ ☐

Completeness

1. Were testing and quality assurance costs separately tracked? — — — —
2. Was the quality of each module measured? — — — —
3. Was system quality measured? — — — —
4. Were errors recorded and tracked? — — — —
5. Were changes recorded and tracked? — — — —
6. Was status effectively controlled and tracked? — — — —
7. Was the full design developed? — — — —

Total ☐ ☐ ☐ ☐

Technical Depth

1. Were effective development tools employed? — — — —
2. Was structured programming required? — — — —
3. Was structured testing required? — — — —
4. Were module test plans used? — — — —
5. Were code walkthroughs effectively held? — — — —
6. Were codes reused from libraries and other applications? — — — —
7. Was a test data base established? — — — —
8. Were the reasons for each test documented? — — — —
9. Was an effective project control methodology employed? — — — —

	Y	MY	MN	N
10. Were the support utilities and libraries effective?	---	—	—	—

Total	☐	☐	☐	☐
II-D Total	☐	☐	☐	☐

E. Implementation

Definition

1. Was an implementation plan and philosophy developed? — — — —
2. Was the order of integration carefully thought out? — — — —
3. Were implementation criteria clearly set? — — — —
4. Was the implementation plan effective? . — — — —
5. Was it reviewed carefully? — — — —
6. Were responsibilities clearly assigned? — — — —
7. Were the right people involved? — — — —

Total	☐	☐	☐	☐

Simplicity and Understanding

1. Was the implication approach understood? — — — —
2. Was simplicity effectively emphasized? — — — —
3. Were the controls understood? — — — —
4. Did the end users understand the implementation plan? — — — —
5. Did the end users understand the acceptance criteria? — — — —

Total	☐	☐	☐	☐

Completeness

1. Were all system tests run as planned? — — — —
2. Were implementation criteria met? — — — —
3. Was the complete system implemented? — — — —
4. Was quality measured and tracked? — — — —
5. Were costs measured and tracked? — — — —
6. Were changes recorded and tracked? — — — —

Total	☐	☐	☐	☐

Technical Depth	Y	MY	MN	N
1. Were all test cases maintained?	—	—	—	—
2. Was a regression plan effectively set up?	—	—	—	—
3. Was the system test technique effective?	—	—	—	—
4. Was a test data base used?	—	—	—	—
5. Was the implementation controlled effectively?	—	—	—	—

Total ☐ ☐ ☐ ☐

II-E Total ☐ ☐ ☐ ☐

Major Project Score Summary

A. *Requirements*
   Definition
   Completeness
   Understanding

D. *Development*
   Definition
   Completeness
   Understanding
   Technical Depth

B. *Specifications*
   Definition
   Completeness
   Understanding

E. *Implementation*
   Definition
   Understanding
   Completeness
   Technical Depth

C. *Design*
   Definition
   Completeness
   Understanding
   Technical Depth

Score 2 for Yes, 1 for Mostly Yes, −1 for Mostly No and −2 for No. Enter the scores as follows:

Component Score
Definition
Understanding
Completeness
Technical Depth

Average ☐

Phase Score
Requirement
Specifications
Design
Development
Implementation

Testing References

Abernathy, D. H. *Survey of Design Goals for Operating Systems*. Report GTIS 72-04. Atlanta: Georgia Institute of Technology, March, 1972.

This paper discusses quality characteristics as well as security. It analyzes the trade-offs and potential conflicts between these characteristics in the context of operating system design.

Adrion, W. Richards, et al, *Validation, Verification and Testing of Computer Software*, ACM Computing Surveys, Vol. 14 #2 June 1982 pg. 159–192.

Akiyama, K. "An Example of Software System Debugging." In *Proceedings of 1971 IFIP Congress*. Amsterdam: North-Holland, 1971.

This paper presents error data correlated to the number of decisions and routine calls and displays the proportion of errors found during each stage of testing (unit, integration, and systems).

Alberts, D. S. "The Economics of Software Quality Assurance." In *Proceedings: 1976 National Computer Conference*, 433–42. Montvale, N.J.: AFIPS Press, 1976.

This paper takes a broad view of the term "quality assurance," which encompasses any software management, design, code, or V&V technique that reduces error incidence. It provides a good summary of the economic justifications for increased early attention to QA activities.

Anderson, Robert B. *Proving Programs Correct*. New York: John Wiley, 1979.

Aron, Joel D. *The Program Development Process*. Reading, Mass.: Addison-Wesley, 1975.

Arthur, Lowell Jay, *Measuring PROGRAMMER Productivity and Software Quality*, John Wiley, 1985.

Baker, A. L., and S. H. Zweban. "A Comparison of Measures of Control Flow Complexity." In *IEEE Transactions of Software Engineering*, SE-6: 506–11. New York: IEEE Press, 1980.

Balbine, B. H. "Better Manpower Utilization Using Automatic Restructuring." In *Conference Proceedings 44*, 313–27. Montvale, N.J.: AFIPS Press, 1975.

Describes a FORTRAN structuring tool.

Barber, R. *Software Reflected*. New York: North-Holland, 1982.

A delightful probe of the software profession as it exists today. Places emphasis on the need for more and better trained professional software engineers. Contains a humorous analogy to the Land of Moc where buildings frequently collapse. Also includes a professional self-test with answers.

Bauer, J. A., and R. Birchall. "Managing Large Scale Development with an Automated Change Control System." In *Proceedings: COMSAC, 1978*. New York: IEEE Press, 1978.

Describes a change control system used on Bell's EES to permit multiple programmers to change the same module.

Bazzichif and I. Spadafora, *An Automatic Generator for Compiler Testing*, IEEE trans SE vol SE-8 July 1982 pg. 343–353.

Beizer, B. *Software System Testing and Quality Assurance*. New York: Van Nostrand, 1984.

The Companion book to Beizer's *Software Testing Techniques*. Covers the broader aspects of system testing and quality assurance.

———. *Software Testing Techniques*. New York: Van Nostrand, 1983.

A comprehensive treatment of unit testing. Heavy emphasis on path testing and graph theory foundations. Some new material, especially in the areas of data validation. Includes author's experiences as director of testing and quality assurance for a telecommunications software producer.

Beizer, Boris, *Personal Computer Quality*, A Guide for Vectoms and Vendors, Van Nostrand Reinhold, New York 1987.

Belady, Laszlo. *Observations, Measurements and Experiments on Operating System Maintenance*. ACM Computing Surveys. New York: Association of Computing Machinery, 1982.

Belford, P. C., and D. S. Taylor. "Specification Verification—A Key to Improving Software Reliability." In *Proceedings: Brooklyn Polytechnic Institute Symposium on Computer Software Engineering*, 66–71. New York: Brooklyn Polytechnic Institute, 1976.

Reports on the use of specification languages and the process of verifying specifications.

Berg, H. K. et al, *Formal Methods of Program Verification and Specification*, Prentice Hall, 1982

Bersoff, A. *Software Configuration Management*. Englewood Cliffs, N.J.: Prentice-Hall, 1980.

Binder, Robert, Application Debugging. Englewood Cliffs, NJ: Prentice-Hall, 1985.

Binder, *Application Debugging: An MVS Abend Handbook.*

Boar, B. H. *Abend Programming for COBOL Programmers*. New York: John Wiley, 1976.

An introduction to debugging principles. How to read and trace IBM system abends. Useful only to the technician who wants to know how to read dumps.

The Boeing Company. *Verification, Validation, and Certification Guidebook*. Software Acquisition Engineering Guidebook Series. Pubn. No. D180-25488-1. Seattle, Wash.: The Boeing Company, August 1980.

Techniques and tools are discussed for evaluating correctness and detecting and correcting errors.

Boehm, B. W. *Characteristics of Software Quality*. TRW Series of Software Technology, vol. 1. New York: North-Holland, 1978.

Reports on a 1973 study performed for the National Bureau of Standards by TRW that sought to identify a set of characteristics of quality software and to define metrics for them. Explored different metrics and then grouped the best ones by desired characteristics. Also summarizes the Air Force CCIP-85 study of 224 errors and considers which metrics would have been likely to locate the particular errors most effectively.

———. "Software Engineering—as it is." In *Proceedings of the 4th International Conference on Software Engineering, Munich, September 1979*. New York: IFIPS Press, 1979.

———. *Software Engineering Economics*. Englewood Cliffs, N.J.: Prentice-Hall, 1982.

———. "Some Steps Toward Formal and Automated Aids to Software Requirements Analysis and Design." In *Proceedings: 1974 IFIP Congress*, 192–97. New York: IFIPS Press, 1974.

This paper presents the requirements-properties matrix discussed in this book. It also discusses the design of automated aids to software requirements analysis and design.

Boehm, B. W., R. L. McClean, and D. B. Urfrig. "Some Experiences with Automated Aids to the Design of Large Scale Software." In *IEEE Transactions on Software Engineering*, SE-1: 125–33. New York: IEEE Press, March 1975.

Discusses the design and development of the Design Assertion Consistency Check tool and reports on experience in its use.

Boies, S. J., and J. D. Gould. *A Behavioral Analysis of Programming—On the Frequency of Syntactual Errors*. IBM Research Report RC-3907. Yorktown Heights, N.Y.: IBM/T. J. Watson Research Center, June 1972.

Boulding, K. *The Image: Knowledge in Life and Society*. Ann Arbor: Ann Arbor Paperbacks, 1961.

Examines the difficult issues of what makes a system.

Bradley, James H. "The Science and Art of Debugging", Computerworld, Vol XIX, #33 (8/19/85).

Brooks, F. R. *The Mythical Man Month: Essays on Software Engineering*. Reading, Mass.: Addison-Wesley, 1975.

A series of insightful essays on various software engineering issues.

Brown, A. R., and W. A. Sampson. *Program Debugging: The Prevention and Cure of Program Errors*. New York: American Elsevier, 1973.

A broad view of debugging that includes testing. Presents a complete program case study for an inventory program in COBOL that goes from design through testing, showing errors made and the program development log.

Brown, G. D. *Advanced ANS COBOL with Structured Programming*. New York: Wiley-Interscience, 1977.

Brown, J. R. "Automated Software Quality Assurance." Chapter 15 in *Program Test Methods*. Englewood Cliffs, N.J.: Prentice-Hall, 1973.

This paper discusses several automated aids and their successful employment on large software projects in performing such QA functions as configuration verification and test thoroughness analysis.

———. *Impact of Modern Programming Practices on System Development*. Report No. RADC-TR-77-121. Rome, N.Y.: Rome Air Development Center, 1977.

This study summarized the modern programming practices used on a very large software project, and presents the results of a survey of 67 project personnel on the impact of the practices on software cost and quality. QA techniques such as automated standards compliance checking were found to have a strong positive impact on maintainability and reliability.

———. *The Quantitative Measurement of Software Safety and Reliability*. TRW Systems Group, One Space Park, Redondo Beach, Calif., 24 August 1973.

Reports on a study conducted to investigate the feasibility of development of a methodology that would permit prediction of the probability that tactical software errors would result in Site Defense missile control and/or nuclear hazards.

Brown, J. R. and M. Lipow, *Testing for Software Reliability*, Prov. of 1975 Intl. Conf. on Reliable Software (April 1975) 32–38.

Bruce, Robert, *Software Debugging for Microcomputers*, Reston, 1980.

Bucher, D. E. W. "Maintenance of the Compute Sciences Teleprocessing System." In *Proceedings of the 1975 International Conference on Reliable Software*, 260–66. New York: IEEE Press, 1975.

Describes the project organization that maintains the INFONET time-sharing system and the testing techniques used to ensure its reliability. The system includes BASIC, COBOL, FORTRAN, a text editor, three data management systems and an extensive library of application packages.

Burch, R. *Computer Control and Audit, A Total Systems Approach.* New York: John Wiley, 1978.

Buxton, J. M., Peter Naur, and Brian Randell. *Software Engineering Concepts and Techniques.* New York: Petrocelli/Charter, 1975.

Chandrasekaran, B., and S. Radicchi, eds. *Computer Program Testing.* New York: North-Holland, 1981

A collection of articles providing a tutorial on the testing field and offering some insight as to research directions in testing computer programs.

Charette, Robert N., *Software Engineering Environments*, McGraw Hill, Hightstown, NJ, 1987.

Chen, E. T. "Program Complexity and Programmer Productivity." In *IEEE Transactions of Software Engineering,* SE-4: 187–94. New York: IEEE Press, 1978.

Chen, Kuec Cho. *An Introduction to Software Quality Control.* New York: John Wiley, 1980.

Applies statistical quality control techniques to software development by specifying the input domain as a symbolic input attribute decomposition (SIAD) tree. Quality control comes from both the tree specification discipline as well as systematic use of statistical sampling for tests. Many complete examples including testing of FORTRAN and COBOL compilers.

Cho, Chen-Kuec, *Quality Programming: Developing and Testing Software with Sttistical Quality Control*, John Wiley & Sons, Somerset, NJ 1987.

Chow, T. S. "Testing Software Design Modeled by Finite State Machines." In *IEEE Transactions on Software Engineering,* SE-4: 78–186. New York: IEEE Press, 1978.

Cicu, A., M. Marocchi, R. Polillo, and A. Sardoni. "Organizing Tests During Software Evolution." In *Proceedings of the 1975 International Conference on Reliable Software.* New York: IEEE Press, 1975.

Clarke, Lori. "Testing: Achievements and Frustrations." In *Proceedings: COMSAC, 1978.* New York: IEEE Press, 1978.

Basic paper with description of ASSET software system.

Clarke, Lou et al, *A Close Look at Domain Testing*, IEEE trans SE, vol SE-8 July 1982—pg. 380–390.

Clarke, Lou, *Final Scientific Research Report*, AFOSR-TR-81-0803, May 1981.

Cooper, John, and Matthew Fisher, eds. *Software Quality Management.* New York: Petrocelli, 1979.

One of the best treatments of the overall topic of quality assurance and quality management. Despite a heavy bias toward government contracting, it is an excellent reference that any testing manager should be familiar with. Includes an index of tools and techniques and a good explanation of various quality-related government publications and directives.

Cougar, Daniel, and Zawacki. *Motivating and Managing Computer Personnel.* New York: John Wiley, 1981.

A broad analysis of survey data from the profession.

Crosby, Philip B. *Quality is Free: The Art of Making Quality Certain.* New York: New American Library (Mentor), 1979.

A paperback book discussing the quality strategies and experiences at ITT Corporation.

Culpepper, L. M. "A System for Reliable Engineering Software." In *IEEE Transactions on Software Engineering,* 174–78. New York: IEEE Press, June 1975.

This paper describes an "audit" program that automatically checks FORTRAN programs for violations of modularity, portability, and consistency standards.

Curtis, B., S. B. Sheppard, and P. Milliman. "Third Time Charm: Predictions of Programmer Performance by Software Complexity Metrics." In *Proceedings of the 4th International Conference on Software Engineering.* New York: IEEE Press, 1979.

Discusses the correlation between McCabe, Halstead, and program-length metrics for small FORTRAN routines.

Curtis, Bill et al, *Measuring the Psychological Complexity of Software Maintenance Tasks with the Halstead and McCabe Metrics,* IEEE trans Soft Eng, vol SE-S March 1979, pg. 99–104.

Data Processing Management Association. "Error Histories in Live Systems." In *Proceedings of 2nd Quality Assurance Conference,* 148. Park Ridge, Ill.: Data Processing Management Association, 1982.

Error statistics for actual production and operation of five application systems covering the period of 10–39 months at Greaterman's Bank, Johannesburg, South Africa.

Dehaan W, RXVP80 *A Software Documentation, Analysis and Test System,* General Research Corp., Santa Barbara, CA.

Demarco, Tom. *Structured Analysis and System Specification.* New York: Yourdon, Inc., 1979.

One of the better treatments of the early stages of systems analysis.

De Millo, Richard A., et al, *Software Testing and Evaluation,* The Benjamin / Cummings Publishing Company, Inc., Menlo Park, CA 94025, 1987.

Demillo, R. A., R. J. Lipton, and F. G. Sayward. "Hints on Test Data Selection: Help for the Practicing Programmer." *Computer,* April 1978.

Deutsch, Michael S. *Software Verification and Validation.* Englewood Cliffs, N.J.: Prentice-Hall, 1982.

Dickman, B. N., S. J. Amster, E. J. Davis, and J. P. Kiconi. *An Experiment in Automatic Quality Evaluation of Software.* Parsippany, N.J.: Bell Telephone Laboratories Internal Report, 1974.

An early effort to develop metrics to "grade" and evaluate programs.

Dijkstra, E. W. *A Discipline of Programming.* Englewood Cliffs, N.J.: Prentice-Hall, 1976.

Dniesirowski, A., J. M. Guillaume, and R. Mortier. "Software Engineering in Avionics Applications." In *Proceedings of the 3rd International Conference on Software Engineering, Atlanta, Ga., May 1978.* New York: IEEE Press, 1978.

Displays statistics on errors found during specification design and coding phases. The effort and type of testing involved is also reported.

Donahoo, J. *A Review of Software Maintenance Technology.* Report No. RADC-TR-80-13, AD/A-082 985. Rome, N.Y.: Rome Air Development Center, 1980.

Dunn, Robert H., *Software Defect Removal*, McGraw Hill, 1984.

Looks at problems originating in software technology as well as those characteristics of management controls. Offers standards that enable the development of QA plans and covers how to organize, implement and staff a QA project.

Ellsworth, L., and B. Claude. *Modern Project Management: Foundation for Quality.* New York: Burrill-Ellsworth Associates, Inc., 1981.

———. *Productivity and Quality Data Processing: The Profit Potential for the '80s.* New York: Burrill-Ellsworth Associates, Inc., 1981.

Elshoff, J. L. "An Analysis of Some Commercial PL/1 Programs." In *IEEE Transactions on Software Engineering,* SE-2. New York: IEEE Press, 1976.

Report of a library profile (static analysis) of commercial PL/1 programs.

Endres, A. "An Analysis of Errors and Their Causes in System Programs." In *Proceedings: 1975 International Conference on Reliable Software,* 327–36. New York: IEEE Press, 1975.

Empirical data on types and distributions of errors in IBM DOS/VS operating system support.

Evans, Michael W., *Productive Software Test Management*, John Wiley Somerset, N.J., 1984.

Evans, Michael W., and Marciniak, John J., *Software Quality Assurance and Management*, John Wiley & Sons, Somerset, NJ 1987.

Fagan, Michael E., "Advances in Software Inspections," *IEEE Transactions on Software Engineering*, VOL.SE-12, NO.7 July 1986.

Fagan, M. E. "Design and Code Inspections to Reduce Errors in Program Development." *IBM Systems Journal* 15(3): 182–211 (1976).

This article reports that substantial improvements in programming quality and productivity have been obtained through the use of formal inspections of design and code. Procedures and the roles of participation in this process are defined. Checklists and data collection formats are also included. It claims that code productivity will be increased significantly, owing to less error rework (examples provided).

Feigenbaum, A. V., *Total Quality Control*, McGraw Hill, 3rd edition, 1985.

Fewer, A. R., and E. G. Fowlkes. "Relating Computer Program Maintainability to Software Measures." In *Proceedings of 1979 National Computer Conference*. New York: AFIPS Press, 1979.

This study presents error data relating complexity measures (Halstead's) to maintainability for 123 PL/1 business routines.

———. "Some Results from an Empirical Study of Computer Software." In *Proceedings of the 4th International Conference on Software Engineering, Munich*. New York: IFIPS Press, April 1979.

Examines error data for 197 PL/1 routines focusing on maintainability.

"Firm Corrects Error Prone Task of Debugging." *Computerworld*, 26 April 1982.

Reports on use of ABENDAID to realize savings of over $100,000 a year at National Life in Nashville.

Fischer, K. F., and M. J. Walker. "Improved Software Reliability through Requirements Verification." In *IEEE Transactions on Software Reliability*, R-28: 233–49. New York: IEEE Press, 1979.

Fisher, D. *A Common Programming Language for DOD: Background and Technical Requirements*. Paper P-1191. Princeton, N.J., Institute for Defense Analysis, June 1976.

This study gives an example of advanced software quality planning and specification. It discusses quality trade-offs (e.g., efficiency and programming ease vs. reliability) involved in developing a DOD common programming language, and identifies language requirements.

Fosdick, L. D., and L. J. Osterweil. "Data Flow Analysis in Software Reliability." *ACM Computing Survey* 8 (1979): 305–30.

Derivation of path expressions from program graphs and an overall survey of symbolic execution methods including the detection of data flow anomalies.

Foster, K. A. "Error Sensitive Test Case Analysis." In *IEEE Transactions on Software Engineering*, SE-6: 258-64. New York: IEEE Press, 1980.

Outlines a structural testing method based on input-data domains that relies on error sensitivity of arithmetic and numerical routines.

Frank, Warner. "The Process and Payoffs of Software Inspections." *Computerworld*, 12 April 1982, 33.

Discusses inspections and gives suggested standards for productivity, cost, and return on investment.

Freedman, Samuel P., and G. M. Weinberg. *Handbook of Walkthroughs, Inspections and Technical Reviews.* 3d ed. Little, Brown, 1982.

> A thorough treatment of what to do and what not to do when conducting technical reviews. Covers both the how and the why of the ideas presented.

Gaines, R. S. "The Debugging of Computer Programs." Ph.D. diss., Princeton University, 1969.

Gane, Chris, and T. Sarson. *Structured Systems Analysis: Tools and Techniques.* Englewood Cliffs, N.J.: Prentice-Hall, 1979.

Gannon, C. "Error Detection Using Path Testing and Static Analysis." *Computer* 12 (August 1979): 26–31.

Gause, Donald, and G. M. Weinberg. *Are Your Lights On?* Cambridge, Mass.: Winthrop Publishers, 1982

> A provocative but light-hearted look at problem definition.

Gelperin D., *Testing Maintainability*, Software Engineering Notes, ACM SIGSOFT, Vol IV #2, April 1979.

Gelperin, David, "Divining Five Types of Testing Tools," *Software News*, August 1987, pp. 42–47.

Gemignani, Michael C. *Law and the Computer.* Boston: CBI Publishing, 1982.

> An overall treatment of computer law with a special emphasis on software liability. The author also produced a five-part in-depth section for *Computerworld* titled "Who's to Blame When the Program Fails?" that was taken from the book's material.

Gilb, T. *Software Metrics.* Cambridge, Mass.: Winthrop Publishers, 1977.

> This book provides useful information on a wide variety of software metrics. Some 44 different candidate metrics are discussed and grouped into the areas of reliability, flexibility, structure, performance, resources, etc.

Gilb, Tom, and Gerald Weinberg. *Humanized Input.* Wellesley, Mass.: QED Information Sciences, Inc., 1984.

Glass, Robert, *Persistent Software Errors*, IEEE trans SE vol SE-7 March 1981 pgs. 162–168.

Glass, R. *Software Reliability Guidebook.* Englewood Cliffs, N.J.: Prentice-Hall, 1979.

> This book considers reliability as the degree to which a software system satisfies its requirements and delivers usable services. The book surveys many methodologies covering the life cycle and rates each as to its reliability value.

Glass, R., and S. Noiseux. *Software Maintenance Guidebook.* Englewood Cliffs, N.J.: Prentice-Hall, 1981.

> A good introduction to maintenance tools and techniques.

Goel, A. L., and K. Okumoto. "Analysis of Recurrent Software Errors in a Real Time Control System." In *Proceedings of 1978 ACM Annual Conference.* New York: Association of Computing Machinery, 1978.

Goodenough, J. B. "A Survey of Program Testing Issues." In *Research Directions in Software Technology*, edited by Peter Wegner. Cambridge, Mass.: MIT Press, 1979.

Goodenough, J. B., and S. L. Gerhart. "Toward a Theory of Test Data Set Selection." In *IEEE Transactions on Software Engineering,* SE-1: 156–73. New York: IEEE Press, 1975.

This paper discusses formal proof methods and the limitations of structure-based testing. Outlines the use of decision tables as a means of designing test cases.

Gould, J. *Some Psychological Evidence on How People Debug Computer Programs.* Report No. RC4542. Yorktown Heights, N.Y.: IBM Corporation, 1973.

Reports on experiments examining different techniques of finding errors in programs.

Gunning, Robert. *How to Take the Fog Out of Writing.* Chicago: Dartuell Press, 1962.

A very readable 64-page booklet that convincingly demonstrates how to quantitatively evaluate written text for understandability.

Gunther, R. *Management Methodology for Software Product Engineering.* New York: John Wiley, 1978.

Contains a chapter devoted to managing software product testing that maps test groups activities into the traditional life cycle phases. It discusses software test documentation and presents a table of contents for test plans and test logs.

Halstead, M. *Elements of Software Science.* New York: Elsevier North-Holland, 1977.

This book summarizes the substantial progress of an effort to establish and validate a general measure of software complexity. It discusses the basic components of the complexity measure and presents results to date in correlating these with program length, language, productivity, and error incidence.

Hanford, K. V. "Automatic Generation of Test Cases." *IBM Systems Journal* 9(1979): 242–47.

Describes the use of syntax-derived test cases for testing PL/1.

Harrison W., et al, *Applying Software Complexity Metrics to Program Maintenance,* Computer Sept. 1982 pgs. 65–79.

Hartwick, R. "Test Planning." In *Proceedings of 1977 National Computer Conference.* Montvale, N.J.: AFIPS Press, 1977.

Heninger, K. L. "Specifying Software Requirements for Complex Systems: New Techniques and their Application." In *IEEE Transactions on Software Engineering,* SE-6: 2–13. New York: IEEE Press, 1980.

Hetzel, W. C. "An Experimental Analysis of Program Verification Methods," Ph. D. diss., University of North Carolina, Chapel Hill, 1976.

Report and analysis of a comprehensive controlled experiment comparing program verification using three different methods: normal, pure black box, and code reading. The experiment showed that even under "ideal" conditions finding errors was difficult. Pure black box testing did not turn out to be statistically inferior to the normal testing approach combining information about code structure with the specifications to derive test cases.

Hetzel, William, ed. *Program Test Methods*. Englewood Cliffs, N.J.: Prentice-Hall, 1973.

A series of papers that grew out of the first conference devoted to program testing held in Chapel Hill, N.C., in 1972. Includes a comprehensive early bibliography (pre-1972) on testing related subjects.

Hibbard, P. G., ed. "Constructing Quality Software." In *Proceedings of the IFIP Working Conference on Constructing Quality Software, Novosibirsk, Russia, 1977*. New York: IFIPS Press, 1977.

A collection of interesting papers prepared for this invited workshop. Also includes a record of participants' discussion and remarks and an excellent conference wrap-up talk.

Holberton, F. E., and E. G. Parker. *NBS FORTRAN Test Program Final Report*. National Bureau of Standards Report No. NBSJR 73-250, June 1973. Bethesda, Md.: U.S. Department of Commerce, June 1973.

Describes the organization and content of a complete test set for FORTRAN containing 180 programs and 75,000 statements. Stresses the test design principle of self-checking tests.

Horowitz, Ellis, ed. *Practical Strategies for Developing Large Software Systems*. Reading, Mass.: Addison-Wesley, 1975.

Includes the often cited paper by Wolverton: "The Costs of Developing Large Scale Software."

Howden, W. E. "An Evaluation of the Effectiveness of Symbolic Testing." *Software Practice and Experience* 8(1978): 381–97.

Howden, W. E., *Symbolic Testing and the DISSECT Symbolic Evaluation System*, IEEE trans Software Eng. vol SE-3, #4, July 1977 pgs. 266–278.

Howden, W. E., *Validation of Scientific Programs, ACM Computing Survey*, vol 14, June 1982 pgs. 193–227.

———. "Functional Program Testing." In *Proceedings: COMSAC, 1978*. New York: IEEE Press, 1978.

Some experience with testing of IMSL numerical routines that indicated functional testing was superior.

———. "Theoretical and Empirical Studies of Program Testing." In *IEEE Transactions on Software Engineering,* SE-4: 293–98. New York: IEEE Press, 1978.

Houghton, and Oakley, eds. *NBS Software Tools Database*. Pubn. No. NBSIR 80-2159. National Bureau of Standards Institute for Computer Science and Technology, October 1980.

A directory and classification of software tools.

Huang, J. C. "An Approach to Program Testing." *ACM Computing Survey* 7(1975): 113–28.

Hung, J. C., *Experience With Use of Instrumentation Techniques in Software Testing*, Proc NSIA National Conference Software Tech. and Management, Oct 1981, pgs. D1–D10.

IBM DP Marketing Group. *Application Program Maintenance Study*. 23 January 1979, Fjeldstad and Harnlen.

IBM Users Group. *A Guide to Implementing Systems Quality Assurance*. GUIDE Project Handbook. New York: IBM Users Group, 1979.

Institute of Electrical and Electronics Engineers. *IEEE Standard Glossary of Software Engineering Terminology*. IEEE Std. 729-1983. New York: IEEE Press, 1983.

———. *IEEE Standard for Software Quality Assurance Plans*. IEEE Std. 730-1981. New York: IEEE Press, 1981.

———. *IEEE Standard for Software Test Documentation*. IEEE Std. 829-1983. New York: IEEE Press, 1983.

———. IEEE Standard for Software Unit Testing, IEEE Std. 1008-1987. New York: IEEE Press, 1987.

———. IEEE Standard for Software Verification and Validation Plans, IEEE Std. 1012-1986. New York: IEEE Press, 1986.

Itoh, Dayu, and T. Izutani. "Fadebug 1, A New Tool for Program Debugging." In *Record of the 1973 Symposium on Computer Software Reliability*. New York: IEEE Press, 1973.

Jackson, Michael. *Principles of Program Design*. New York: Academic Press, 1975.

Describes the Jackson technique of data-driven design.

Jarrah, L., and B. Torsun. "An Empirical Analysis of COBOL Programs." *Software Practice and Experience* 9(September 1979): 341–59.

Jensen, ed., Software Verification and Validation, Prentice-Hall, 1982.

Jones, T. C. "Measuring Programming Quality and Productivity." *IBM Systems Journal* 17(1): 69–78 (1978).

Juran, J. M., and Fran Gryna. *Quality Planning and Analysis*. New York: McGraw-Hill, 1980.

Kapor, G. "Quality of Specifications." *Computerworld*, 26 April 1982, 22.

An examination of 68 completed program specifications from various organizations. The reasons for changes made were recorded and tabulated, showing that more than 80% of the changes were due to the "quality" of the specifications, not the user changing his mind.

Keravnou, E. T. and Johnson L, *A Case Study in Fault Diagnosis*, McGraw Hill, Hightstown, NJ, 1987.

Kernighan, B. W., and P. J. Plauger. *The Elements of Programming Style*. New York: McGraw-Hill, 1974.

This book attempts to define "good programming style" and show how programs written with good style will be easier to read and understand, often smaller, and more efficient. Programs may be "structured" but still not have these qualities. Over 50 examples are presented and explained clearly.

————. *Software Tools*. Reading, Mass.: Addison-Wesley, 1976.

King, James, *Symbolic Execution and Program Testing*, CACM, Vol 19 #7 July 1976 pgs. 385–394.

Kopetz. *Software Reliability*. Deerfield Beach, Fla.: Verlag, 1979.

Short paperback addressing a variety of topics related to producing high-reliability software. Good coverage of errors and error classification.

Kosy, D. W. "Air Force Command and Control Information Processing." In *The 1980 Trends in Software Technology*. Report No. R-1012-PR. Santa Monica, Calif.: Rand Corporation, June 1974.

This report is an expanded version of the CCIP-85 software technology assessment. It discusses the current and projected state-of-the-art in assuring such software quality attributes as reliability, acceptability, adaptability, and integrity, along with cost and schedule.

Laemel, A. E., *Software Modeling Studies, A Statistical Theory of Computer Program Testing*, Rome Air Devel Ctr Report RADC TR 81-183 vol. IV.

Lehman, J. "How Software Projects are Really Managed." *Datamation*, January 1979, 131–35.

A study report analyzing 57 software projects and looking at techniques actually used. Includes a table showing testing tools and techniques and the percentage of projects that used them.

Leibholz, S. W., and L. D. Wilson. *User's Guide to Computer Crime*. Radnor, Pa.: Chilton, 1974.

Lientz, Bennet P., and E. Burton Swanson. *Software Maintenance Management*. Reading, Mass.: Addison-Wesley, 1980.

A major study of the maintenance of computer application software in 487 data processing organizations.

Linger, D., H. D. Mills, and N. Wirth. *Structured Programming: Theory and Practice*. Reading, Mass.: Addison-Wesley, 1979.

Methodology for reading, writing, and proving programs correct. Concept that programs are mathematical objects. Several case studies of program examples developed using the concepts.

Lipow M. and T. A. Thayer, *Prediction of Software Failures*, Proc. 1977 Annual Reliability and Maintainability Synposium, IEEE Cat. #77CH1161-9RQC, pgs. 489 –494.

Litecky, C. R., and G. B. Davis. "A Study of Errors, Error Proneness, and Error Diagnosis in COBOL." *Communications of the ACM* 19(1976): 33–37.

Loeckx J, Sieber K, and Stansifier R. D., *The Foundations of Program Verification* Second Edition, John Wiley & Sons Somerset, NJ, 1987.

London, R. *A View on Program Verification: Proceedings of the 1975 International Conference on Reliable Software.* New York: IEEE Press, 1975.

A pragmatic look at proof of program correctness.

McCabe, See attached fed. pub. NBS 500-99.

McCabe, T. J. "A Complexity Metric." In *IEEE Transactions on Software Engineering,* SE-2: 101–11. New York: IEEE Press, 1976.

This paper contains the complexity metric definition and derivation for program graphs.

———. *Structured Testing.* Catalog No. EHO 200-6. New York: IEEE Computer Society Press, 1983.

A tutorial collection of papers that focus on the relationship between testing and program complexity. Cyclomatic complexity is defined as a program graph measure and techniques for developing program test cases are outlined. General guidelines on program verification and program reliability are also covered.

McCabe, Tom and Associates. *Software Quality Assurance: A Survey.* Columbia, Md.: Tom McCabe and Associates, 1978.

McCabe, Thomas J. Structured Testing, Silver Spring, MD, IEEE Computer Society Press, 1983.

McClure, C. L. *Managing Software Development and Maintenance.* New York: Van Nostrand Reinhold, 1981.

McCracken, D. D., and G. M. Weinberg. "How to Write a Readable FORTRAN Program." *Datamation,* October 1972, 73–77.

Stresses the need that programs be adequately documented, so that someone studying them can determine what they were intended to do. Defines a complete package of documentation as containing: a precise statement of what the program is supposed to do; a complete set of sample input and output, including test cases; a set of operating instructions for the computer operator; and a complete set of flowcharts. Other factors affecting software quality are examined.

McFarlan, F. W., and R. L. Nolan, eds. *The Information Systems Handbook.* Homewood, Ill.: Dow Jones Irwin, Inc., 1975.

A group of 40 papers covers all aspects of information systems management and administration.

Manley, J. H., and M. Lipow. *Findings and Recommendations of the Joint Logistics Commanders' Software Reliability Work Group.* Vols. 1 and 2. Report No. AFSC TR-75-05. Washington, D.C.: Department of the Air Force, November 1975.

This report presents the deliberations of a group of 30 software and computer system professionals from government, industry, and the academic community meeting during the period October 1974–May 1975. Problems in United States Department of Defense computer resource acquisition were defined and solutions developed. The SRWG plan for improving the software acquisition process was adopted almost in its entirety by the DOD. Heavy emphasis is given to technology programs that will lead to effective software quality assurance programs and methods for providing more reliable and maintainable software.

Manna, Zohar, and Richard Waldinger. "The Logic of Computer Programming." In *IEEE Transactions on Software Engineering*, SE-4: 199–229. New York: IEEE Press, 1978.

Surveys the methodology and limitations of formal proofs of program correctness referred to in this book as the testing principle that complete testing is not (theoretically or practically) possible.

Mayeda, Wataru. *Graph Theory*. New York: John Wiley, 1979.

An excellent basic treatment of graph theory concepts and applications.

Metzger, Phillip. *Managing a Programming Project*. 2d ed. Englewood Cliffs, N.J.: Prentice-Hall, 1981.

A fine overall treatment of the project life cycle and basic project management. Includes checklists and sample management control reports.

Mili, Ali, *An Introduction to Formal Program Verification*, QED Information Sciences, Wellesley, MA, 1987.

Miller, E. F. "Program Testing." *Computer*, April 1978.

An introductory overview of testing with an emphasis on unit testing and path analysis.

———. "Program Testing: An Overview for Managers." In *Proceedings: COMSAC, 1978*. IEEE Catalog No. 78C-H1338-3C. New York: IEEE Press, 1978.

Some basic concepts and rules of thumb for size of testing budget and tests required to achieve 90% segment coverage.

Miller, E. F., and W. E. Howden, eds. "Software Testing and Validation Techniques." In *IEEE Computer Society Tutorial*. Catalog No. EHO 180-Q. 1981.

Miller, E. F., and R. A. Melton. "Automated Generation of Test Case Data Sets." In *Proceedings of the 1975 International Conference on Reliable Software*. New York: IEEE Press, 1975.

Mills, H. D. *Safeguard Code Certification Experimental Report*. IBM Federal Systems Division Systems Assurance Report. Gaithersburg, Md.: IBM, 1970.

The classical error-seeding experiment.

———. "Software Development." In *IEEE Transactions on Software Engineering*, SE-2(4): 265–73. New York: IEEE Press, 1976.

Mo Hanty, Siba, *Models and Measurements for Quality Assessment of Software*, ACM Computing Surveys, vol. 11 Sept. 1979 pgs. 251–275.

Moranda, P. B. "Limits to Program Testing with Random Number Inputs." In *Proceedings: COMSAC, 1978*. New York: IEEE Press, 1978.

Moriconi, M. S. "A Designers/Verifiers Assistant." In *IEEE Transactions on Software Engineering*, SE-5: 387–401. New York: IEEE Press, 1979.

Describes a tool called the designers/verifiers assistant that embodies a theory of how to reason about changes to a design or verification. Includes excerpts from a sample session.

Muchnick, and T. C. Jones, eds. *Program Flow Analysis Theory and Applications*. Englewood Cliffs, N.J.: Prentice-Hall Software Series, 1981.

Fairly advanced treatment of program flow and data flow analysis techniques. Does not include practical examples or case history data.

Myers, G. J. *The Art of Software Testing*. New York: John Wiley, 1979.

———. *Composite/Structured Design*. New York: Van Nostrand Reinhold, 1978.

This book discusses the process of structured design including stepwise refinement, coupling, and design criteria.

———. "A Controlled Experiment in Program Testing and Code Inspections." *Communications of the ACM*, September 1978.

Compares black box testing, combined testing, and code inspections with a group of 59 experienced programmers in a controlled experiment.

———. *Software Reliability—Principles and Practices*. New York: John Wiley, 1976.

This book covers concepts of software reliability, design of reliable software, software testing, and some miscellaneous related topics such as management techniques, effects of programming languages and computer architecture on reliability, proving program correctness, and reliability models.

Naftaly, S. M., and M. C. Cohen. "Test Data Generators and Debugging Systems . . . Workable Quality Control." *Data Processing Digest* 18(February–March 1972).

An early survey of test data generation tools.

NBS SP 500-75, "Validation, Verification and Testing of Computer Software," W. Richards Adrion, Martha Branstad, and John C. Cherniavsky, National Bureau of Standards, February, 1981.

NBS SP 500-93, "Software Validation, Verification and Testing Technique Tool and Reference Guide," Patricia B. Powell, Editor, National Bureau of Standards, September, 1982.

NBS SP 500-98, "Planning for Software Validation, Verification, and Testing," Patricia B. Powell, Editor, National Bureau of Standards, November, 1982.

NBS SP 500-99, "Structured Testing: A Software Testing Methodology Using the Cyclomatic Complexity Metric", Thomas J. McCabe, National Bureau of Standards, December, 1982.

NBS SP 500-136, "An Overview of Computer Software Acceptance Testing," Dolores R. Wallace, National Bureau of Standards, February, 1986.

NBS SP 500-146, "Report on the NBS Software Acceptance Test Workshop, April 1–2, 1986", Dolores R. Wallace and John C. Cherniavsky, National Bureau of Standards, March, 1987.

Noll, Paul. *The Structured Programming Cookbook*. New York: Mike Murach Associates, 1978.

Structured design and programming for small programs.

Osterweil, L. J., J. K. Brown, and L. Stucki. "ASSET: A Lifecycle Verification and Visibility System." In *Proceedings: COMSAC, 1978*. New York: IEEE Press, 1978.

Osterweil, L. J., and L. D. Fosdick. "DAVE: A Validation Error Detection and Documentation System for FORTRAN Programs." *Software Practice and Experience*, October–December 1976, 66–71.

Overton, R. K. *Research Toward Ways of Improving Software Maintenance*. Hanscom Air Force Base Electronic Systems Division Report Nos. ADA005827 and AD760819. Bedford, Mass.: Department of the Air Force, 1974.

An empirical study examining how maintenance programmers actually spend their time.

Page-Jones, ? The Practical Guide to Structured Systems Design, New York, Yourdon Press, 1980.

Paige, M. R. "An Analytical Approach to Software Testing." In *Proceedings: COMSAC, 1978*. New York: IEEE Press, 1978.

Paige, M. R., and M. A. Holthouse. "On Sizing Software Testing." In *Proceedings: 1977 International Symposium of Fault Tolerant Computing*. New York: IEEE Press, 1977.

Panzl, David. "Automatic Software Test Drivers." *Computer*, April 1978, 44–70.

Parikh, Garish. *Techniques of Program and System Maintenance*. Lincoln, Nebr.: Ethnoteck, 1980.

Parikh, Garish, and Nicholas Zvegintzov. *Tutorial on Software Maintenance*. IEEE Catalog No. EH0201-4. New York: IEEE Computer Society Press, 1983.

A collection of papers on maintenance, in six parts: the world of software maintenance; understanding software; the modification of software; the evolution of software; the death of software; and the management of software maintenance.

Parnas, D. L. "Some Conclusions from an Experiment in Software Engineering Techniques." In *Proceedings: 1972 Fall Joint Computer Conference*, 325–29. Montvale, N.J.: AFIPS Press, 1972.

Students were each to write a program as well as a second program to be used to check out someone else's program using only specification information. Combinations of the student programs were then integrated and compared.

Perry, W. *Effective Methods of EDP Quality Assurance*. Wellesley, Mass.: QED, 1977.

Includes a sample software QA manual and presents software testing as one activity requiring a QA review.

Perry, William E., A Structured Approach to Systems Testing, Wellesley, MA, QED Information Sciences, 1983.

Perry, William E., *How to Test Software Packages*, John Wiley & Sons, Somerset, NJ 1986.

Persig, R. M. *Zen and the Art of Motorcycle Maintenance.* New York: Bantam Paperbacks, 1974.

A delightful look at the concepts of quality and maintenance from a completely different perspective.

Peters, L. J., and L. L. Tripp. "Software Design Representation Schemes." In *Proceedings: Symposium on Computer Software Reliability.* New York: Polytechnic Institute of New York, April 1976.

A comparative analysis of different methods of representing programs including comments on use and experience with each alternative.

Petschenik, Nathan "Practical Priorities in System Testing," IEEE Software Vol 2 #5 (September), 1985.

Powell, Patricia B., ed. *Planning of Software Validation, Verification, and Testing.* Special Publication 500-98. Rockville, Md.: National Bureau of Standards, 1982.

This document explains the selection and use of various testing tools and techniques and discusses how to develop a plan to meet specific validation, verification, and testing goals.

———., ed. *Software Validation, Verification, and Testing Techniques and Tool Reference Guide.* Special Publication 500-93. Rockville, Md.: National Bureau of Standards, 1982.

Thirty techniques and tools are described, giving basic features and an assessment of applicability and effectiveness.

Putnam, R., and R. W. Wolverton. *Quantitative Management: Software Cost Estimating.* IEEE Tutorial. New York: IEEE Press, November, 1977.

A thorough state-of-the-art treatment on cost estimation as of 1977.

Pynn, Craig, *Strategies for Electronics Test*, McGraw Hill, Hightstown, NJ, 1987.

Ramamoorthy, C. V. et al, *Software Engineering Practices in the U.S. and Japanese Organizations Computer*, June 1984.

Ramamoorthy, C. V. et al, *A systematic Approach to the Development and Validation of Critical Software for Nuclear Power Plants*, 4th International Software Engineering Conference Proceedings.

Ramamoorthy, C. V., and S. F. Ho. "Testing Large Software with Automated Software Evaluation Systems." In *IEEE Transactions on Software Engineering*, SE-1: 46 –58. New York: IEEE Computer Society Press, 1975.

Ramamoorthy, C. V., S. F. Ho, and W. T. Chen. "On the Automated Generation of Program Test Data." In *IEEE Transactions on Software Engineering*, SE-2: 293–300. New York: IEEE Press, 1976.

Rasmussen and Roose eds, *Human Detection and Diagnosis of System Failures*, Plenum 1981.

Redwine, Samuel T. "An Engineering Approach to Software Test Data Design." In *IEEE Transactions on Software Engineering*, SE-9(2). New York: IEEE Computer Society Press, 1983.

This paper outlines a systematic approach to test data design based on the five coverage spaces or domains of processing functions, input, output, interaction among functions, and the code itself.

Reifer, D. J. "Automated Aids for Reliable Software." In *Proceedings of the 1975 International Conference on Reliable Software*. New York: IEEE Press, 1975.

Reifer, D. J., and S. Trattner. "A Glossary of Software Tools and Techniques." *Computer*, July 1977.

Rodwine, Samuel T. An Engineering Approach to Software Test Data Design, IEEE Transactions on Software Engineering, Vol SE-9 No. 2 (March) 1983.

Roth, *Computer Logic Testing and Verification*, Computer Science 1980.

Rubey, R. J., J. A. Dana, and P. W. Biche. "Quantitative Aspects of Software Validation." In *IEEE Transactions on Software Engineering*, SE-1: 150–55. New York: IEEE Press, 1975.

Rudner B., *Seeding/Tagging Estimation of Software Errors: Models and Estimates*, Rome Air Develop Ctr. Report RADC TR 77-15.

Rustin, R., ed. *Debugging Techniques in Large Systems*. Englewood Cliffs, N.J.: Prentice-Hall, 1971.

Describes debugging tools and approaches, and defines the distinction between debugging and testing.

Sadowski, W. L., and D. W. Lozier. "A Unified Approach to Algorithm Testing." In *Program Test Methods*, edited by W. C. Hetzel, 277–90. Englewood Cliffs, N.J.: Prentice-Hall, 1973.

The chapter discusses how portability of fundamental algorithms in terms of desired level of accuracy is achieved by using primary, transfer, and working standards to "calibrate" the subject software.

Sardinas. *EDP Auditing: A Primer*. New York: John Wiley, 1981.

Scherr, A. L. "Developing and Testing a Large Programming System, OS/360 Time Sharing Option." In *Program Test Methods*, edited by W. C. Hetzel. Englewood Cliffs, N.J.: Prentice-Hall, 1973.

Presents an overview of the process used to design, develop, and test the Time Sharing Option of Operating System 360.

Schick, G. J., and R. W. Wolverton. "An Analysis of Competing Software Reliability Models." In *IEEE Transactions on Software Engineering*, SE-4: 104–20. New York: IEEE Press, 1978.

Provides an overview of the development and experience with various software reliability models.

Schneiderman, N. F. *Software Psychology: Human Factors in Computer and Information Systems*. New York: Winthrop Publishers, 1980.

Schneiderman, N. F. "Analysis of Error Processes in Computer Software." In *Proceedings of the 1975 International Conference on Reliable Software*. New York: IEEE Press, 1975.

———. "Application of Program Graphs and Complexity Analysis to Software Development and Testing." In *IEEE Transactions on Software Reliability*, R-28: 192–98. New York: IEEE Press, 1979.

Provides a basic overview of graph applications to programs. Includes a discussion of experiments on ALGOL code using McCabe's metric and describes several semiautomatic test tools.

Schneiderman, N. F., and H. M. Hoffman. "An Experiment in Software Error Data Collection and Analysis." In *IEEE Transactions on Software Engineering*, SE-5: 276–86. New York: IEEE Press, 1979.

Four programs were written in ALGOL by the same individual with error data collected and correlated to structural complexity measures.

Shedley, Ethan I. *The Medusa Conspiracy*. New York: Viking Press, 1980.

A provocative spy novel that involves software errors leading up to nuclear war in the Middle East.

Sheppard, S. B., W. Curtis, P. Milliman, M. A. Borst, and T. Love. "First Year Results from a Research Program on Human Factors in Software Engineering." In *Proceedings of the 1979 National Computer Conference*. Montvale, N.J.: AFIPS Press, 1979.

Describes an experiment involving programmers modifying small FORTRAN routines. Results include correlation of complexity metrics to the ease of modification and the subject's ability to remember the program control structure.

Skidmore, Len. *COBOL Testing for Business Applications*. Boston: CBI Publishing Co., 1983.

Describes overall testing concepts and stresses the unit test plan.

Smith, Truck, Secrets of Software Debugging, Blue Ridge Summit, PA, TAB Books Inc., 1984.

Sorkowitz, Al, *HUD Gains Control with Testing Procedures*, GCN Dec. 1984.

Spier, M. J. "Software Malpractice—A Distasteful Experience." *Software Practice and Experience* 6(1976): 293–99.

Describes a (negative) case history of how an initially well-conceived and cleanly implemented compiler went wrong. Describes how an initial "optimization" implanted a latent bug, how the bug was subsequently activated through innocent compiler modification, and how the compiler then deteriorated because of bad "corrections" to the bug manifestation.

Stauffer, B. C., and Roger U. Fujii, "Security Evaluation of Mission Critical Systems," *Proceedings of COMPASS'86*, Georgetown University, Washington, D.C., IEEE, E. 47th St., New York, NY 10017.

Stepczyk, F. M. *Requirements for Secure Operating Systems*. TRW Software Series. Pubn. No. TRW-SS-74-05. June 1974.

This study discusses the component attributes of computer security, including isolation, identification, controlled access, surveillance, and integrity/maintainability. It presents detailed requirements for the above and analyzes techniques for addressing them.

Stevens, R. J., *Operational Test and Evaluation*, New York, John Wiley 1979.

Stucki, L. G. "A Prototype Automatic Testing Tool." In *Proceedings: 1972 Fall Joint Computer Conference*, 829–35. Montvale, N.J.: AFIPS Press, 1972.

Swanson, E. B. "The Dimensions of Maintenance." In *Proceedings: Second International Conference on Software Engineering*, 492–97. New York: IEEE Computer Society, 1976.

Thayer, T. A., M. Lipow, and E. C. Nelson. *Software Reliability Study*. TRW Software Series. Pubn. No. TRW-SS-76-03. March 1976.

This document is the final technical report for the Software Reliability Study, performed by TRW for the United States Air Force System Command's Rome Air Development Center. It presents results of a study of error data, collected from four software development projects.

———. *Software Reliability, A Study of Large Project Reality*. New York: North-Holland, 1978.

An important early reference work on error data. Examines errors, sources, and causes. Very carefully documents five major projects within TRW including the four cited in the previous reference.

Thompson, W. E. and P. O. Chelson, *On the Specification and Testing of Software Reliability*, Proc 1980 Annual Rel & Maint. Symp., IEEE Cat. #80 CH1513-R pgs. 379–383.

TRW Defense and Space Systems Group. *Software Tools: Catalogue and Recommendations*. Redondo Beach, Calif.: TRW Defense and Space Systems Group, 1979.

Tsui, Frank F, *LSI/VSLI Testability Design*, McGraw Hill, Hightstown, NJ, 1987.

Tucker, A. E. *The Correlation of Computer Programming Quality with Testing Effort*. SDC Report TM 2219. Santa Monica, Calif.: System Development Corp., January 1965.

Errors and testing effort were collected for five projects and displays were prepared showing errors found vs. effort and time.

U.S. Air Force. *Information Processing/Data Automation Implications of Air Force Command and Control Requirements in the 1980s(CCIP-85): Highlights.* Vol. 1, SAMSO/ SRS-71-1. Rome, N.Y.: April 1972.

U.S. Department of the Air Force. *Acquisition and Support Procedures for Computer Resources in Systems.* Air Force Regulation 800-14. Vol. 2. Rome, N.Y.: Department of the Air Force, 1975.

Contains a chapter specifying policy for software testing at the following levels: informal testing, preliminary qualification testing, formal qualification testing, and system level testing. It also identifies the required contents for test plans and procedures and discusses methods for computer program verification.

U.S. Department of the Army. *Testing of Computer Software Systems.* Department of the Army Technical Bulletin TB 18-104. Ft. Belvoir, Va.: Department of the Army, September 1981.

Defines the Army's software testing methodology including required tests and test documentation.

U.S. Det. of Commerce FIPS 99/10/

U.S. Department of Defense. *Test and Evaluation.* Department of Defense Directive No. 5000.3. December 26, 1979.

Describes the scope and applicability of DOD T&E activities and outlines policies and responsibilities for both development and operational testing.

U.S. Department of the Navy. *Weapon System Software Development.* Military Standard MIL-STD-1679. Department of the Navy, 1978.

Describes required quality assurance procedures at each stage of development and specifies software trouble reporting procedures.

U.S. General Accounting Office. *Federal Agencies' Maintenance of Computer Programs: Expensive and Undermanaged.* Pubn. No. AFMD-81-25. Washington, D.C.: U.S. GAO, 26 February 1981.

U.S. General Services Administration. *Government Software Contracts.* General Services Administration Bulletin 51. Washington, D.C.: USGSA, 19 May 1981.

Report of a GAO study of nine completed software contracts that failed with analysis of key failure costs.

United States Professional Development Institute. "Software Quality Assurance." *Government Computer News*, April 1984, 29–50. Special Section.

An overview of quality assurance, especially as it relates to government agencies. Includes special feature articles and interviews.

Van Tassel. *Program Style, Design, Efficiency, Debugging and Testing.* New York: Van Nostrand, 1981.

Vick, Charles R. and Ramamoorthy, C. V. Eds, *Handbook of Software Engineering*, Van Nostrand Reinhold, New York 1983.

Voges, U., L. Gmeiner, and A. A. Von Mayhauser, "SADAT—an Automated Test Tool." In *IEEE Transactions on Software Engineering*, SE-6: 286–90. New York: IEEE Press, 1979.

Describes the SADAT testing tool and experiences with its use.

Walsh, T. J. "A Software Reliability Study using McCabe's Complexity Measure." In *Proceedings of 1977 National Computer Conference*. Montvale, N.J.: AFIPS Press, 1979.

McCabe complexity is measured for 276 routines in the AEGIS system and experiences are reported.

Warren, J. C., Jr. *Software Portability*. Stanford Digital Systems Laboratory Technical Note No. 48. Palo Alto: Stanford University Press, September 1974.

This paper discusses the basic concepts and considerations in software portability (e.g., abstract machines, bootstrapping, simulation, emulation, higher-order languages, pseudo-code), the use of such concepts to date, and suggestions for research into further concepts to improve portability.

Watkins, Marvin, *A Technique for Testing Command and Control Software*, CACM vol 25 April 1982 pg. 228–232.

Weinberg, G. M. *An Introduction to General Systems Thinking*. New York: Wiley Interscience, 1975.

———. "The Psychology of Computer Programming." New York: Van Nostrand Reinhold, 1971.

The classic reference on programmer teams and the influence of groups on programming work. Source of egoless programming.

———. "The Psychology of Improved Programmer Performance." *Datamation*, November 1972, 82–85.

This paper summarizes the results of some experiments that show the high leverage involved in setting quality objectives. Several groups of programmers were given the same assignment but different quality attribute objectives. For each attribute the highest performance was achieved by the group given that attribute as its success criterion.

———. *Rethinking Systems Analysis and Design*. Boston: Little, Brown & Co., 1982.

A delightful collection of essays and fables on many of the issues affecting software development. Includes a description of the black box general problem-solving computer model used in Weinberg's workshops.

White, L. J., and E. I. Cohen. "A Domain Strategy for Computer Program Testing." In *IEEE Transactions on Software Engineering*, SE-6: 247–57. New York: IEEE Press, 1980.

Williams, M. S. "The Advanced Data Processing Testbed." In *Proceedings: COMSAC, 1978.* New York: IEEE Press, 1978.

Describes the ADAPT testbed tool at Huntsville, Alabama.

Wirth, Niklaus. *Systematic Programming: An Introduction.* Englewood Cliffs, N.J.: Prentice-Hall, 1976.

Woolridge, S. *Systems and Programming Standards.* New York: Petrocelli/Charter, 1977.

One chapter addresses systems testing and presents the table of contents for a system test plan as well as a checklist for system testing.

Wulf, W. A. "Report of Workshop No. 3, 'Methodology'." In *Symposium on the High Cost of Software, Carnegie-Mellon University, September 17, 1973,* 1–12. Pittsburgh, Pa.: Carnegie-Mellon University Press, 1983.

This paper discusses the qualitative difference among programs and explores means for consistently producing better programs. Also noted are the absolute cost of software, its cost relative to hardware and its escalation as time goes by. A number of software attributes are defined; maintainability, modifiability, robustness, clarity, performance, cost, and portability.

Yeh, R., ed. *Current Trends in Programming Methodology.* Vol. 1, *Software Specification and Design.* Englewood Cliffs, N.J.: Prentice-Hall, 1977.

———. *Current Trends in Programming Methodology.* Vol. 2, *Program Validation.* Englewood Cliffs, N.J.: Prentice-Hall, 1977.

A series of papers with a few of special interest to testing, including "Structured Program Testing" by Pete Henderson, which was one of the first published papers using this title. Includes an extensive annotated bibliography.

Yeh, R. T., and P. Zave. "Specifying Software Requirements." In *Proceedings of IEEE* 68: 1077–85. New York: IEEE Press, 1980.

This paper examines specification errors and outlines a suggested methodology for specification design.

Youngberg, E. P. "A Software Testing Control System." In *Program Test Methods*, edited by W. C. Hetzel. Englewood Cliffs, N.J.: Prentice-Hall, 1973.

Describes the design of a particular test control vehicle called VCS (Validation Control System) for testing of parts of the UNIVAC operating system software.

Yourdon, Ed. *Managing the System Life Cycle.* New York: Yourdon Press, 1982.

Yourdon, Ed, and Larry L. Constantine. *Structured Design.* Englewood Cliffs, N.J.: Prentice-Hall, 1979.

Describes the Yourdon structured design methodology and approach. Surveys the history of structured design concepts.

Yourdon, E. N., *Structured Walkthroughs*, Englewood Cliffs, N.J. Prentice-Hall, 1979.

INDEX

Index